Supernatural
Shakespeare

MAGIC AND RITUAL
IN MERRY OLD ENGLAND

Praise for
Supernatural Shakespeare

"The perfect comprehensive introduction to the supernatural as represented by Shakespeare, a gift to all students in its clarity, with some good moments for colleagues as well."
— Ronald Hutton, Author of *Pagan Britain*

"Fairies and dwarves, ghosts and magic, rites and rituals, wizards and weirdos, natural and supernatural: these are the topics of Supernatural Shakespeare. *Snodgrass argues that it would be a mistake to look for coherence in Shakespeare's English fairy-lore because Shakespeare wrote for his audiences and "cherry-picked from a wide range of folk and literary traditions" to please those audiences. Contemporary audiences and readers (and perhaps especially academics) may have very different expectations than Shakespeare's original audiences. Like Shakespeare's works,* Supernatural Shakespeare *itself aims at a broad audience. While the Shakespearean solemnity drilled into so many of us from elementary school onward has in some ways produced a Shakespeare accessible only to an educated elite, Snodgrass playfully discusses how Shakespeare gives characters (and narratives) a 'compelling interiority' and, never falling short of academic rigor, does so in ways that keep the material accessible, refreshing, and readable rather than opaque, tedious, and snobbishly academic."*
— Simon C. Estok, Author of *Ecocriticism and Shakespeare* and *The Ecophobia Hypothesis*

"From the fairies of A Midsummer Night's Dream *to the witches of* Macbeth, *from* Hamlet's *ghost to* The Tempest's *Ariel, Shakespeare's plays teem with supernatural beings and events. These speak to the popular understanding of Shakespeare's day, on one hand, while on the other hand investing his works with an air of the magical and divine. Snodgrass's* Supernatural Shakespeare: Magic and Ritual in Merry Old England *studies this material intently, teasing out its basis in ritual and lore while also placing it within the practices and conventions of Shakespeare's theater itself. The result is an engaging, readable, and informative study."*
— Bruce Boehrer, Author of *Shakespeare Among the Animals* and *Environmental Degradation in Jacobean Drama*

"The style of the book is playful and will certainly appeal to younger people and curious beginners. It certainly provides a lot of fascinating insights, and I can only hope that it will encourage more interest in Shakespeare and in the English Renaissance."
— François Laroque, Author of *Shakespeare's Festive World*

"Supernatural Shakespeare demonstrates, in an entertaining and highly readable style, the ways in which ideas about 'magic' suffused Shakespeare's world, his plays, and his performance practice. The book evokes the spirit of Shakespearean England as an exciting era that consistently blurred boundaries between the natural, the religious, and the supernatural."
— Dr. Jason Gleckman, Author of *Shakespeare and Protestant Poetics*

Supernatural Shakespeare

MAGIC AND RITUAL
IN MERRY OLD ENGLAND

j. SNODGRASS

A City of Light imprint

New Idea Press
A City of Light imprint

City of Light Publishing
266 Elmwood Ave. Suite 407
Buffalo, New York 14222

info@CityofLightPublishing.com
www.CityofLightPublishing.com

Book design by Ana Cristina Ochoa

ISBN 978-1-942483-92-2 (paperback)
ISBN 978-1-942483-93-9 (ebook)

10 9 8 7 6 5 4 3 2 1

Library of Congress Cataloging-in-Publication Data
Names: Snodgrass, j., author.
Title: Supernatural Shakespeare : magic and ritual in merry old England / j. Snodgrass.
Description: Buffalo : New Idea Press, a City of Light imprint, [2021] | Includes bibliographical references and index. | Summary: "Immerse yourself in Shakespeare's magical world, filled with supernatural encounters with faeries, ghosts and witches. Frolic with royalty, wander through forests, and experience love layered with enchantment. The Bard's use of these fantastical phenomena has had a tremendous and enduring influence on authors and audiences for more than four centuries. But what are their origins? Explore the folk beliefs and literary sources that influenced Shakespeare and discover how he assembled his own masterful portraits of these phenomena, giving his plays vibrant life and his characters unforgettable personalities. This exploration of magic and mystery is enlivened by Shakespeare's wit and brilliance and illuminated with scholarly insights from Shakespeare's time to the present. Supernatural Shakespeare is both an approachable introduction for casual readers and a contribution to the canon that scholars will find valuable. The author's lively and humorous approach enhances the joy of studying Shakespeare. For the reader and playgoer alike, Supernatural Shakespeare enhances the experience of entering this world of magic and wonder. Shakespeare's characters make many references to magical beliefs about seasons, holidays and folk traditions that celebrate the natural cycles of death and renewal. Some of his comedy plots are structured around the victory of springtime youth over cold, wintery antagonism. And in his tragedies we see the triumph of dark winter, with a ray of spring light approaching. Supernatural Shakespeare progresses through an Elizabethan calendar, from cold tragedies to warm comedies"-- Provided by publisher.
Identifiers: LCCN 2021021255 (print) | LCCN 2021021256 (ebook) | ISBN 9781942483922 (paperback) | ISBN 9781942483939 (adobe pdf) | ISBN 9781942483939 (ebook) | ISBN 9781942483939 (epub) | ISBN 9781942483939 (kindle edition) | ISBN 9781942483939 (mobi) | ISBN 9781942483939 (pdf)
Subjects: LCSH: Shakespeare, William, 1564-1616--Knowledge. | Supernatural. | Manners and customs. | Supernatural in literature. | Manners and customs in literature.
Classification: LCC PR3004 .S66 2021 (print) | LCC PR3004 (ebook) | DDC 822.3/3--dc23
LC record available at https://lccn.loc.gov/2021021255
LC ebook record available at https://lccn.loc.gov/2021021256

*"There are more things in heaven and earth, Horatio,
than are dreamt of in your philosophy."*
(Hamlet I.v)

*"If all the year were playing holidays,
To sport would be as tedious as to work;
But, when they seldom come, they wish'd-for come,
And nothing pleaseth but rare accidents."*
(1 Henry IV I.ii)

Dedicated to Ellen Scherer and Madison Sedlor.

To Elizabeth, Jackson, Sarah, Malcolm and William-Wallace.

Thank you, Mike Scott,
for the songs and the inspiration to keep exploring.

And thank you Marti Gorman, Hannah Gordon, Emily Yancey, Andrew Zuccari, Shawnell Tillery, Joyce Stilson, Carly Weiser, Neal Radice, Chris Handley, Becky Globus, Jenni Attea, Matt Boyle, Michael Fanelli, Melissa Leventhal, Peter Snodgrass, Dominick Patrone, Katie Mallinson, Jon Elston, Emma English, Nick Edwards, Sarah Emmerling, Elliott Fox, Leyla Gentil, Zack Hatrick, Emrald Ja'Ciel, Leonardo LiPomi, Rachel Tschari, Amanda Vink, Emma Tryon, Zoe D. Kiriazis, Matt Rittler, Jessica K. Rasp, Renee Ronan, Tara Potzler, Dawn Greene, Summer Harris, Rachel Wach and other people I worked with this year and idiotically left off this list.

Contents

Afterlife and Ghosts

Introduction

he writings of William Shakespeare have a certain supernatural aura about them. They are timeless, immortal, definitive, like a sacred scripture. His poetry reaches angelic heights and demonic depths. He's even got that "thee" and "thou" authority that can make him sound like God. His works have been referred to as "secular scripture," and poet Ted Hughes wrote that Shakespeare's canon is the emergence of modernity from medievalism, "modern England's creation story, our sacred book, closer to us than the Bible."[1]

There's a myth that he never changed a word after writing it, that his works are a product of semi-divine inspiration. The term "bardolatry" describes someone who idolizes Shakespeare as the perfect mind. It's been said that he formulated every plot that could be told. The title of literary critic Harold Bloom's magnum opus on Shakespeare gives him credit for no less than "The Invention of the Human."

Scholars have debated for centuries about what mere mortal could have spontaneously generated all this perfection. Did the small-town glove-maker's son really know all this stuff? Or was it some educated noble hiding behind a second-rate actor? I don't know or care in the slightest "who *wrote* Shakespeare's plays." My interest is in "who *heard and understood* Shakespeare's plays." How much did *they* know? What was the common knowledge of the time, the cultural assumptions everyone took for granted to the point that they did not need to be explained? The inside jokes that would have been ruined by exposition? I'm particularly interested in folk beliefs about the supernatural and rituals intended to communicate with unseen powers.

"Supernatural" in the title of this book is meant in a couple of different ways. The obvious meaning is the paranormal panorama of fairies, ghosts and witches, familiar folklore beings that pop up in Shakespeare's plays. In Reginald Scot's 1584 *Discoverie of Witchcraft*, he wrote:

> *Our mothers' maids have so frayed us with Bull-beggars, Spirits,*
> *Witches, Urchins, Elves, Hags, Faeries, Satyrs, Pans, Faunes, Sylvens,*
> *Kit-with-the-Canstick, Tritons, Centaurs, Gyants, Impes, Calcars,*
> *Conjurors, Nymphs, Changelings, Incubus, Robin Goodfellow, the*
> *Spoorn, the Mare, the Man-in-the-Oak, the Hell-wain [wagon],*
> *the Firedrake, the Puckle, Tom-thombe, Hobgoblin, tom-tumbler,*
> *Boneless, and other such Bugs, that we are afraid of our shadow.* [sic]

This is only a partial inventory. From the distance of history we could add "kings and queens" to this list, since they were believed to possess certain magical powers of healing and control over weather. Sure, the royalty physically existed, but so did the women who were called "witches."

A coronation ritual could imbue someone with supernatural energy. One minute you're drinking with your pal Hal, and the next a priest says some words and puts a gold crown, like a halo, around his head and he's Henry V. You've joked with him in darkened taverns, but now when he moves his lips, thousands of Englishmen obediently march themselves into a meat-grinder to invade France.

"Nature" as we know it today was *super*natural in the ancient world, created and constantly tinkered with by God or gods. The whole idea of a sun-centered universe turning like clockwork and rotating cyclical seasons was just a rumor when Shakespeare lived and wrote. In *Romeo and Juliet*, Juliet speaks of the sun being drawn around the Earth by a chariot:

> *Gallop apace, you fiery-footed steeds,*
> *Towards Phoebus' lodging. Such a waggoner*
> *As Phaeton would whip you to the west*
> *And bring in cloudy night immediately.* (R&J III.ii)

Rosalind in *As You Like It* says "*The poor world is almost six thousand years old,*" (AYL IV.i) based on a medieval reckoning that the Biblical creation story took place in 4004 BCE.

Like his contemporaries, Shakespeare's idea of a "natural habitat" for humanity was not Earth, but Eden, a paradise of ease and equality. He considered the world as he knew it to be a supernaturally cursed obstacle course, a grim arena for testing souls, some of which could escape into an otherworldly paradise after death, although Shakespeare himself was very pessimistic about this prospect. When his ghosts and characters talk about the afterlife they usually speak of a punishing Purgatory.

Shakespeare's plays contain many references to folk rituals intended to incite changes of season. Religion scholars call this "Sympathetic Magic," like dancing in a circle to signal to the superpowers that it's time to turn the wheel of the year. That he never fully explains these rituals or what they're meant to accomplish is a sign that his audience already knew them well. When a young lady in *Midsummer Night's Dream* calls her rival *"thou painted Maypole"* or when the duke discovers four sleeping teenagers on the edge of the forest and guesses they've been observing *"the Rite of May,"* there is no explanation of this object or ritual, or what they have to do with growing enough food to keep a community alive. The original audience already knew that dancing around a maypole and getting frisky in the woods was humanity's way of reminding unseen powers to usher in spring fertility.

"Supernatural" in this book also refers to folk beliefs that certain actions can influence the future, what we might call "superstition," and that certain specialists can contact the spirit world to learn about what's coming.

> *Look how the world's poor people are amazed*
> *At apparitions, signs, and prodigies,*
> *Whereon with fearful eyes they long have gazed,*
> *Infusing them with dreadful prophecies.* (V&A 925-928)

These lines seem at first to say that the lower classes are easily duped by superstition and astrology, but actually say that all people are unfortunate to obey these signs–or disobey them. In Shakespeare's world, the predictions of witches and soothsayers always turn out to be correct. And shooting stars and tempests and apparitions are warnings to be ignored at great peril. "Folk belief" is not just for the illiterate peasants—nobles and royals pay attention to them too.

In our desire to remake Shakespeare in our own image as a "modern" man, we might want to see him debunk magical thinking. He doesn't, first of all, because magic makes for a better story. Second, because of his audience. Yes, there were a few renaissance readers, but the majority of the people in the crowd were still medieval (defiantly medieval and resentful of the new Renaissance intellectual globalism, that was selling out the old farm and village life. I think our current political climate allows us to understand this pretty well).

We might imagine that Shakespeare would confine magical thinking to his light comedies and long-ago fairy tales, but this is also untrue. Linda Woodbridge writes, "Despite the common assumption that Shakespearean comedy deals in unreal and fantastical worlds, it is interesting that overt magic and supernatural beings occur in only about a quarter of Shakespeare's comedies, while they appear in 60 percent of his history plays and 60 percent of his tragedies."[2] Magic is often strangely absent in his comedies. Magic doesn't show up in *Love's Labour's Lost* to suspend the ladies' disbelief; it doesn't show up to make *All's Well That Ends Well* end well.

After Shakespeare died, his rival contemporary playwright Ben Jonson snarled, "I remember the players have often mentioned it as an honor to Shakespeare that in his writing, whatever he penned, he never blotted out a line. My answer hath been, 'Would he had blotted a thousand.'"[3] The myth of Shakespeare's divine inspiration had already taken hold, which is silly because he didn't even publish definitive versions of his scripts during his lifetime. The manuscripts we have now are pieced together from variant transcripts that circulated after his death. Some are like "bootleg" concert recordings—someone in the audience wrote down the lines of a play and sold copies of it!

There is no "perfect" manuscript of *Hamlet*, for example. Three different versions were floating around, and editors have bickered for four hundred years over how to assemble a single master script. One of them says:

> *To be, or not to be, aye there's the point.*
> *To die, to sleep, is that all? Aye all:*
> *No, to sleep, to dream, aye marry there it goes.*

Macbeth is Shakespeare's shortest tragedy, but some scholars argue that the script we have was edited down from its full length to make room for musical numbers that seem to have been copied out of *another* play, and were then removed without restoring whatever the deleted scenes had been.[4]

Jonson's response to the myth that Shakespeare never blotted a line was that he should have crossed out a thousand of them. Any modern playwrighting teacher would agree: Shakespeare's plays are over-written and should be sharpened by some serious editing. But we who experience the works on stage or film don't need to worry about that because directors (almost) always cut out about a third of the script before starting rehearsals. You'll know when they didn't–*Hamlet* will be four hours long, as it was in Kenneth Branagh's 1996 film. But generally, Shakespeare's plays keep getting better as directors diligently carve and shape them down. Branagh cut more than half of *Love's Labour's Lost* and it was better than the original. Directors keep the "greatest hits" of the script, the memorable lines and scenes, but often eliminate side characters and whole side plots.

We don't possess "perfect" versions of Shakespeare's plays. The serious scholars know it, but they're in no hurry to leap up and shout it to the masses because their jobs depend on a public belief that every word was written down by Shakespeare himself, and that every word is intentional (or even *un*-intentional, a glimpse into Shakespeare's subconscious!). Every year, professors and scholars publish heaps of essays, articles, and books examining newly discovered patterns in the words of the plays, sometimes balancing a giant thesis on a single line.

The scholar Northrop Frye felt secure enough in his position to write: "His plays bring us close to the oral tradition, with its shifting and kaleidoscopic variants, its migrating themes and motifs, its tolerance of interpolation, its detachment from the printed ideal of an established text."[5] No pure "perfect" specimen of a Shakespeare script seems to exist, and if we possess numerous drafts of something, we must conclude that the writing process was organic, not supernatural.

Shakespearean English

amille Paglia writes: "The sixteenth century transformed Middle English into modern English. Grammar was up for grabs. People made up vocabulary and syntax as they went along… Shakespearean language is a bizarre super-tongue; alien and plastic; twisting, turning, and forever escaping. It is untranslatable, since it knocks Anglo-Saxon root words against Norman and Greco-Roman importations sweetly or harshly, kicking us up and down rhetorical levels with witty abruptness. No one in real life ever spoke like Shakespeare's characters."[6]

"Shakespearean English" is the bane of high school and college students assigned to read *Romeo and Juliet*. How can you get into the emotional flow of the story when you've got to translate most of the lines? Even the famous *"wherefore are thou Romeo?"* is a stumbling block: Juliet is not asking *where* he is but *why* his name is Romeo! The "thees" and "thous" are a bother, and readers probably don't even notice that Juliet blandly calls him "you" until flights of romance elevate her speech into poetry. Shakespeare's characters don't speak "Shakespearean English" all the time, only when they think they're saying something really important.

Shakespeare often wrote in a verse pattern called iambic pentameter: "pentameter" meaning ten syllables, "iambic" meaning an alternation of stresses, like saying "I *am*, I *am*, I *am*, I *am*, I *am*," sometimes arranged in rhyming pairs like "Two *house*holds, *both* a*like* in *dig*nity, / In *fair* Verona, *where* we *lay* our *scene."* But even this pattern can be obscured by words with an unclear number of syllables: *"For never was a story of more woe / Than this of Juliet and her Romeo."* In this last line, one or the other of the tragic lovers has a two-syllable name–Julyet or Romyo–but which is it?[7] Of course a modern actor doesn't have to make this decision, since they're instructed to break up Shakespearean verse to make it sound more "natural" (although clearly William Shakespeare tore out his hair struggling to make his verse sound *un*-natural, or *super*-natural). And then there are all those Shakespearean characters, generally of the lower social classes, whose informal speech is not constrained by verse at all.

So now suppose some bedraggled high school student is assigned to read *Romeo and Juliet*, but instead watches a video of it. Ahhhh, what a relief! The story makes sense! You can figure out what they're trying to say! This is because Shakespeare's writing was not *meant* to be read on a page. Other writers in his day published their scripts to be studied by the folks at home, but Shakespeare did not; his words were meant to be heard while watching performers move on a stage. And a good number of the peasants who paid a penny to see the original performances understood little more than a modern high school sophomore, but they could still enjoy the story as though it were a dance piece: two teens get together but keep getting pulled apart, his friend dies, her cousin dies, everybody dies, the end. Or not quite… Original productions would conclude with the bloody dead lovers leaping back onto the stage to close the evening with a lively folk dance.

Prince Hamlet, while directing some actors for a performance, mentions *"the groundlings, who, for the most part, are capable of nothing but inexplicable dumb shows and noise."* (HAM III.ii) By *"groundlings,"* Shakespeare meant the people in what we today would call "the pit"— the best spots at a rock concert! But in Shakespeare's time, the best spots were elevated box seats, where the elite could experience the event without having to rub elbows with the sweaty peasants in general admission. *"Groundlings"* was actually a polite word--they were more commonly known as the "Penny Stinkers" or just "Stinkards." By *"dumb shows,"* Shakespeare means pantomime. He understood that the peasants would not understand his elevated language but could still get a good show out of it. *Hamlet* is a perfect example; the basic plot would make sense even without understanding a word.[8]

The 1500s were a turbulent time for language in Europe. The only real stronghold of education and literacy was the Roman Catholic Church, which conducted its business and services in Latin. Meanwhile the peasantry of European nations spoke local bastardized versions of Latin that we now call Romance Languages: Spanish, French, Italian, etc., or (in those places that the Roman Empire had failed to conquer) Germanic languages. English was a crazy mixed-up mutt combining elements of German, Latin, various indigenous British languages decorated with fancy bits of Greek. From these languages it inherited not only words but grammatical rules, which is why English today is one of the hardest languages to learn, even for people who grow up surrounded by the English language.

The Protestant Reformation unleashed many pent up frustrations in Europe, one of which was that Catholic scripture and ritual, all in Latin, did not allow local peasantries to make up their own minds about how to attain salvation. In the times of Henry VIII, Queen Elizabeth, and King James, there was a strong interest in making scripture and ritual accessible in the English language. And by historical coincidence, in the midst of all this, there is the sudden birth of what we now call "Mass Media" and "Information Technology:" the printing press! Instead of a book being hand-copied by monks and costing the equivalent of a Ferrari, pamphlets (like magazines or blog posts) could be run off in the thousands and purchased for a penny.

Then in 1604, King James launched the massive project of producing an English translation of the entire Bible, to be mass-produced and used all over England. But for this to be accomplished, the English language itself had to be standardized with a unified set of grammatical rules. And in yet another historical coincidence, Shakespeare's plays were being written at this same time, so Shakespeare sounds Biblical (and for those of us who read the Bible in modern translations, Shakespeare can sound even *older* than the Bible[9]). When Shakespeare wrote, the letters "J" and "V" were brand new! There were only 24 letters in the Elizabethan English alphabet; "U" and "V" were the same letter, as were "I" and "J," and the letter "Y" could be used as shorthand for "Th," as in "ye."

Here's a famous passage from the 1623 folio version of *Romeo and Juliet*, with "U" and "V" often reversed, no letter "J," even the word "sun" spelled two different ways:

He ieasts at Scarres that neuer felt a wound,
But soft, what light through yonder window breaks?
It is the East, and Iuliet is the Sunne,
Arise faire Sun and kill the enuious Moone...
See how she leanes her cheeke vpon her hand.
O that I were a Gloue vpon that hand,
That I might touch that cheeke. (R&J II.ii, "ieasts" is "jests," jokes)

As English emerged from under the shadow of Latin as a language of intellectual exploration and sacred scripture, there was an interest among the elite in seeing what this ambitious, young bastard language could do. Renaissance literary and artsy types developed an appetite for novel "new" words, like the Medieval elite appetite for foreign spices. William Shakespeare capitalized on this, peppering his writings with zesty imports like "bandit," "critic," "lonely," "addiction," "assassination," "lackluster"... well it sounds lackluster now, but at the time these words were new to the English language—he "bedazzled" it. He introduced new words in poetic repetitions, following them with a parallel word or sentence to explain the meaning. The poet Ted Hughes calls it a "prodigiously virtuoso pidgin. It never loses the extempore, unpredictable quality of something being put together, out of everything within reach, in an emergency."[10] His writings demonstrate a vocabulary of about 29,000 words,[11] whereas a modern college graduate may know 3,000-4,000 words (or in the U.S., maybe 200 words and 400 emojis, and oddly enough, that's a source of national pride).

There's an irony that Shakespeare played such a prominent role in elevating the English language to the point where it has eclipsed Greek and Latin as the language of elite discourse. And yet now "Shakespearean English" has become an elite foreign language that high school students need to translate or read summaries of...or just watch the movie.[12]

In 1853, an exasperated scholar wrote:

Shakespeare is the great poet he is from his skill in discerning and firmly conceiving an excellent action, from his power of intensely feeling a situation, of intimately associating himself with a character; not from his gift of expression, which rather even leads him astray, degenerating sometimes into a fondness for curiosity of expression, into an irritability of fancy, which seems to make it impossible for him to say a thing plainly, even when the press of the action demands the most direct language... Shakespeare appears in his language to have tried all styles except that of simplicity.[13]

Yes, Shakespeare could learn a lot from Hemingway. But he'd lose something, too. Shakespeare's enduring power is not just in his plots (most of which were borrowed from other writers anyway), but in wrapping these stories and characters in poetry. Some might find Hamlet's speech patterns to be an obstacle to our understanding, and certainly his monologues slow down what could have been a lightning fast stunt show, but the Shakespearean poetry of *Hamlet* does more than just hold up a mirror to nature, it gives us a glimpse into the *super*-nature of the soul.

Stage Magic

Pardon, gentles all,
The flat unraised spirits that hath dar'd
On this unworthy scaffold to bring forth
So great an object. Can this cockpit hold
The vasty fields of France? Or may we cram
Within this wooden O the very casques
That did affright the air at Agincourt?
...And let us, ciphers to this great accompt,
On your imaginary forces work...
Think, when we talk of horses, that you see them
Printing their proud hoofs i' th' receiving earth;
For 'tis your thoughts that now must deck our kings,
Carry them here and there, jumping o'er times,
Turning th' accomplishment of many years
Into an hour-glass; for the which supply,
Admit me Chorus to this history. (H5 I.i)

heater requires a suspension of disbelief. You don't have to *believe* the stage is the battlefield of Agincourt, but you've got to silence that inner voice that keeps telling you it's not. It's sort of like turning off your phone before the show starts: "brain, mute all updates of how implausible this is." Often there's some plot point right at the base of the structure, something not credible, and if you pull out the pin the whole plot would

collapse: Identical twins can't be male and female! There's no way he thinks she's a boy! That's not a real lion! Or maybe it is! Not to mention the little things: They didn't speak English in Verona!

Shakespeare's characters also suspend their disbelief in ways that can try *our* suspension of disbelief. The restrictive father has a blind spot big enough for his daughter and her unapproved wooer to waltz right through it. The jealous husband will accept *anything* that confirms his suspicions, but he's deaf to anything that would disprove them. Shakespeare's characters have no sense of smell: if the man she's dancing with wears a mask, she can't distinguish her lover from some other guy. Or perhaps Shakespearean masks also change a person's musk.

Suspension of disbelief is likewise an essential element of religious ritual. If someone in the back of the church shouts, "That's not *really* blood in that chalice," or "Maybe he was only *pretending* to be dead when they laid him in the tomb," it's obvious they've come to the wrong place. When you're walking out of a musical and someone snarls, "In real life people don't burst into song," they've come to the wrong show and should have bought a bus ticket to eavesdrop on some downtrodden couple arguing about their household budget and other dreary logistics of real life.

We go to the theater to watch people play make believe, but it doesn't work unless *we play along* and let ourselves be swept up in the magic. The term "suspension of disbelief" is architectural, as if we're holding up the roof or girding some imaginary bridge for characters to walk across. In ritual terms, we could also call it a "sacrifice of disbelief." Our nit-picking rationality is a gift we (temporarily) lay on the altar of theater. It's the cost of admission into the magical ritual that can transform us. We pay this cost as individuals, and we are initiated into a congregation, "the audience," with a very important role in the show.

The performers *feel* us, and it fuels their performance. Backstage in the dressing rooms, actors grade the audience: "We had a really good audience tonight" is determined by audience energy more than by size. "They were right there *with* us." *Together* we created the illusion that we *really were* in an ancient Athenian forest. Or the performers warn each other: "Before you go on stage, it's a dull audience tonight so you'll need to expend more energy." The interplay between audience and performers creates a transformative alchemy or chemistry that theater people call "magic." And it *is* magic in the sense of something scientists haven't charted yet. This magic is the source of Puritan hostility against the theater, in both Shakespeare's time and our own.

After a powerful theatrical performance, people can walk out glowing, feeling fortified and healed. The technical term for this is "catharsis," a release of repressed emotional energy, and it can be as powerful as a massage or a visit with the chiropractor, albeit without being physically touched. But this obviously won't happen to the person at the musical who tenses up as each a song starts. The audience can't be "touched" unless they choose to expose their emotions.

Theater as Ritual

ir James Frazer wrote: "Myth changes while custom remains constant; men continue to do what their fathers did before them, though the reasons on which their fathers acted have been long forgotten. The history of religion is a long attempt to reconcile old custom with new reason, to find a sound theory for an absurd practice."[14]

Theater was born of ritual. "Ritual" is the enaction of a programmed sequence of words and actions intended to invite supernatural forces to stabilize the rhythm of time by creating a connection with the past and future. Here's an easy example: If you go to church, you witness basically the same ritual every week and annual holiday (time marches consistently) and it's likely the same ritual that your great-grandmother attended, and your great grand-daughter will attend (so symbolically, past and future generations are there *with* you). This can make rituals feel dull, just "going through the motions," but it's also what gives them their power. If you've ever been to a church service and if you've ever attended a production of *Hamlet,* it should be easy to see the connection: A priest can add nuance to the Eucharist and an actor can add nuance to Hamlet, but we know how the story's going to end. Not to spoil the surprise, but the Prince dies.

Ritual begins with folk pageants designed to magically influence changes of season. Scholars call this "Sympathetic Magic": If I light this bonfire the night before the summer solstice, then the sun will sympathetically rise and shine through the longest day of the year. Today we live in a clockwork universe where cosmic events and seasonal cycles run on time and remind us of what we're supposed to be doing.

But our primitive ancestors believed that changes of time and tide and celestial signs were handled manually by gods who needed humans to remind them when to turn the sun, send the rains, open the blossoms one by one, etc.

In the modern industrial world, many of us have career routines that are unaffected by seasonal changes. Our livelihood (how we get our food) slogs on regardless of winter or spring, and food availability is also unchanged–we can buy strawberries all year 'round, and eating an egg on Easter Sunday is no big deal. The weather is always the same on the Internet (perpetual pink sunset with storm-clouds on the horizon), and changes in "climate" are political puppet shows manipulated by unseen plutocrats driven by super-appetite, ironically similar to Greek gods. Meanwhile, somewhere in the background, this arrangement is causing a climate disaster and seasons are getting wacky. Our escapism (*from* nature) is actually changing the climate—but then we can plug in and hide from that on the Web. It can be hard for us to understand an agricultural life in which work and food availability were controlled by seasons. Perhaps the nearest we can get to this is an annual yearning to watch *It's a Wonderful Life* in winter, and then in spring to re-watch whatever old romantic comedy film we loved the most when we were thirteen.

The most important seasonal cycle in human life is the annual change from winter sterility to spring fertility, and back again. Rituals to encourage the coming of spring tend to involve fruitfulness: human conception and the celebration of natural abundance–sex and sugar. Rituals of bracing for winter tend to be dour: the contemplation of human mortality (since not everyone would survive until next spring) and repentance (sadness and sacrifice), sweetened a bit by the understanding that, if we do our penance correctly, sex and sugar will return. In theatrical terms we would classify these rituals by their Greek names: Comedy and Tragedy. The Greeks didn't invent them. We give "the Greeks" credit for inventing *everything* because they were white, but they really stole their best ideas from Iraq, Egypt, Turkey and Africa. The Greeks *named* Comedy and Tragedy, *classified* them and *inscribed* some scripts, but these same basic rituals could be found anywhere in the world.

An overly ambitious man breaks the chain of law or succession, strives to gain immortality by becoming a legendary king or hero, then gets crushed in the gears of his own selfish devices. That's a Tragedy, a winter ritual, a reminder that we're all going to die but the sun will keep rising and setting, so it's best to go with the flow. Two young (human) lovebirds want to mate, they flap their wings and tweet at each other, but some manifestation of Old Man Winter keeps pushing them apart. Then they go over his head and hatch some babies. That's a Comedy, a spring ritual, a reminder that life will find a way to go on. These basic narratives can be conveyed in any number of ways: dance, song, puppets, masks, improvised or scripted dialogue. And the names and details can be filled in with local heroes or legends: Oedipus, Macbeth, Coyote, etc.

Ritual personae are archetypes: the man whose ambition brings winter, the teenagers whose love brings spring, etc. The playwright and performers' task is to turn these archetypes into individuals, to "flesh them out" with personal histories and motivations and dreams. The hope is that the audience will identify with these individuals, and by extension, with the archetypes, thereby becoming participants in the ritual. If we emotionally hitchhike on Macbeth's quest, then the sacrifice of his ambition becomes a penance for our own. If we attend *Much Ado About Nothing* with our spouse, then Beatrice and Benedick's mating dance becomes our foreplay and we're expected to go home and conceive vivaciously talkative children.

Most of Shakespeare's plots come from histories (his royalty plays) or other plays and stories descended from old wives' tales and ultimately seasonal rituals. This would be like inheriting a fully choreographed mime routine and then adding dialogue. "Shakespeare's method was not to change implausible story material, but to invent characters and motives which would make it more acceptable and credible, moment by moment, on the stage."[15] Shakespeare's particular ability to give psychological and emotional interiority to these pre-programmed automatons is the reason for his enduring success: *Othello* is a car-crash in slow motion, but four hundred years later we *still* can't look away. Shakespeare makes us care about the characters, even the evil clown Iago who grabs the steering wheel.

Festivity comes from a seasonal surplus, a surplus of wealth/food (like the need to finish off winter supplies before Lent) and surplus energy (like the restlessness of an indoor winter being released in the spring). Surplus is celebrated as a sign that the community can accomplish more than bare survival, and times of revelry tend to involve more food and less sexual restriction than usual. In Shakespeare's time this was generally celebrated with a limited period of misrule. In festival time, everything is distended;

limits are tested, and often people are reminded of what's good about restriction (by hangover, or an unplanned pregnancy). But this pushing of limits can also reveal which restrictions are needlessly strict or outdated, and lead to a reexamination of regulations. Many of Shakespeare's comedies begin with an outdated restriction that's getting in the way and must be relaxed or revoked.

William Shakespeare the businessman wrote plays that could be put on during any season. The title of *Twelfth Night* refers specifically to a Christmas festival, but the staging can be springtime and the story can be enjoyed at any time of year. And yet there is a lurking festivity that animates the play with gender-bending, drunken pranks and scapegoating–elements of the Twelfth Night holiday. The festive spirit elevates the useless alcoholic Toby Belch into a mastermind conspirator. It possesses Olivia; we know from the start that the woman who mourns her brother and father will find a man, but it's a shock at the end when she marries a guy she's only met five minutes earlier. She hasn't become stupid; she is possessed by the spirit of festivity. This spectre of festivity haunts the uptight puritan Malvolio, turning him into a clown-puppet and then beating him. In this story the spirit is playful and generally benevolent (except toward Malvolio who leaves the stage cursing and vowing revenge). But the spirit will return, charged with malice, in *Othello*, and festive pranks will be deadly.

Festivity stalks Shakespeare's characters, and the plots he chose to write can be likened to elaborate mazes leading to mass-murder or mass-marriage. His comic lovers seek the festivity of fertility and conception, Hamlet seeks a macabre day-of-the-dead, but other characters are led blind into it. C.L. Barber writes that Shakespeare steers his characters into festivity's path: "If they do not seek holiday it happens to them."[16] So in this book we'll be paying close attention to when a character is unknowingly manipulated into enacting a role from a holiday pageant.

Besides seasonal festivals, ritual is also about safeguarding the steady succession of generations: the wisdom of age must guide the energy of youth and the promise of babies to ensure the survival of the family line. Many of Shakespeare's romantic comedies involve a struggle with parents and/or laws (from dead ancestors) which must be resolved before conception can be blessed. Shakespeare generally heightens the conflict by disposing of the mother beforehand since she might be more likely to speak for compromise, and by making the hero and/or heroine an only child. Many of the plays begin with a father commanding his only son or daughter *not* to marry so-and-so. And then the kids work it out. Linda Woodbridge observes that Shakespearean tragedies also tend to feature a youthful rebellion against the older generation, but it goes too far and brings destruction. *King Lear, Macbeth,* and *Hamlet* all have this in common, and *Othello* and *Romeo and Juliet* are variations of it.

The generational struggle in Shakespeare's plays also links with seasonal rituals of tug-of-war between old winter and young summer. Comedies end with a victory for springtime fertility, tragedies feature a (temporary) victory of winter sterility. In other plays, the older generation is represented by law: the wisdom of dead ancestors. Tragedies feature a rigid legalism that must break the criminal hero so that law and cultural continuity can survive. In comedies the old law is firm at the beginning, but then in the last five minutes, some authority figure suddenly decides it can be bent (*Comedy of Errors, Midsummer Night's Dream,* and *Measure for Measure* all begin with an inflexible law, and end with a somewhat arbitrary decision not to enforce it; or we could say they end with the authority figure suddenly becoming possessed by festivity). *"Young blood doth not obey an old decree."* (LLL IV.iii)

Like rural fertility ritual, professional theater was highly sexualized. Shakespearean comedy is foreplay and almost always ends with the characters exiting the stage toward wedding-and-bedding. Original productions of Shakespearean tragedies would generally end with the characters jumping onto the stage for a festive and erotic dance, like the conclusion of "Pyramus and Thisbe" in *Midsummer Night's Dream.* The theater was a popular place for prostitutes to pick up their next trick, sometimes dressed as boys to capitalize on a transvestite comedy. Urban theaters were no less popular than brothels as targets for Puritan resentment, as an angry Christian ranted in 1583:

> Mark the flocking and running to Theatres and Curtains,
> daily and hourly, night and day, time and tide, to see Plays and
> Interludes; where such wanton gestures, such bawdy speeches,
> such laughing and fleering, such kissing and bussing, such
> clipping and culling, such winking and glancing of wanton
> eyes, and the like, is used, as is wonderful to behold. Then, these
> goodly Pageants being done, every mate sorts to his mate, every

one brings another homeward of their way very friendly, and in their secret conclaves (covertly) they play the Sodomites, or worse. And these be the fruits of Plays and Interludes for the most part. And whereas you say there are good Examples to be learned in them, truly so there are: if you will learn falsehood; if you will learn cozenage; if you will learn to deceive; if you will learn to play the hypocrite, to cog, lie, [and] become a Bawd, unclean, and to devirginate Maids, to deflower honest Wives: If you will learn to murder, slay, kill, pick, steal, rob, and rove... If you will learn to play the Whoremaster, the Glutton, Drunkard, or Incestuous person: If you will learn to become proud, haughty, and arrogant; and, finally, if you will learn to contemn God and all his laws, to care neither for heaven nor hell, and to commit all kind of sin and mischief, you need to go to no other school, for all these good examples may you see painted before your eyes in Interludes and Plays.[17]

Before we jump to theater's defense, we should note that Shakespeare's characters do all these things and more. And yet I would argue that it was not so much the sensationalism of theater that drew Puritan rage, but the ritualism, particularly the ritualistic belief that the workings of the universe can be influenced by willful human actions.

Christian ritual affirms that problems will be solved, the humble will be exalted, and the exalted will be humbled, *after death*. But theater affirms that these things can happen in life through human ingenuity and trickery, sometimes assisted by pagan gods. God and Jesus never solve anybody's problems in Shakespeare's plays, but Greco-Roman deities appear in several (Juno, Ceres and Iris in *The Tempest*, Hymen in *As You Like It* and *Two Noble Kinsmen*, Diana in *Pericles*, Jupiter in *Cymbeline*). And then there's a whole host of Shakespeare's supernatural agents: the ghosts, fairies, witches and soothsayers whose predictions always come true.

Tragedy

he word "Tragedy" comes from the Greek *tragos*, the goat that was sacrificed or driven away to cleanse the human community–what we might call the "scapegoat." Greek Tragedies involved a character, generally driven by pride, who committed some crime. The gods would punish this crime with blight, the human community would face the prospect of starvation, and then the death of the criminal would restore order. The audience participated by vicariously enjoying the central character's ambitious rise, then resenting their power, and finally cheering when they were torn apart. In this way the audience purged their own ambition and reaffirmed their devotion to their humdrum routine and social class.

Shakespeare's tragedies are named after individuals, like *Hamlet, King Lear, Macbeth, Othello*, etc., while his comedies have more general names like *Much Ado About Nothing, As You Like It, All's Well That Ends Well*. Every individual life will end while life, in general, will go on. We all know, walking into a tragedy, that the hero will be broken. Shakespeare adds to this by giving his tragic heroes an interiority. We see (and hear) their insides, and once they've been hollowed out they're killed. It's highly ritualistic, like a vivisection culminating in a sacrifice. The Globe Theatre was a bloody temple, its stage an altar.

"A sad tale's best for winter," (WT II.i) says a boy in *Winter's Tale*, and then he dies of a broken heart. The bleak sterility of winter was long considered a punishment for human ambition (in Eden) or for rigid legalism (in the Greek myth of Hades and Persephone). In Shakespeare's universe, winter is a punishment for bad leadership. Macbeth's ambition

throws Scotland into a long dark night, Lear's folly causes a storm in Britain, Leontes' insane jealousy establishes the climate for *The Winter's Tale*. And these plays all end with the coming of spring.

"Nowadays," wrote an unhappy theater critic in 1606, "they put at the end of every Tragedy (as poison into meat) a comedy or jig." A tragedy must end with a return of fertility, and also a restoration of order. If a character's ambition toward social mobility or revenge threatens to throw the world into chaos, there must be some reminder at the end that life will go on, and human relations will still be structured. *Hamlet*, for example, ends with the coming of Fortinbras. He seems to come out of nowhere, but actually it's been established that his father was killed by Hamlet's father, which makes him, in a sense, another Hamlet. But unlike the sarcastic and bipolar prince of Denmark, the dull, marching Fortinbras represents stability in leadership. Shakespeare's tragedies follow dreamers and idealists, but end with political realists in control.

Comedy

he word "Comedy" comes from the Greek word for "village singing," and celebrates the survival of community. In Shakespeare's time, the word "Comedy" was interchangeable with "Comonty," for the commoners. While tragedy focuses on the doomed individual, comedy focuses on the continuity of community. This is why Shakespeare's comedies are not named after their main characters.[18] We may think a Shakespearean comedy is all about a pair of lovers going off to make a baby, but the ritual of comedy only works if the *community* is healed at the end.

"For revels, dances, masks, and merry hours, / Forerun fair Love, strewing her way with flowers." (LLL IV.iii) A comedy has three parts corresponding to the coming of spring. The story begins with a rigid law or cold parent obstructing the release of youthful energy. Then comes a carnivalesque period when pent-up energy distorts itself in tricks, disguises, partner-swapping, gender-bending. And finally, the energy is reintegrated into community through a ritual—a wedding blessed by the parents, the laws, the community. This is when the girls change out of their boy-clothes and become Moms.

The most distinctive trait of the stage comedy is its ending: an affirmation that problems can be solved and life will continue. Often in Shakespeare's comedies, all is lost and hopeless until the last five minutes, when everything is suddenly resolved: the irrational law is lifted, the obstacle-father changes his mind or gets pushed out of the way, Benedick stops Beatrice's insults with a kiss, etc. And this ending retroactively corrects the gloom that has hung over the characters from the start. The reverse is true as well: *Romeo and Juliet* rolls along like a comedy until the last five minutes. In 1681, Nahum Tate wrote an alternate "happy" ending to *King Lear*, where Edgar and Cordelia marry, and this was the more popular version of the play for almost 150 years, until 1823 when a depressive, drug-addled actor demanded to play the original tragic ending. Audiences hated it, but the tragic ending eventually caught on.

Comedy does not necessarily entail laughter—plenty of Shakespeare's comedies aren't funny. *Measure for Measure* has fewer punchlines than *Othello*. The comic structure does *enable* laughter by letting us know that the characters are protected from serious harm. And laughing along with a comedy heightens our sense of connection: by laughing we symbolically become wedding guests, sharing in the ritual. Laughter can also be a form of sacrifice and communion, to lambaste a constipated authority figure. I don't personally laugh at Shylock in *Merchant of Venice*, but refusing to laugh at him turns the comedy into a tragedy. The play is designed so that our laughter tears him to pieces and we feast on his figurative dismemberment.

The word "humour" comes from chemicals, sometimes noxious, that build up in the human body. And unsurprisingly "humor" is often associated with bodily secretions (urine and feces), sounds (flatulence) and sexual effluvia—natural lubrications and emissions. "Potty humor." I think that "humor" still comes from a sort of bile, something toxic that builds up in the body seeking release. A laugh, like a belch or gas, is something that must come out and then we feel healthier. But like these other involuntary noises, a laugh can cause some insult or embarrassment in certain social settings. So, bawdy humorous displays create a safe space for this. William Shakespeare loved dirty jokes. We no longer recognize many of his puns and don't look for them because his plays have become a sort of sacred scripture, but they pop up here and there if we're paying attention.

Shakespeare's comedy is never satirical. He never calls the emperor naked, never goes hacking at the roots of the patriarchal or hierarchical structure. Even his royalty plays are remarkably apolitical. He wrote in a time of government censorship, under the Orwellian-sounding "Revels Office," where a bureaucratic "Master of Revels" checked scripts for subversive content before they could be played on city stages. In place of satire, Shakespeare favored *Saturnalia*, temporary festive role-reversals where master and servant trade hats, a duke disguises as a monk, women try on the trousers and do the wooing, clowns instruct kings, the patriarch regresses into a whiny toddler, kids sneak out at night and sleep during the day, the drunkard calls the shots and the sober man is locked in an asylum, etc. But before the curtain closes, the festival of fools must end—the blurry carnival merry-go-round stops spinning and everyone gets back in line, in their own clothes. Or perhaps a more appropriate metaphor would be a ferris wheel which turns a revolution and then rights itself.

Pastoral

hen Polonius introduces the traveling theater troupe in *Hamlet*, he calls them: *"The best actors in the world, either for tragedy, comedy, history, pastoral, pastoral-comical, historical-pastoral, tragical-historical, tragical-comical-historical-pastoral, scene individable, or poem unlimited."* (HAM II.ii) Of the eight theatrical genres he lists, four include "Pastoral." This was a major theatrical trend in Shakespeare's time, a specific type of play with rules and structure like Comedy and Tragedy. A Pastoral play would generally focus on a banished princess who disguises herself as a shepherdess, falls in love with a prince, and then the revelation of her royalty removes all obstacles to their marriage. We may recognize these core conventions from Disney's *Sleeping Beauty* film.

The basic moral of the Pastoral was that urbanization creates problems that can be solved in the countryside or forest. And in Shakespeare's time, when subsistence farmers were losing their lands and being driven to the cruel cities, Pastoral comedies could gently satire urban capitalism (while safely maintaining that royal marriages could fix economic problems). The population shift from country to city was also creating a nostalgia for the simple peasant life: "Under the Stuarts, people set about retrospectively re-creating the myth of 'Merry England' and began to hark back nostalgically to a joyful, festive England in which the morose boredom of Sundays had been a thing unknown."[19] The popularity of Pastoral is likely the reason Shakespeare called one of his Pastoral Comedies *As You Like It* – he knew the plot was in fashion.

Shakespeare's strictest Pastoral is *Winter's Tale*. The banished princess disguised as a shepherd falls in love with the prince, who can't marry her unless she's a princess—and she is! *As You Like It* is more flexible, but basically fits the same pattern. The banished daughter disguises herself as a woodland boy and falls in love with the son of a nobleman. In *Cymbeline*, the king's daughter flees a wicked stepmother, dresses as a boy and reunites with her banished husband. By the time Shakespeare wrote *The Tempest* he was pretty much checking off boxes: Duke's banished daughter, check. Prince, check. Identities revealed and marriage sealed, check.

At times he got more playful, mixing Pastoral conventions with elements of other genres. *A Midsummer Night's Dream* begins with problems of the city which are resolved in the forest. In *All's Well That Ends Well* a jilted bride stalks her husband on a military campaign and uses a disguise to seduce him. It bends all the rules and takes place mostly indoors, but still functions pretty well as Pastoral.

And then there's the case of *King Lear*. Shakespeare took the plot from a Pastoral Comedy in which the banished princess disguises herself as a shepherdess and marries a disguised French King, and they then return from their honeymoon to rescue Lear from his two evil daughters.[20] But Shakespeare steered the story into a ditch of madness and death. I had the good fortune to see an outdoor performance of *King Lear* which was interrupted and called off due to rain twenty minutes before the end (ironic, since a good deal of the play is supposed to take place in a storm). It was quite a different play. Edmund got the queens, Cordelia lived—it was a lot of fun. It should have been called *A Comedy of Errors*. *King Lear* has many of Shakespeare's most darkly comical lines and is certainly funnier than *All's Well* or *Measure for Measure*. I can get through those without smiling once but can never get through *King Lear* without laughing.

Folk Pageantry

hakespeare seldom strictly adheres to the rules of a genre. "To judge...Shakespeare by Aristotle's rule is like trying a man by the Laws of one Country who acted under those of another."[21] His unconventional deviations earned some sneers from more formal writers and critics of his time, but delighted audiences. Sir Philip Sidney complained about "mongrel tragicomedy" in his 1595 *Apology for Poetry*, but it is Shakespeare's genre-bending that makes his characters seem so spontaneous and free, and the corresponding mix of audience reactions is surely a central factor in the longevity of these plays. *Coriolanus* is Shakespeare's most formally correct tragedy, but it's nobody's favorite.

Secular theater and its Classical conventions were relatively new in England when Shakespeare lived. Likewise, the emergence of professional theater was largely a by-product of urbanization (rural folks moving to the city) and the declining power of the Roman Church.

Theatricality had always existed in England, and in the Medieval period there were two main branches of it. The "professional" show was the Catholic Church, whose clergy was made up largely of unmarriageable sons, sons who could not inherit, or sons who weren't interested in women. When we envision the decorations, costumes, pageantry and musicality of the Mass, it doesn't seem like a stretch to imagine the Medieval Church as probably about as gay as the modern theater.[22] The church also sponsored traveling companies to do "Mystery Plays," street spectacles with elaborate sets to give the paupers a glimpse of heaven, hell and purgatory.

The other branch of theatricality was rural folk pageants. For certain holidays, villagers would get together and put on skits. If you've been to a sleep-away camp where they do skits, that's probably a good approximation of it. These could be improvised around a basic plot like an improv comedy show, or be memorized and a little more formal like a church Christmas Pageant—but put on by drunken adults. And in some instances, a particularly entertaining village group could tour other villages during the agricultural off seasons, and maybe even be called to play before royalty. Unlike the Catholic clergy and later the professional theater, these village groups could be a mix of men and women. In *Two Noble Kinsmen*, the folk pageant cannot proceed until it has the required number of female performers. But sometimes for entertainment purposes it was found funnier for women to be played by men in drag.

In *Henry IV, Part I*, two drunken buddies put on a little comedy sketch in a tavern where they take turns playing the king and prince, and an observer laughs, *"He doth it as like one of these harlotry players as ever I see!"* (1H4 II.iv). Satirical nightclub sketch comedy may have been a form of advertising for prostitutes. In *Love's Labour's Lost*, a handful of villagers (teacher, police officer, clown, etc.) present the "Nine Worthies," an improvisational pageant of legendary heroes. In *Midsummer Night's Dream*, some local artisans (tinker, tailor, carpenter, etc.) memorize and rehearse a play to enter a royal talent show. And *Hamlet* features a touring troupe of players who show up at the castle with a menu of available shows they can perform on request.

What Shakespeare's play-within-a-play pageants have in common is that they're highly interactive; the audiences keep heckling the performers, and the performers talk back to them. While on stage, a commoner could publicly admonish a duke or king without penalty. Prince Hamlet, for all his theatricality, is a terrible audience member. He talks through the entire show and keeps fidgeting in his seat. The pageants tend to have classical sources: the "Nine Worthies" are mostly Greek and Roman heroes; "Pyramus and Thisbe" is a story from Ovid's *Metamorphoses*; Julia in *Two Gentlemen of Verona* tells of a folk pageant about Ariadne of Crete.[23] Was this the commoners' way of joking about a classical education? Or perhaps performing Greco-Roman myths was less controversial than playing Biblical stories. Shakespeare concludes these amateur shows with sing-along folk dances which also became a common practice in the professional theater. A 1612 order by Justices of the Peace banned "certayne lewde Jigges songs and daunces...at the'end of everye playe, many tymes causing tumultes and outrages." [sic][24] But the law was not heeded.

Shakespeare threw folk pageantry into the mix of his plays, often on the margins. Serious nobles pursue tragic ambition or comic romance in lofty verse, and then there's some interlude of the commoners giving commentary or pursuing their mundane goals in ordinary English. And we may note that, regardless of whether a play is set in Greece, Rome, Italy or Denmark, the commoners are always *English* commoners. This in itself is a supernatural element of Shakespeare's writing: the deliberate anachronism of putting the "groundlings" of his audience onto the stage. But these intrusions of English amateur folk pageantry into classical structures of Comedy and Tragedy make the plays feel more *natural*, and the settings seem more lived-in.

C.L. Barber writes:

> Shakespeare creates [the sense] of people living in a settled group, where everyone is known and to be lived with, around the clock of the year... The braggart and his quick zani, the pedant, the parasite priest, the rustic clown–the group functions together to present "his lordship's simple neighbors." Through them we feel a world which exists before and after the big moment of the entertainment, and we see the excitement of the smaller people about the big doings.[25]

It's the side characters, the "extras" who keep reminding us that life will go on, which is the point of the whole ritual. The ambitious killer will die, the lovers will wed, and life will continue.

Dramatis Personae

MACBETH:
Tomorrow, and tomorrow, and tomorrow
Creeps in this petty pace from day to day
To the last syllable of recorded time;
And all our yesterdays have lighted fools
The way to dusty death. Out, out, brief candle!
Life's but a walking shadow, a poor player
That struts and frets his hour upon the stage
And then is heard no more. It is a tale
Told by an idiot, full of sound and fury,
Signifying nothing. (MAC V.v)

odern creative writing courses instruct authors to invent a character, think about some need this character has, and then create a situation in which this character can pursue this need. But Shakespeare's plays clearly did not begin this way. He started with a situation (usually borrowed from another writer), like a clockwork machine or labyrinth. *Then* he crafted the characters (again, usually borrowed, but retooled) and developed motivations that would keep them moving through the maze, either to be snapped at a dead end or to be released into marital bliss.

Most of Shakespeare's characters were already famous *before* he wrote the plays, and the audience already knew how the story would end. In modern times, each generation gets a new film of Peter Parker becoming Spider-Man, and even before it's released, we know he'll learn a lesson about power and responsibility, and that the film will make money. Shakespeare did the same thing with Hamlet, except with a twist at the end (he doesn't win the throne). Shakespeare's particular skill was to create the illusion that Hamlet was *steering* the story, but Elsinore was always an elaborate mousetrap. And even centuries later, *Hamlet* always ends the same, with the hero crushed in the gears of this clockwork. But it's also true that the character of Hamlet can still *seem* spontaneous and autonomous.

The great literary critic Harold Bloom's magnum opus of bardolatry was called *Shakespeare: The Invention of the Human.* As a summation of a lifelong exploration of Shakespeare, I think that this title deserves some attention. The "human" as we think of one—an individual with a drive toward social and intellectual betterment—is a fairly new construct. In tribal cultures, the person is a single cell of a tribal organism, which regenerated itself by continuously growing new cells and flaking off old ones. In the ancient Empires, most people were a cog in a sort of machine. Then, with the spread of Christianity, a person became a soul temporarily stranded on an inferior earth struggling back toward the perfected world of paradise. The Catholic era was an intellectual Dark Age, and social elevation existed only in old wives' tales.

The Protestant Reformation challenged Rome's monopolistic control over salvation and introduced an individual responsibility to discern and live the sort of life that could earn salvation. Instead of paying Roman priests for God's forgiveness, each person was encouraged to negotiate an individual contract with God, and if they kept their spiritual end of the deal, they could expect God to look after their worldly welfare. Some of us may recognize this as stale, old-timey parental advice: work hard and say your prayers, and you'll succeed in business and go to heaven. But it was revolutionary news in Shakespeare's day. The "Individual" as a concept could finally be explored. I would not say that Shakespeare *invented* the "Individual," but in his plays we see a vibrant, hungry curiosity about what the "Individual" might be, and in the plays' immediate success we see that audiences wanted this exploration.

Shakespeare also expressed some anxiety about the logical outcome of individualism. Edmund in *King Lear* is a self-made man, a "rugged individual," but his desire for social advancement is toxic. When we think of Shakespeare's great Individuals; Hamlet, Macbeth, Cleopatra, Othello, etc.; we can't help but notice that these are the titles of tragedies.

Shakespeare lived during the Renaissance, a period when Western Europe re-appropriated long-lost Greek and Roman documents (these had been destroyed in the early days of Catholicism, but the Muslims had kept their copies and eventually shared some during the Crusades). Some Greek philosophers had pursued the concept of the Individual: the idea that our responses to new situations should be dictated by personal character suppositions. And Greek theatrical scripts contained stories about individuals either pursuing or fleeing their fixed destiny.

During the Reformation, ideas about fate and astrology, long suppressed by the Catholic Church, were allowed back into the mainstream cultural debate.[26] Shakespeare took a quick look at this and decided to go in another direction. *Romeo and Juliet* begins with *"star-crossed lovers,"* but then Romeo defies the stars and allows his own internal character flaws to cause his downfall. He's astrologically doomed, but helps this along by being impulsive, rash and suicidally over-reactive (he would have killed himself early in the play had not the Friar and Nurse stopped him). This was Shakespeare's answer to the Greek tragedians: *"The fault, dear Brutus, is not in our stars / But in ourselves."* (JC I.ii) In Shakespeare's writing, the future is set but the past is changeable; although each character's end is predetermined by the conventions of comedy or tragedy, the author would retroject internal strengths and flaws to plausibly drive them there.[27] This interiority of character is Shakespeare's most distinctive signature.

In *Twelfth Night*, the butler Malvolio receives a letter (supposedly from the lady he serves) that says:

> *In my stars I am above thee; but be not afraid of greatness. Some are born great, some achieve greatness, and some have greatness thrust upon 'em. Thy Fates open their hands; let thy blood and spirit embrace them; and, to inure thyself to what thou art like to be, cast thy humble slough and appear fresh.* (TN II.v)

He fantasizes about social elevation and recreates himself, but the letter was just a chambermaid's cruel prank and the play ends with him impotently cursing. Shakespeare invites us in on the joke—the Puritan is easily seduced by *"stars"* and *"fates,"* but he can't get away from his own tiresome and stodgy personality. Shakespeare is far more flexible with his young female protagonists, including the chambermaid who pranked Malvolio, who earns marriage to a nobleman!

Janet Spens observes: "Shakespeare's delineation of women is almost entirely from the external point of view. We know Ophelia, Imogen, Cordelia, as we know our intimate friends, perhaps as a man knows the woman he loves, but not as we know ourselves."[28] Shakespeare liked femininity, but not femaleness. "Feminine" is (or at least was) a cultural set of expectations about how a non-man should act. Femaleness is natural, biological: menstruation, pregnancy, childbirth, lactating—all that stuff that Shakespeare found really gross. He enjoyed creating feminine characters to be played by boys, and he often bent the rules of expected "feminine" behavior, to a certain extent. But he clearly found women terrifying.

Shakespearean comic heroines can change themselves in order to seize the reins of destiny...except to the extent that they're destined to get pregnant just after the curtain falls. But from the start of the play, anything goes. We can almost imagine that some of these girls know they're in a comedy play and will be married in five acts, so it's a wild game of musical chairs to see who'll get who. *"Jack shall have Jill,"* Puck says at the end of *Midsummer Night's Dream*, but usually it's Jills who get their Jacks. They also have to shape their Jacks a bit. Modern women might hear time and again that you can't train your man, but Rosalind tutors the hopeless Orlando in *As You Like It*, Portia humbles the frivolous Bassiano in *Merchant of Venice*, and by feigning submission, Kate tames the wild Petruchio in *Taming of the Shrew*.

"Apparel oft proclaims the man," says Polonius in *Hamlet*, and in Shakespeare's world, clothes can literally make a man. *"It is the lesser blot, modesty finds, / Women to change their shapes than men their minds."* (TGV I.iv) Shakespearean heroines will often stalk their prey using disguises, and the author was surely aware of the comic effect of having a boy play a woman playing a boy. Or in *As You Like It* and *Two Gentlemen of Verona*, a boy playing a woman playing a boy playing a woman. Shakespeare's transvestite comedies really dig into the fluidity of gender.[29] Camilla Paglia calls him "a metamorphosist...He shows *process*, not objects. Everything is in flux–thought, language, identity, action. He enormously expands the inner life of his personae and sets them into the huge fateful rhythm which is his plot, an overwhelming force entering the play from beyond

society... He is the first to reflect upon the fluid nature of modern gender and identity."[30]

"*All the world's a stage,*" says Jaques in *As You Like It,* "*And all the men and women merely players; They have their exits and their entrances; And one man in his time plays many parts.*" (AYL II.vii) But then a strange thing happens when the curtain closes. We've watched these characters change during the play, but then we are meant to believe that once the curtain falls they will stay the same forever–the four superficial dandies of *Love's Labour's Lost* will suddenly be able to keep their word for a year (after breaking their initial oaths in minutes), couples who find love will always be in love. Really, the only characters we know for sure will stop changing after the curtain are Romeo, Juliet, Hamlet, Ophelia–those who die. In real life, courtship is a lifelong process.

Some of Shakespeare's most enduring characters actually direct the action from on stage. The easiest example is Hamlet, a theater enthusiast and performer. When the traveling players arrive, he requests a specific play he knows will torment his mother and stepfather, and even inserts "*A speech of some dozen or sixteen lines which I would set down.*" It's not explicitly clear which speech this is, but it's likely the one where the player-queen "*protests too much*" that she deserves to be "*accurst*" if she ever remarries. He then proceeds to direct them on how to perform it:

> *Speak the speech, I pray you, as I pronounced it to you, trippingly on the tongue... Nor do not saw the air too much with your hand, thus, [but] suit the action to the word, the word to the action, with this special observance, that you o'erstep not the modesty of nature; for anything so overdone is from the purpose of playing, whose end, both at the first and now, was and is, to hold as 'twere the mirror up to nature...And let those that play your clowns speak no more than is set down for them. For there be of them that will themselves laugh, to set on some quantity of barren spectators to laugh too, though in the meantime some necessary question of the play be then to be considered. That's villainous, and shows a most pitiful ambition in the fool that uses it.* (HAM III.ii)

Hamlet declares early on that he'll be performing the role of the madman and is aware of when he's being watched. He stage-manages the scene with Ophelia when Claudius and Polonius spy on them, and later when he breaks character while scolding his mother, he kills the audience (Polonius listening from behind the curtain) to protect the consistency of his role. His last words are a command that his friend Horatio share behind-the-scenes details of his performance in a specific way.

Rosalind in *As You Like It* spends a good deal of the play disguised as a boy, directing Orlando on how to play the role of an ideal lover.[31] Petruchio in *Taming of the Shrew* puts on a show of madness until the leading lady Katherina learns to trust his directorial instincts. Prospero in *The Tempest* is a master of theatrical magic (it helps that his stage manager is the shape-shifting fairy Ariel). He produces an elaborate spectacle for the shipwrecked nobles, then a goddess pageant for his daughter, and finally instructs the audience directly about how to applaud. Prospero is such a successful showman that commentators for centuries have argued this is Shakespeare himself.

Other Shakespearean characters direct atrocity shows, like Iago micromanaging an immersive theatrical experience for Othello, including many winking asides to the audience, and Lady Macbeth who stage-manages her husband. In modern times we'd call her his agent. The history plays are, naturally, full of kings who order people around, and sometimes give overblown speeches to rile up the troops (convincing peasants to die in their idiotic wars, for example: *"Imitate the action of the tiger... / Disguise fair nature with hard-favour'd rage; / Then lend the eye a terrible aspect,"* H5 III.i) but none are particularly theatrical except for Richard III, who knows there is a theater audience out there and gleefully invites us to enjoy his pageant of butchery.[32] Like Iago, he seems to genuinely think he's in a comedy play.

Shakespeare's most theatrical character must be Cleopatra, queen of *"infinite variety."* With a seasoned performer's fluidity she flows between her private and celebrity personae. Camille Paglia writes: "For Cleopatra, life is theater. She is a master propagandist. Truth is inconsequential, dramatic values are supreme. Cleopatra shamelessly manipulates others' emotions like clay."[33] She plays the players, toys with the investors and stages her own death—*twice*. Most of her show is for an audience of one, Antony, from whom she elicits a series of emotional responses: adoration, indignation, murderous rage.[34] But she is tragically vulnerable to reviews, which take the form of Roman gossip. She rages against the epithets they apply to her performance and the dull understudy they try to replace her with (Caesar's own sister).

In the end she is cornered, cast in the role of aging seductress, defeated witch-queen in a parade produced and directed by Caesar Augustus, followed by theatrical productions where:

> *Mechanic slaves,*
> *With greasy aprons, rules, and hammers, shall*
> *Uplift us to the view; in their thick breaths,*
> *Rank of gross diet, shall we be enclouded,*
> *And forc'd to drink their vapour...*
> *Saucy lictors*
> *Will catch at us like strumpets, and scald rhymers*
> *Ballad us out o' tune; the quick comedians*
> *Extemporally will stage us, and present*
> *Our Alexandrian revels; Antony*
> *Shall be brought drunken forth, and I shall see*
> *Some squeaking Cleopatra boy my greatness*
> *In th' posture of a whore.* (A&C V.ii)

Refusing to act in someone else's show and horrified by the idea of being played by a boy, she costumes and poses herself for a final performance: suicide. An artist even in death, she poses for a dramatic painting. Or a selfie.

Shakespeare also wrote his audience into his plays—the "groundlings" who paid a penny to stand for three or four hours in front of the stage. They didn't necessarily hang on every word of these lofty sagas about doomed kings and aristocratic courtships, and it's possible they could understand Shakespearean verse about as well as today's high school students. But knowing them he added interludes about peasant side-characters and their "little" issues (Launce berating his dog for urinating on noblemen steals the show in *Two Gentlemen of Verona*. This two-minute stand-up comedy cameo might be the only part of that script worth keeping). And whether the play takes place in Venice, Elsinore, Athens, wherever or *when*ever, "of whatever nationalist and historical period the main characters are represented as being, the lower classes are always portrayed as Englishmen of Shakespeare's own time."[35] *Midsummer Night's Dream* takes place in ancient Athens about 1400 BCE, but then into the forest stumble a bunch of English craftsmen from 1600 CE (three thousand years later) and wacky comedy ensues without audience complaint.

Shakespeare's plays are all pantomime acts in which the motions and endings of the central characters are predetermined by his sources, histories and short stories he read, or other popular plays he saw. His heroes, heroines and villains are preprogrammed automatons, and yet his genius was to give them a compelling interiority, a reason for doing these things. And the enduring popularity of his writing is ample evidence that he succeeded.

Witches

here is no single definitive Shakespearean stance on "Witches." As with fairies, ghosts and other supernatural phenomena, Shakespeare fits each "witch" to the structure of the story being told. The trinity in *Macbeth* is the most famous, but lesser known Shakespearean witches include a widowed queen in *Richard III*, a door-to-door medicine woman in *The Merry Wives of Windsor*, Joan of Arc in *Henry VI Part 1*, and some male characters as well. Although he reserves the word "Witch" for women, Prospero in *The Tempest*, King Lear, and even Friar Lawrence in *Romeo and Juliet* enact functions associated with witchcraft.

Old Europe had always had medicine women and shamans, people with special knowledge of medicinal plants and weather patterns, and who were believed to make contact with spirits (of nature and ghosts of the dead) through ecstatic trances brought on by ritual incantations and psychedelics. When Christianity arrived and "Religion" became an exclusively male affair, the shamaness or "witch doctor" still retained her position as the local midwife and Planned Parenthood: the person who knew about womens' health and childbirth, as well as contraception and abortion. This darker side of the job led to the re-imagining of the shamaness as an enemy of fertility, we thus begin to see a belief in the witch as someone who magically blights livestock, curses men with impotence, and causes stillbirths and birth defects.

In Shakespeare's time, an elaborate mythology developed saying that "witches" had allied themselves with the Christian Devil and were purely malicious in their intentions. Popular images of the witch-god

Robin Goodfellow, with his goat-legs and horns, made this equation seem logical enough (although really, popular imagery of the Christian Devil had been shaped by images of this indigenous goat-man-god, so it's a circular argument). For resisting the misogyny of the Church, these women were viewed as enemies of God. Fertility rituals led by women, sometimes involving premarital sex, and a knowledge of contraception and abortion, were certainly crimes against paternity and the rising might of patriarchalism, so the demonization of these rites and priestesses followed.

"Witches" also became a popular target for public frustration. As cash-crop capitalism put a greater strain on farmlands (causing famine) and rural farmers were displaced into city slums (full of the plague), the local medicine woman became a convenient scapegoat. This continues into modern electoral politics, as pawns of big business distract voters from economic injustices by making campaign promises to persecute women for having premarital sex.

Shakespeare's writing about witches displays a fascinating diversity, each portrait shaped by the needs of a particular story. Some are helpful, some are harmful, and others are entirely ambiguous. There is an intriguing pattern—witches in his plays are neither persecuted nor punished. He wrote only one "witch-trial," and that was of Joan of Arc in *Henry VI, Part I*. And as we'll see, her trial and execution had more to do with being French than being a witch.

Weird Sisters

MACBETH

The weird sisters, hand in hand,
Posters of the sea and land,
Thus do go about, about,
Thrice to thine, and thrice to mine,
And thrice again, to make up nine.
Peace! The charm's wound up. (MAC I.iii)

"Weird" has come to mean strange or frightening, largely because of these witches in *Macbeth*. But *Wyrd* is an old Anglo-Saxon word for "becoming," related to the Latin *vertere*, "to turn," and the Old High German *wirtel*, "spindle." In native European belief, the *Wyrd* is a web of strands connecting all destinies into a fabric that is constantly being woven at one end and unraveling at the other. The mythical weaving and cutting of these individual life-strands is done by a female trinity. The Greeks called these Fates, and in Viking belief they are Norns. Likewise, the primary function of the Weird (destiny) Sisters in *Macbeth* is predicting deaths and births—mostly deaths.

Shakespeare encountered the *Macbeth* witches in Raphael Holinshed's *The Chronicles of England, Scotland, and Ireland* (1587). In reporting on the Scottish king Macbeth, Holinshed wrote, "The common opinion was that these women were either the weird sisters, that is (as ye would say) the goddesses of destiny, or else some nymphs or fairies, imbued with knowledge of prophecy by their necromantical science." Necromancy is communication with spirits of the dead.

The triple goddess of fate, determining the length of a thread and cutting someone's life line, is mentioned in *A Midsummer Night's Dream*, when Thisbe weeps over her dead lover and calls out:

> *O Sisters Three,*
> *Come, come to me,*
> *With hands as pale as milk;*
> *Lay them in gore,*
> *Since you have shore*
> *With shears his thread of silk.* (MND V.i)

And in *Henry IV, Part 2* a battle-weary soldier lunges into a suicidal charge with a cry of:

> *What! Shall we have incision? Shall we imbrue?*
> *Then death rock me asleep, abridge my doleful days!*
> *Why, then, let grievous, ghastly, gaping wounds*
> *Untwine the Sisters Three! Come, Atropos, I say!* (2H4 II.iv)

In Greek myth, Atropos was the sister holding the scissors.

A close look reveals that each *Macbeth* witch has a particular function. The first asks questions and speaks for the past; the second speaks for the present; and the third for the future. For example, in their prophecy about Macbeth's rise to power, the first calls him what he's been: Thane (like a duke) of Glamis; the second calls him what he is presently becoming: Thane of Cawdor; and the third calls him King, which he will soon be.

The witches in *Macbeth* are musical, they *"go about, about,"* performing their *"antic round"* in a circle dance, and their song is catchy. When Macbeth repeats their prophecy, Banquo refers to the *"selfsame tune"* by which they sang it. Their songs tend to be built around threes: in the fourth act they sing a song with three refrains of *"Double, double, toil and trouble; / Fire burn and cauldron bubble"* (MAC IV.i) while cooking a stew of nasty things. They sing, sometimes individually and sometimes in unison.

Their music is contagious. Macbeth and Lady Macbeth will soon start speaking in triplicate. After waffling a bit about killing the king, Macbeth becomes resolute with the done-done-done of *"If it were done when 'tis done, then 'twere well / It were done quickly."* (MAC I.vii) and: *"Tomorrow, and tomorrow, and tomorrow."* (MAC V.v) in his climactic speech, delivered to his servant Seyton (Satan?). Although Lady Macbeth has only heard their message second hand, she gives a triple invocation: *"Come, you spirits [and] fill me...come to my woman's breasts...come, thick night,"* (MAC I.v) and her last words in the play will be *"To bed, to bed, to bed."* (MAC V.i)[36] Whether or not spirits do possess her (and then kill her) is open to interpretation. Certainly, her sleep-walking hints in this direction. And her three invitations may shed some light on the mysterious scene of the Porter at the gate, calling three times: *"Knock, knock, knock! Who's there?"* and describing three ghosts of the damned. (MAC II.iii)

The Weird Sisters are complex characters. They are not the murderers in the play, and Macbeth observes that their prophecy will come true whether he kills Duncan or not. Furthermore, they prophesy that Duncan's murder will be avenged. Their brew does contain human body parts, but the implication is that these have been exhumed, not that the witches killed to obtain them. We do once hear their report of casting a curse on a sailor's rude wife, yet it's not lethal. The primary function of the Weird Sisters in *Macbeth* is not to represent evil, but rather inevitability.

Hecate

MACBETH

Productions of *Macbeth* will generally feature three witches, but the play actually has four. The ringleader, called Hecate, is distinct from the nameless three. Macbeth refers to her as *"pale Hecate"* and later as *"black Hecate."* Other references in Shakespeare imply that Hecate is some manifestation of night, or specifically the moon which could shine pale or be blacked out by clouds. Lear swears by the sun, then Hecate, then the stars:

> *By the sacred radiance of the sun,*
> *The mysteries of Hecate and the night;*
> *By all the operation of the orbs,*
> *From whom we do exist and cease to be.* (KL I.i)

and in *A Midsummer Night's Dream*, Puck sings:

> *We fairies, that do run*
> *By the triple Hecate's team*
> *From the presence of the sun,*
> *Following darkness like a dream,*
> *Now are frolic.* (MND V.i)

When the players present their atrocity show in *Hamlet*, the murderer says his poison has been strengthened by Hecate's triple curse:

> *Thou mixture rank, of midnight weeds collected,*
> *With Hecate's ban thrice blasted, thrice infected,*
> *Thy natural magic and dire property*
> *On wholesome life usurp immediately.* (HAM III.ii)

Hecate seems to have originated in Egypt (*Heqit* may mean "intelligence" or "tribal ruler" in Egyptian) and was then adopted into Hesiod's theological genealogy *Theogony* as a pre-Olympian Titaness who ruled with Zeus. Once established in Greek mythology she was sometimes divided in three to correspond with phases of the moon and a woman's life: the virginal Artemis/Diana, the maternal Phoebe/Luna, and the widow Hecate.[37] Or, in statuary representations she could be one body with three faces and six arms. In Roman Christianity, the virginal and maternal aspects of Hecate were appropriated for Mary, leaving only the sterile crone elements of the goddess to be associated with the name Hecate. And still today, the words "Hecate, witch goddess" would more likely conjure the image of an old hag than a blushing virgin or nursing mother.

The trinitarian nature of Hecate implies that her stage representation should be three witches together. In the third act of *Macbeth*, a fourth witch called "Hecate" does show up and scold the weird sisters for appearing to Macbeth without her (but this section is generally considered an addition to Shakespeare's script).[38]

> FIRST WITCH. *Why, how now, Hecate? You look angerly*
> HECATE. *Have I not reason, beldams as you are,*
> *Saucy and overbold? How did you dare*
> *To trade and traffic with Macbeth*
> *In riddles and affairs of death?*
> *...And you all know security*
> *Is mortals' chiefest enemy.*
> *(Music and a song within, "Come away, come away.")*
> *Hark! I am call'd; my little spirit, see,*
> *Sits in a foggy cloud and stays for me. Exit.*
> FIRST WITCH. *Come, let's make haste; she'll soon be back again.*
> *(Exeunt.)* (MAC III.v)

Then Hecate returns a couple of scenes later to commend the sisters on a potion they are making:

> HECATE. *O, well done! I commend your pains,*
> *And everyone shall share i' the gains.*
> *And now about the cauldron sing,*
> *Like elves and fairies in a ring,*
> *Enchanting all that you put in.*
> *(Music and a song, "Black spirits." ["Black spirits and white, red*

spirits and gray; / Mingle, mingle, mingle, you that mingle may"]
Hecate retires.) (MAC IV.i)

Returning to the Egyptian origin of the name Hecate, Shakespeare will create a sort of three-in-one witch goddess in Cleopatra: human and divine, she is a being of *"infinite variety,"* living simultaneously in past, present and future (aware that after death she will be resurrected as a character in a play). Ted Hughes sees her as a reincarnation of Lady Macbeth, apparently fortified by the power of all of *Macbeth's* witches, and with a hardier consort: the fun-loving hyper-masculine Antony, to replace the insecure and mopey Macbeth. She is called a witch, even by Antony himself.

> From the Roman point of view she [is] not only the black African Queen of serpents, witchcraft, magicians, poisons, the river of the dead and the Underworld, but also a 'gypsy', a 'trull', a 'whore', a 'boggler', 'filth', 'errors', 'confusion', [yet she] incorporates also Divine Mother, Sacred Bride, the whole of the Goddess.[39]

In Cleopatra's dramatic death scene, flanked by two acolytes, she is nursing a poisonous serpent: a thought-provoking reflection of Lady Macbeth's speech about killing a toothless infant.

Sycorax
THE TEMPEST

In the *Tempest*, the wizard (male witch) Prospero reigns over an island between Italy and North Africa, which was previously ruled by Sycorax, *"a witch, and one so strong / That could control the moon, make flows and ebbs."* (TEM V.i) The name might be Shakespeare's invention, and there's some scholarly debate about its etymology, but *korax* is Greek for "raven," and this is the most probable origin. There's also a possibility that the name comes from Circe, a witch-goddess from Coraxi, who inhabited an enchanted island in Homer's *Odyssey.* When Odysseus and his men land on her island, she presents them with a great feast and a good deal of wine, and the drunken sailors are transformed into swine.[40] Going further out on a limb, there's a possible connection with the Gaelic winter-witch-goddess Cailleach (pronounced something like "Kilyax," meaning old hag) who gathers firewood on the second of February, as Sycorax's son Caliban does in *The Tempest*.

We find out about Sycorax only from Prospero's report, yet they've never met – she died before he arrived. And we know he's a deceiver, and a bit of a misogynist. But he describes:

> *The foul witch Sycorax, who with age and envy*
> *Was grown into a hoop... For mischiefs manifold, and sorceries terrible*
> *To enter human hearing, from Argier* [Algeria, North Africa]
> *Was banish'd; for one thing she did They would not take her life...*
> *This blue-ey'd hag was hither brought with child...*[41]
> *Thou, my slave* [were] *then her servant;*
> *And, for thou wast a spirit too delicate*
> *To act her earthy and abhorr'd commands,*
> *Refusing her grand hests* [orders], *she did confine thee,*
> *By help of her more potent ministers,*
> *And in her most unmitigable rage,*
> *Into a cloven pine.* (TEM I.ii)

She then died, leaving the fairy Ariel trapped in the tree until Prospero released him. Sycorax sounds pretty bad but then again, Prospero has also enslaved Ariel, and threatens to encase him in an oak, much stronger than pine. Shakespeare seems to have inserted Sycorax into the background to make Prospero look kind by comparison, but really there's little distinction between the two: they were both banished for witchcraft, and both would have been executed had they not had children. Sycorax birthed the *"hag-born"* fish-man Caliban, who Prospero surmises was sired *"by the devil himself / Upon thy wicked dam."* (TEM I.ii, Caliban names his mother's god "Setebos") but it's fascinating that Shakespeare, who believed so strongly in hereditary traits, gives Caliban no power: he couldn't charm Miranda, he can't perform or detect magic, and his curses are ineffectual. A good deal of scholarly effort has gone into expounding upon the significance of Syrocax, but Shakespeare gives us very little to work with—she never appears or gets to speak for herself, we receive only a sketchy outline from the unreliable Prospero.

Familiars
Macbeth | Tempest | Henry VI:I

Isaac Asimov writes that witches have "spirits as companions and servants. The Latin word for servant is *famulus*. A spirit who acts as a servant is thus a 'familiar spirit,' or simply a 'familiar.' These familiars were thought to take the shape of animals so that they might exist in the neighborhood without being detected. A cat was one favorite shape of this sort (based, perhaps, on no other reason than that old ladies who had survived their families and were forced to live on in isolation found cats to be quite agreeable company.)"[42] The Weird Sisters' familiars are a cat called Graymalkin ("Malkin" being a shortened form of "Matilda"), "Paddock," an old word for toad, and a rat without a tail. Hecate in her pale form has a wolf as her sentinel, and in her black form her familiars are a bat and a beetle.

The cat and toad were inspired by witch confessions extracted under torture by King James, after his ship nearly sank during a storm at sea in 1589. Agnis Sampson confessed that she and other witches christened a cat, tied pieces of a dead man's body to it and threw it into the sea to curse James' voyage. She also confessed to hanging a toad upside down and collecting its drippings as a venomous poison. But we should keep in mind that she said this as her head was being wrenched with a rope and "pilliwinks were laid on her fingers," while her accomplice was having his fingernails torn out and his legs crushed in iron boots.[43] I don't know what a "pilliwink" is, but I do know that confessions under torture lack credibility. King James himself wrote a couple of pamphlets about witchcraft, and Shakespeare, eager to please his new patron, incorporated elements of these into *Macbeth*.

The most famous familiar in Shakespeare's work must be Ariel, the fairy held hostage by Prospero in *The Tempest*. Prospero is never definitively labeled a wizard but he spends the whole play casting spells and conjuring illusions with his magic books, robes and staff. Whether or not we consider Caliban a familiar as well depends on where we stand regarding his humanity. If we view both as Prospero's familiars, they make a complementary set: Ariel representing air/fire and Caliban representing earth/water.

In *Henry VI, Part I*, Shakespeare presents Joan of Arc, whom French characters in the play call *"Joan la Pucelle* [the Maiden/Virgin] *A holy prophetess new risen up."* But from the English perspective she is *"Pucelle, that witch, that damned sorceress."* Remember, she was a French enemy of the English, they burned her for witchcraft, and she was not officially canonized as a Catholic Saint until 1920. When she loses a battle and is captured by the English, her defeat is presented as a sign that she has been abandoned by her familiars. Shakespeare dramatizes their rejection of her in a powerful scene:

> *[JOAN] PUCELLE. Now help, ye charming spells and periapts;*
> *And ye choice spirits that admonish me*
> *And give me signs of future accidents; (Thunder)*
> *Under the lordly monarch of the north,*
> *Appear and aid me in this enterprise!*
> *(Enter FIENDS)*
> *This speedy and quick appearance argues proof*
> *Of your accustom'd diligence to me.*
> *Now, ye familiar spirits that are cull'd*
> *Help me this once, that France may get the field.*
> *(They walk and speak not)*
> *O, hold me not with silence over-long!*
> *Where I was wont to feed you with my blood,*
> *I'll lop a member off and give it you*
> *In earnest of a further benefit,*
> *So you do condescend to help me now.*
> *(They hang their heads)*
> *No hope to have redress? My body shall*
> *Pay recompense, if you will grant my suit.*
> *(They shake their heads)*
> *Cannot my body nor blood sacrifice*
> *Entreat you to your wonted furtherance?*
> *Then take my soul – my body, soul, and all,*
> *Before that England give the French the foil.*
> *(They depart)*
> *See! they forsake me. Now the time is come*
> *That France must vail her lofty-plumed crest*
> *And let her head fall into England's lap.*
> *My ancient incantations are too weak,*
> *And hell too strong for me to buckle with.*
> *Now, France, thy glory droopeth to the dust.* (1H6 V.iii)

Joan's invocation of these "fiends" sheds a fascinating light on Lady Macbeth's *"Come, you spirits"* speech. And her offer of an exchange—blood, body, soul—is a keen acknowledgment that magic always comes with a price.

Joan is led away into captivity, and a couple of scenes later Shakespeare shows a witch trial, omitting any reference to tortures inflicted on the Maid of Orleans. She pathetically pleads for mercy because of her virginity, then claims to be pregnant by three different Englishmen, and is finally led off to be burned alive. Again, not the Saint Joan of Arc we may be accustomed to, but as character assassinations go it's remarkably sympathetic.

Winds and Curses
MACBETH | RICHARD III

FIRST WITCH. Where hast thou been, sister?
SECOND WITCH. Killing swine.
THIRD WITCH. Sister, where thou?
FIRST WITCH. A sailor's wife had chestnuts in her lap,
And mounch'd, and mounch'd, and mounch'd. 'Give me,' quoth I.
'Aroint thee, witch!' the rump-fed ronyon cries.
Her husband's to Aleppo gone...
SECOND WITCH. I'll give thee a wind.
FIRST WITCH. Thou'rt kind.
THIRD WITCH. And I another.
FIRST WITCH. I myself have all the other,
And the very ports they blow...
I will drain him dry as hay:
Sleep shall neither night nor day
Hang upon his penthouse lid;
He shall live a man forbid.
Weary se'nnights nine times nine
Shall he dwindle, peak, and pine;
Though his bark [boat] cannot be lost,
Yet it shall be tempest-toss'd. (MAC I.iii)

In Shakespeare's plays, witches, fairies and kings have limited control over weather.[44] The witches here summon a tempest to punish a sailor for his wife's inconsiderate behavior, similar to the punitive storm in *The Tempest*. We also hear reports of the witches in flight: *"Infected be the air whereon they ride."* (MAC IV.i) It's not revealed from this whether they can fly by themselves; presumably they ride on something.

The only actively malicious things we see the Weird Sisters do are cursing livestock—*"killing swine"*—and casting a curse on a sailor's wife who refused to share some chestnuts with the first witch (we'll never know how this might have gone if she'd used the magic word "please"). Tales of witch-curses generally begin with someone refusing charity to an impoverished elderly woman, and thus contained a constructive lesson about sharing. The witch then makes a wax figure, like a Voodoo-doll, of the sailor and causes him to *"dwindle, peak, and pine"* during a storm at sea, but says that he'll survive. (MAC I.iii)

The best (or worst) curses in Shakespeare are delivered by Queen Margaret in *Richard III*. The widow of Henry VI appears from the shadows as Richard consolidates his power (considering that, historically, she was in France at the time, we could almost see her apparition as an astral projection). Richard quickly calls her a *"foul wrinkled witch"* and she launches into a series of dire predictions:

> QUEEN MARGARET. *Can curses pierce the clouds and*
> *enter heaven?*
> *Why then, give way, dull clouds, to my quick curses!*
> *... That none of you may live his natural age,*
> *But by some unlook'd accident cut off!*
> [RICHARD] GLOUCESTER. *Have done thy charm,*
> *thou hateful wither'd hag.*
> QUEEN MARGARET. *And leave out thee?*
> *Stay, dog, for thou shalt hear me.*
> *If heaven have any grievous plague in store*
> *Exceeding those that I can wish upon thee...*
> *The worm of conscience still be-gnaw thy soul!*
> *No sleep close up that deadly eye of thine,*
> *Unless it be while some tormenting dream*
> *Affrights thee with a hell of ugly devils!*

Thou elvish-mark'd, abortive, rooting hog...
The slave of nature and the son of hell. (R3 I.iii)[45]

This goes on and on, it's one of Shakespeare's most entertaining scenes and she curses almost everyone in great detail. Then the rest of the play is the gradual unfolding of her gloomy prophesies coming to bloody fruition. Shakespeare was clearly not writing in support of witchcraft, but in his plays a witch's prophecy/curse always comes true.

Wizards
COMEDY OF ERRORS | KING LEAR

When Lady Macbeth begins to sleepwalk and weaken, a doctor is summoned. We're probably better off not knowing what procedures he tried, since medieval Scottish medicine was not much better than medieval torture. But at last the doctor's helpless diagnosis is *"More needs she the divine than the physician."* (MAC V.i) Here he's not talking about the "divine" power of prayer or whatnot, but about a diviner: someone who can communicate with spirits to locate something, in this case a cure. The word "diviner" is interchangeable with shaman, necromancer, medicine person, or witch.

Shakespeare describes one of these in *A Comedy of Errors*, when the mistaken identity between identical twins leads the townspeople to believe a man is insane or possessed by demons:

> *They brought one Pinch, a hungry lean-fac'd villain,*
> *A mere anatomy, a mountebank,*
> *A threadbare juggler, and a fortune-teller,*
> *A needy, hollow-ey'd, sharp-looking wretch,*
> *A living dead man. This pernicious slave,*
> *Forsooth, took on him as a conjurer,*
> *And gazing in mine eyes, feeling my pulse,*
> *And with no face, as 'twere, outfacing me,*
> *Cries out I was possess'd. Then all together*
> *They fell upon me, bound me, bore me thence,*
> *And in a dark and dankish vault at home*

There left me and my man, [servant] *both bound together;*
Till, gnawing with my teeth my bonds in sunder,
I gain'd my freedom. (COE V.i, see also the treatment of Malvolio
in *Twelfth Night*)

Shakespeare also gives the clergy elements of witchcraft. King John
accuses the Roman Catholic priesthood of *"juggling witchcraft"* for selling
Indulgences (coupons for God's forgiveness of sins).[46] And in *Romeo
and Juliet* the Franciscan Friar Lawrence concocts potions, speaking of a
"powerful grace that lies in herbs, plants, stones, and their true qualities" (R&J
II.iii) Linda Woodbridge observes that "vegetives, herbs, and plants are
one thing—one might grant such herbalism the status of protoscience
rather than magic—but 'stones,' mentioned by both Cerimon [in *Pericles*]
and Friar Lawrence, are quite another."[47]

King Lear refers to his two scheming daughters as *"unnatural hags,"*
but in the play they are calculating capitalists, and it is Lear himself who
invokes Hecate and gives his beloved Cordelia a curse for her dowry. Later
he blights his daughter Goneril:

Hear, nature, hear; dear goddess, hear
Suspend thy purpose, if thou didst intend
To make this creature fruitful!
Into her womb convey sterility! (KL I.iv)

And after realizing his daughter Regan is just as bad, he goes running
around the forest with a crown of weeds, commanding winds to blow. Like
all curses in Shakespeare, Lear's will come true: his ungrateful daughters
will perish childless, and Cordelia will be drawn back in the end to die
proving she loved her father best. King Lear, named after a Celtic sea god
(the Welsh Llyr, Irish Lir or Ler) turns out to be one of the great witches
of Shakespeare.[48]

In *Julius Caesar* and *Antony and Cleopatra* fate is voiced by male
soothsayers: *"Beware the Ides of March,"* Caesar is warned, and though he's
superstitious about everything else he dismisses this famous warning. *"In
nature's infinite book of secrecy / A little I can read,"* says the palm-reader in
Antony and Cleopatra, and when the unsatisfied customer demands a better
fortune, he responds *"I make not, but foresee."* (A&C I.ii) This soothsayer

can also see a person's aura or genius (what some might call a guardian angel), as he tells Antony:

> *Thy daemon, that thy spirit which keeps thee, is*
> *Noble, courageous, high, unmatchable,*
> *Where Caesar's is not; but near him thy angel*
> *Becomes a fear, as being o'erpow'r'd.* (A&C II.iii)[49]

Shakespeare uses Soothsayers as a dramatic convention, almost a form of audience participation. We in the audience already know Caesar will die and Antony will lose the battle of Actium, and would love to warn them, but the author affirms that these headstrong characters would not have listened anyway. But it's also fascinating that, however we may wish to adopt Shakespeare as a skeptical modern, in his writings the fortune-teller's visions and predictions always come true.

Charms
MIDSUMMER | AS YOU LIKE IT | OTHELLO

In *A Midsummer Night's Dream*, Egeus accuses his daughter's sweetheart Lysander of using witchcraft to charm her (in the original sense of "charm:" to manipulate through magic):

> *This man hath bewitch'd the bosom of my child [with] rhymes,*
> *And interchang'd love-tokens...*
> *Bracelets of thy hair, rings, gawds, conceits,*
> *Knacks, trifles, nosegays.* (MND I.i, "nosegay" meant a bouquet)

This all sounds like harmless stuff you might find for two bucks at the pre-teen shop in the mall, but in Shakespeare's time trinkets were still handmade, and there is a certain magic in giving someone a gift you've crafted with your own hands (or woven of your own hair).

Poetic writings can function as love charms. Orlando carves Rosalind's name into trees and hangs poems from them in *As You Like It* (they end up married), Berowne writes a bad sonnet for a different Rosaline in *Love's Labour's Lost* (she banishes him), and Hamlet disowns the poems he wrote for Ophelia (they both end up dead). Orlando's love charms are especially significant in his invocation of the triple goddess representing the full sway of life from virginity's *"chaste eye"* to pregnancy's lunar *"pale sphere"* to death's *"huntress' name"*[50]:

> ORLANDO. *Hang there, my verse, in witness of my love;*
> *And thou, thrice-crowned Queen of Night, survey*
> *With thy chaste eye, from thy pale sphere above,*
> *Thy huntress' name that my full life doth sway.*
> *O Rosalind! these trees shall be my books,*
> *And in their barks my thoughts I'll character,*
> *That every eye which in this forest looks*
> *Shall see thy virtue witness'd every where.*
> *Run, run, Orlando; carve on every tree,*
> *The fair, the chaste, and unexpressive she.* (AYL III.ii)

Shakespeare's most tragic and ill-fated love charm appears in *Othello*, a handkerchief from an Egyptian (in English slang a "gypsy"), not as a charm of seduction, but rather of protection, as Othello explains:

> *That handkerchief*
> *Did an Egyptian to my mother give;*
> *She was a charmer, and could almost read*
> *The thoughts of people. She told her, while she kept it,*
> *T'would make her amiable and subdue my father*
> *Entirely to her love, but if she lost it*
> *Or made a gift of it, my father's eye*
> *Should hold her loathed and his spirits should hunt*
> *After new fancies.* (OTH III.iv)[51]

Desdemona loses this talisman and the honeymoon turns to a mass funeral, the marriage bed piled high with cadavers. Rationally, we can say that Iago manipulated Othello's hanky superstition. But by Shakespearean logic, it's equally valid to say that Desdemona's loss of the protective love charm invokes her gruesome death.

Flowers

HAMLET | WINTER'S TALE

Ophelia's madness in *Hamlet* is portrayed in striking images: she brings Hamlet his love letters and he throws them back at her, and a few scenes later we see her handing flowers out to her family and friends. In some film and stage productions her flowers are only make-believe, or straw or twigs and this really lets the audience know she's gone mad, but the script itself says she enters *"fantastically dressed with straws and flowers,"* (HAM IV.v[52]) and it seems likely enough that in original productions she held the flowers she was talking about.

Audiences would have expected a girl of Ophelia's age and station to have a certain "education," some literacy, sewing, which we see her do in the second act, and also some knowledge of plants for both cooking and herbal medicine, natural remedies. "For the early modern audience, the image of Ophelia holding flowers and herbs thus implies a potential attempt at self-administered medicine...a last futile attempt at recovering from this tragic vision."[53] Natural medicine may seem a poor fit in this exploration of witchcraft, but we should recall that "witch" was a title often thrust upon medicine women ("witch doctors") who specialized in womens' medicine. The "witch" was like the medieval version of Planned Parenthood, today's target of medieval suspicion and violence.

The particular herbs and flowers that Ophelia carries were all well known as home remedies and had recently appeared in John Gerard's popular 1597 book *Herball*:

> *There's rosemary, that's for remembrance; pray love, remember.*
> *And there is pansies, that's for thoughts. There's fennel for you, and*
> *columbines. There's rue for you; and here's some for me. We may call it*
> *herb of grace o' Sundays. O you must wear your rue with a difference.*
> *There's a daisy. I would give you some violets, but they wither'd all*
> *when my father died.* (HAM IV.v)

Gerard wrote that the fragrance of rosemary was good "for all infirmities of the head and braine [and] comforteth the braine, the memorie

[and] inward senses." Inhaling the juices of daisies could "mitigate all kinde of paines [and] purgeth the head mightilie of foule and filthie slimie humours." Fennel could ease obstructions in the lungs, liver and kidneys, and a columbine perfume could be sprinkled around a room to put people at ease. Violets were ground with sugar into a syrup "most pleasant and wholesome, especially it comforteth the hart, and the other inward parts." [sic]⁵⁴ When Ophelia says the violets have withered, this means a loss of hope and comfort. They will be mentioned again at her funeral, when her brother says:

> Lay her i' th'earth,
> And from her fair and unpolluted flesh
> May violets spring. (HAM V.i)

Besides their positive psychological effects, fennel, and rue were also used to terminate pregnancies (the flower's name, "rue," means regret). This, and her Valentine song about the nobleman who lost interest in marrying the maiden because she'd already slept with him, would have sparked an audience debate about whether Ophelia was or had been pregnant by Hamlet.⁵⁵ The debate remains open.

Ophelia is self-medicating. Today's Ophelias may look for these comforts in pill-form, but she must concoct her own herbal medicines. Ophelia seeks relief in nature but too late, she's already been terminally poisoned by the cold, dark, dreary castle, which is essentially a tomb. But Shakespeare reincarnates Ophelia as Perdita in The Winter's Tale and banishes her from the castle at birth (just when the kingdom of Sicilia is being cursed to endless winter). She's raised by humble shepherds and this time, the prince she meets is not a melancholy Dane but a well-adjusted Bohemian. Perdita repeats Ophelia's flower-distribution, but in its natural habitat, the sunny countryside.

The prince's father has come disguised to witness the rural sheep-shearing pageant, and in particular to spy on his son and the young shepherdess. Perdita appears, *"most goddess-like prank'd up"* like the flower deity Flora⁵⁶ (perhaps a clue to Ophelia's appearance *"fantastically dressed with straws and flowers"*) and approaches the disguised king. First she offers rosemary and rue, but after the he antagonizes her with a botanical debate, she alters the gift:

> Here's flow'rs for you:
> Hot lavender, mints, savory, marjoram;
> The marigold, that goes to bed wi' th' sun,
> And with him rises weeping; these are flow'rs
> Of middle summer, and I think they are given
> To men of middle age. Y'are very welcome. (WT IV.iv)

These mid-year flowers were used to treat various maladies of middle-age: lavender to strengthen the bowels and ease flatulence, mint to aid digestion (and soothe gonorrhea), savory to dull aching joints, marjoram for memory-loss, and marigolds for heart palpitations. Sharon Kelley comments, "Perdita's list of cures reads like a modern AARP advertisement... Listening to this list of beneficial flowers, many in Shakespeare's audience would either be rubbing their sore, aging bodies empathetically or laughing at the endless list of physical ailments that Perdita is subliminally suggesting plague, or may soon assault, the King of Bohemia."[57]

After listing summer flowers for the disguised king, she turns to the prince and wishes she had spring flowers for him:

> Now, my fair'st friend,
> I would I had some flow'rs o' th' spring that might
> Become your time of day [like] daffodils,
> That come before the swallow dares, and take
> The winds of March with beauty; violets, dim...
> Pale primroses...bold oxlips, and
> The crown-imperial; lilies of all kinds,
> The flow'r-de-luce being one. O, these I lack
> To make you garlands of, and my sweet friend
> To strew him o'er and o'er!
> ...Like a bank for love to lie and play on. (WT IV.iv)

While the flowers she gave the king were medicinal, perhaps a joke on the ailments of old age, the flowers she names for the young prince are aesthetic; she sees no ailment in him but only wishes she could play with him in a bed of roses. This image is a powerful contrast with the drowned Ophelia, her dress blooming in the weeping brook and dragging her down to muddy death, her *fantastic garlands* [of] *weedy trophies* floating to the surface.

The Good Witch
MERRY WIVES OF WINDSOR

Shakespeare's *The Merry Wives of Windsor* is about women shaming men for their lust and jealousy. The merry knight Falstaff rides into town fantasizing about adulterous affairs with two married women and they publicly humiliate him. The insanely jealous husband, Mr. Ford, is also set up for ridicule.

Into this play where men are chaotic and women restore order, Shakespeare inserts three references to a historical witch, Jyl or Gillian of Braintford, a tavern-keeper and apparently a celebrity. She is attested in contemporary sources for her fearful curses and comical flatulence, but no surviving document suggests that she was brought to trial for witchcraft. In the fourth act, Mrs. Ford and Mrs. Page have lured the lusty Falstaff to a secret meeting at the Ford home. When Ford returns, they dress Falstaff in womens' clothing.

> MRS. FORD. *My husband...cannot abide the old woman of Brainford; he swears she's a witch, forbade her my house, and hath threat'ned to beat her...*
> MRS. PAGE. *He'll be here presently; let's go dress him* [Falstaff] *like the witch of Brainford.* (MWW IV.ii)

The first thing we may notice is that these women, fine upstanding members of the community, do not fear this "witch." That she's forbidden to go inside lets us know that she makes house calls. Ford's threat of violence shows that he considers her a threat to his masculinity and patriarchal control, but he does not say he'll report her to the authorities to be burned at the stake. He doesn't want the witch empowering his wife, but he doesn't consider her dangerous.

When Mr. Ford comes home and hears that the witch is upstairs, we hear his opinion on her: *"A witch, a quean, an old cozening quean!"* (*"cozening"* means swindling and *"quean"* here means whore):

> Have I not forbid her my house? She comes of errands, does she? We are simple men; we do not know what's brought to pass under the profession

*of fortune-telling. She works by charms, by spells, by th' figure, and such
daub'ry as this is, beyond our element. We know nothing. Come down,
you witch, you hag you; come down, I say.* (MWW IV.ii)

The disguised Falstaff scampers down the stairs and Mr. Ford thrashes
him as he runs out the door.

Here we have an inventory of the witch's house-call services:
"Fortune-telling," predictions about future gossip. *"Charms"* might mean
magical trinkets or could mean spells to make someone more noticeable.
"Spells," incantations or symbolic actions to influence natural phenomena.
"By th' figure" could mean wax Voodoo-dolls like the one mentioned in
Macbeth. And *"daub'ry"* likely involved ointments: aphrodisiacs, skincare
and cosmetic products (like a door-to-door Avon saleswoman). *"Beyond
our element"* refers to divination, contact with a spirit world hidden from
basic human senses.

The play climaxes with Mrs. Page and Mrs. Ford inviting Falstaff to
a nighttime forest rendezvous under an oak, and they instruct him to wear
antlers like the legendary Herne the Hunter. There he finds himself at the
center of a fairy pageant of disguised singing, circle-dancing children. "We
see the wives of Windsor going into the woods at night to meet a horned
man, a devil: the central stage action images a witches' sabbath."[58] The
Sabbath here is not presented as evil, it is performed to symbolize womens'
protection from male exploitation. Ironically this dance is choreographed
by the local parson. But the ringleader is Mistress Quickly, local busybody
(who appears as a prostitute in the Henry IV plays), not Jyl of Brainford.

We never see the "witch" of Brainford on stage, only Falstaff disguised
as her. And between Mrs. Ford accepting her house-calls and Mr. Ford
wanting to beat her, we could have a neat symmetry: women trust her, and
men don't. However, hearing she's in town, a male character seeks the witch
to inquire who will marry a local girl. (MWW IV.v) "What we do not see
in *The Merry Wives* are evil hags who cast malevolent spells on innocent
targets or consort with the devil," writes Colleen Marie Knowlton-Davis.
"Instead, Shakespeare shows women and some men seeking the advice and
knowledge of the local witch, while jealous or authoritative men react to
her with fear and anger—not because she is an agent of Satan, but because
she has power in the secret, domestic realm where he cannot meddle."[59]

The Witches' Tale
THE WINTER'S TALE

Shakespeare will return to the triple nature of the witch near the end of his career, making a trinity consisting of the maiden, mother, and widow, the heroes of *The Winter's Tale*. The story begins like a fairy tale with the king becoming sick with a jealousy that will plunge his realm into sixteen years of winter sterility. He's convinced that his wife Hermione has been engaged in a long-term affair with his best friend, and that his son and soon-to-be-born daughter are illegitimate. The king orders Hermione to be thrown into prison (their young son dies of the shock and their daughter is born in the prison-underworld) and then has her dragged before the court for what reads like a witch trial.

Leontes considers that if his wife were *"given to the fire"* he might be able to rest more soundly. And when her friend Paulina enters with the newborn baby, the king cries:

> *Out!*
> *A mankind witch! Hence with her, out o' door!*
> *A most intelligencing bawd!...A callat* [scold]
> *Of boundless tongue...*
> *This brat is none of mine...*
> *Hence with it, and together with the dam*
> *Commit them to the fire.* (WT II.iii)

Paulina invokes the *"good goddess Nature"* who made the child in her father's image, but the king calls her *"A gross hag... I'll have thee burn'd."* She responds, *"I care not. / It is an heretic that makes the fire, / Not she which burns in't."* ("witch" pun probably intended). Leontes then momentarily sees how crazed he's become:

> *I am a feather for each wind that blows.*
> *Shall I live on to see this bastard kneel*
> *And call me father? Better burn it now*
> *Than curse it then. But be it; let it live.* (WT II.iii)

He commands Paulina's husband to abandon the newborn in a forest. The servant complies, hoping *"Some powerful spirit instructs the kites and ravens / To be thy nurses!"* (WT II.iii)

No sooner has he left but messengers from the Oracle of Delphi arrive. This is Pythia, the python priestess of Apollo's temple in Greece, who induces visions by inhaling fumes in a cavern. Mythically these fumes come from the decomposition of a primeval chaos-serpent, but in reality it was probably natural gas. We may doubt this sort of divination, but in Shakespeare's world the witch/oracle/soothsayer is always right. Pythia's messengers confirm what the audience knows: everyone is innocent except Leontes, who is a tyrant, and he will have no heir until the abandoned baby is found. But the king refuses to believe it and his wife collapses. Paulina re-enters, still assuming she'll be tried as a witch:

> *What studied torments, tyrant, hast for me?*
> *What wheels, racks, fires? What flaying, boiling*
> *In leads or oils? What old or newer torture*
> *Must I receive, whose every word deserves*
> *To taste of thy most worst?* (WT III.ii)

She declares the queen dead and curses the king (and, by extension, the whole kingdom) to a barren *"winter in storm perpetual."* Leontes repents but it's too late, and the play itself abandons his blighted realm to follow the adventures of his daughter Perdita, adopted and raised by a shepherd in fertile Bohemia. Sixteen years later she plays the role of the nature goddess Flora at a fertility pageant, and this sets in motion the chain of events in which she will be reunited with her father. Then the aging Paulina will lead them into a tomb to view a statue of the dead queen Hermione, and after a magical incantation *"Music, awake her; strike! 'Tis time; descend; be stone no more; approach,"* (WT V.iii) the frozen queen is resurrected and Leontes exclaims, *"If this be magic, let it be an art lawful as eating."* (WT V.iii) Shakespeare throws in a half-hearted hint that she's been alive all along, but the sighting of her ghost midway through the play makes this doubtful. In the end, this trinity of Paulina, Hermione and Perdita heal the sterile winter-king Leontes, summoning a new era of fertility and abundance in the nation.[60]

The Good, the Bad and the Ugly

Shakespeare's plays contain a good deal of diversity on the topic of witches—diverse types of witches and diverse attitudes toward them. Shakespeare himself does not seem to have borne them any particular ill will. Even the Weird Sisters in *Macbeth*, pumped up with King James' cartoonish stereotypes, are presented as complex and ambiguous characters. And although the witch-hunting King himself was in the audience, the Weird Sisters are never captured or brought to trial. The only witch trial/burning in Shakespeare's plays is Joan of Arc, who is really punished for being French.

When it comes to curses and prophecies, they are never proven wrong. Having the curse come true makes good dramatic sense and doesn't by itself prove that Shakespeare had any faith in them. And yet, the last piece of writing he's suspected to have done is a curse, to mark his own grave:

> *Good friend, for Jesus' sake forbear*
> *To dig the dust enclosed here*
> *Blessed be the man that spares these stones*
> *And cursed be he that moves my bones.*[61]

Fall and Winter Festivals

Halloween | Samhain

MACBETH

> *Now o'er the one half-world*
> *Nature seems dead, and wicked dreams abuse*
> *The curtain'd sleep; witchcraft celebrates*
> *Pale Hecate's offerings; and wither'd Murther,*
> *Alarum'd by his sentinel, the wolf,*
> *Whose howl's his watch, thus with his stealthy pace,*
> *With Tarquin's ravishing strides, towards his design*
> *Moves like a ghost.* (MAC II.i)

Before the Roman Christian invasion, the English Pagan year had begun and ended with a day of the dead called Samhain. This night, a portal between one year and next, was also believed to be the time when the veil between the living world and spirit world was at its thinnest. It is from Samhain that we inherit customs associated with Halloween, in Shakespeare's time known as Hallowmas.[62]

In *Two Gentlemen of Verona*, a man can tell his friend is in love because he looks *"like a beggar at Hallowmas,"* (TGV II.i), a reference to what we now call Trick or Treat, but which used to involve grownups asking for alcohol. Shakespeare also refers to the English practice of carving scary faces on root vegetables (as Americans do with pumpkins), when Falstaff describes a lean and frightening police officer *"like a fork'd radish, with a head fantastically carved upon it with a knife."* (2H4 III.ii)

If Shakespeare wrote a Halloween play, *Macbeth* would be the most obvious candidate, not only because of its witches and ghosts. Isaac Asimov muses that the historical Macbeth seems to have been the last of Scotland's Pagan kings. "The Scottish church may have looked back on Macbeth as one of the last representatives of the old Celtism and might have considered him in league with vague old magical and pagan practices. Can it be that the dim tales of his league with the powers of darkness (only his Celtism, really) crystallized at last into the tale of witches?"[63]

Samhain, the Celtic New Year, was traditionally the end of the warring season in which thanes and kings would jockey for political positions and the right to tax the harvests of surrounding villages. The play *Macbeth* begins with an armistice and a promotion for its title character. "Thane of Cawdor" was not only a title, but also a license to extort agricultural tribute from farmers in that area. This is a fine promotion, but then he stumbles into a Wiccan Sabbat and sets his sights on the crown of Scotland.

The weather in *Macbeth* certainly sounds like late autumn, with references to harvest storage and falling leaves: *"Though bladed corn be lodged and trees blown down...nature's germaines* [or seeds] *tumble all together."* (MAC IV.i) The play begins with a murky, chaotic mix of *"Fair is foul, and foul is fair."* (MAC I.i) Macbeth himself makes the same observation: *"So foul and fair a day I have not seen."* (MAC I.iii) But once the butchery begins, the weather settles into an ominous darkness.

As a king, Macbeth brings the sterility of winter—he can sire no offspring and kills other peoples' children, and the dreadful weather continues until at last the march of Birnam Wood, like a May Day procession, heralds the coming of summer. The historical Macbeth ruled for seventeen years, but in this play it's all condensed down to one unpleasant winter.

On the Christian calendar, Halloween is the evening before All Saints Day, a celebration of the saints not popular enough to have a feast day of their own, followed by All Souls Day, a celebration of all other sundry dead believers. Shakespeare's *Richard III* features All Souls as the day on which the king orders the execution of his murderous henchman Buckingham, who muses *"All-Souls' day is my body's doomsday."* (R3 V.i) Shakespeare then uses that night to terrify the doomed King Richard with a series of ghostly visions, a grim parade of everyone he's killed, each one cursing him to *"Despair and die."* (R3 V.iii)

Christmas | Yule

> *Blow, blow, thou winter wind,*
> *Thou art not so unkind*
> *As man's ingratitude;*
> *Thy tooth is not so keen,*
> *Because thou art not seen,*
> *Although thy breath be rude.*
>   *Heigh-ho! Sing heigh-ho! unto   the green holly.*
>   *Most friendship is feigning, most loving mere folly.*
> *Then, heigh-ho, the holly!*
> *This life is most jolly.*
> *Freeze, freeze, thou bitter sky,*
> *That dost not bite so nigh*
> *As benefits forgot;*
> *Though thou the waters warp,*
> *Thy sting is not so sharp*
> *As friend rememb'red not.*
>   *Heigh-ho! sing, &c. (AYL II.vii)*

There are no merry Christmases in Shakespeare, on or off stage.

Like his contemporaries, Shakespeare seems to have viewed winter as unnatural, an annual punishment imposed because of humanity's fall from grace in Eden.[64] Winter in Shakespeare's plays is a usurper, hijacking the weather. It often comes as a result of bad rulership, as in *The Winter's Tale, Hamlet, King Lear and Macbeth,* and can be ended by a restoration of

good leadership: the approach of the green forest ends a cruel winter in
Macbeth, and Richard III famously begins with:

> *Now is the winter of our discontent*
> *Made glorious summer by this sun* [son] *of York...*
> *And all the clouds that lour'd upon our house*
> *In the deep bosom of the ocean buried.*
> *Now are our brows bound with victorious wreaths.* (R3 I.i)

In all of Shakespeare's work there are only seven references to
December, six of which highlight its cold, dark barrenness in contrast
with bright, fertile spring.[65] The darkness and cold of the season, bringing
feelings of isolation and depression, gave rise to indoor festivities of
warmth and light and family connections. As the summer solstice was
celebrated with an outdoor bonfire, the winter solstice centered around
the hearth: holly and mistletoe would be hung indoors and a large
oak stump called the "Yule Log" would be dragged inside and burned
through twelve days of indoor festivity (if this fire went out it was taken
as a bad omen for the coming year). The word "Yule" is attested in various
Northern European languages and its origin is unknown, but it's from
"Yule" that we get the English word "Jolly." *"Heigh-ho, the holly! This life is
most jolly."* (AYL II.vii) Yuletide was a period of alcoholic wassail, over-
eating, and various hijinks culminating on the "Twelfth Night." Although
none of Shakespeare's plays explicitly takes place on Christmas, he refers
to numerous Yuletide traditions.

A winter song at the end of *Love's Labour's Lost* refers to a warm
hearth and a bowl of hot wassail with crab-apples in it:

> *When icicles hang by the wall...*
> *And Tom bears logs into the hall...*
> *While greasy Joan doth keel* [stir] *the pot...*
> *When roasted crabs hiss in the bowl,*
> *Then nightly sings the staring owl:*
> *'Tu-who;*
> *Tu-whit, To-who'- A merry note.* (LLL V.i)

Christmas Hamlet

HAMLET

Shakespeare didn't write a Christmas play. Oddly enough, his most Christmas-y piece is *The Tragedy of Hamlet, Prince of Denmark*. The college students are home on vacation, the king is wassailing and theater companies are on tour. When the ghost appears, an officer refers to an old folk-belief about Christmas Eve:

> *Some say that ever 'gainst that season comes*
> *Wherein our Saviour's birth is celebrated,*
> *The bird of dawning singeth all night long;*
> *And then, they say, no spirit dare stir abroad...*
> *No fairy takes, nor witch hath power to charm;*
> *So hallow'd and so gracious is the time,* (HAM I.i)

And Horatio responds, *"So I have heard, and do in part believe it,"* (HAM I.i) which implies that the appearance of a ghost on this night contradicts the belief – it might be Christmas Eve.

Hamlet, home on break from his university studies in Wittenberg, has the gloomy attitude of a kid who saw Mommy kissing Santa Claus, and sneers at the festivity:

> *The King doth wake tonight and takes his rouse,*
> *Keeps wassail, and the swaggering upspring reels;*
> *And as he drains his draughts of Rhenish down,*
> *The kettle-drum and trumpet thus bray out*
> *The triumph of his pledge.* (HAM 1.iv)

"Wassail" was a bowl of warm ale flavored with roasted apples (in *Midsummer Night's Dream*, Puck says *"and sometime lurk I in a gossip's bowl / In very likeness of a roasted crab,"* meaning an apple.) The word "Wassail" likely derives from "wish-health," a song that tenant farmers would sing at their landlord's door at Christmastime in the hope of being invited inside for a party. This tradition would eventually become Christmas Caroling, and some songs like "Here We Come a-Wassailing" and "We Wish You a Merry Christmas" still retain this function of a neighborly blessing in exchange for sixpence or figgy pudding. A Wassail song from 1660 begs pardon for drunken indecencies:

> Give to the King
> and Queen wassailing;
> And though with ale ye be whet here;
> Yet part ye from hence,
> As free from offense,
> As when ye innocent met here.[66]

This likely refers to the mock royalty of a Christmas party, and Santa-Claudius is, in many ways, like the mock king of a holiday festival, a creature of appetite. "In carnival time the lower half of the body (belly, digestive tract, genitals) are given preeminence over the upper half (heart and head, emotion and intellect)."[67] The intellectual Hamlet is obsessed with the notion that Claudius, Gertrude and Ophelia are guided only by their lower appetites.

The touring of theater troupes was also traditional at this time of year. Amateurs would go door-to-door offering Mummer pageants, and professional theater companies would do private performances in royal courts (as Shakespeare and company did for several of Queen Elizabeth's Christmas parties). In *Love's Labour's Lost*, Berowne snidely refers to a *"Christmas comedy,"* and in *Taming of the Shrew*, an audience member asks, *"Is not a commonty a Christmas gambold or a tumbling-trick?"* (TS Ind. ii)

Hamlet is persuaded to not return to school at the end of his break, and there is a lapse of time. Ophelia sings a Valentine's Day song and hands out flowers. And then the May Day ritual combat between Hamlet and Laertes beckons the coming of spring. Of course, it's hard to say anything for sure about seasons in Hamlet. Somehow, in the midst of the play, the sarcastic schoolboy prince takes a cruise to England, spends some time among pirates, and returns as a weary 30-year-old.[68]

Twelfth Night

TWELFTH NIGHT

The concept of "Twelve Days of Christmas" mainly survives in the modern world as a cloying and repetitive song about someone whose true love gives them a whole lot of birds and milkmaids. Nobody knows when Jesus was born. May 20th was popular for a while in Western Christianity, while Eastern Christianity celebrated on January 6th. Then, about three hundred years after killing Jesus, the Roman Church decided on December 25th. Since many solar religions of Egypt, Rome, Iran, and Northern Europe were already celebrating at this time of year with gifts, feasts and decorations, the Church Fathers decided to drop this holiday on top of all that as a way to *stop* people from feasting, gifting and decorating. However, it took a while for the Eastern church to accept this, and so from December 25 to January 6 became known as the twelve days of Christmas.

Shakespeare's play, *Twelfth Night, or What You Will*, contains no reference to Christmastime, and the story (mourning followed by weddings) is more suited the end of winter than its middle. The title may derive from the night of the play's debut. On January 6th, 1601, an Italian Duke named Virginio Orsino was visiting Queen Elizabeth's court, and wrote a letter home reporting that after the Twelfth Night banquet,

> Her Majesty mounted the stairs, amid such sounding of trumpets that methought I was on the field of war, and entered a public hall, where all round were rising steps with ladies, and diverse consorts of music. As soon as her Majesty was set at her place many ladies and knights began a Great Ball. When this came to an end, there was acted a mingled comedy, with pieces of music and dances, and this too I am keeping to tell by word of mouth.

Unfortunately, he does not give the title, but with this having been the Twelfth Night, there's a clear possibility that Shakespeare had been commissioned by the Queen to write this play, incorporating the name of the visiting Orsino. The count's opening line, *"if music be the food of love, play on"* may even refer to this show as an interlude in an evening of song and dance.

Shakespeare the businessman was shrewd enough to not explicitly tie any play to any particular holiday. But *Twelfth Night* does contain many elements of Twelfth Night tradition. Coming just after the Winter Solstice, these were some of the shortest days and longest nights of the year, a time when villagers were depressed, farm-work was near impossible, and thus a natural time for mischievous festivity. François Laroque comments that in the play, "the world is nothing but a hall of mirrors. With disguises and misunderstandings abetting, sexes can be swapped, as can identities (but not, except in Malvolio's wishful dreaming, social positions). This was indeed a crossroads of the year, where night won out over day and the interplay of misunderstandings brought forth a comedy of errors and metamorphoses. It was a period that was placed under the aegis of the two-headed Janus, but in this case he is, rather, an androgynous Janus who embodies the junction of two times and two sexes. The theme of an upside-down world is also illustrated, in this interval of mysterious time, by the fact that it is the women who are laying down the law."[69]

Twelfth Night revelries often centered around a mock nobleman known as the Lord of Misrule or "King of the Bean"—whoever found the dried bean in his piece of cake would play this role. The traditional nobleman was ruled by his head and heart, and the Lord of Misrule was an inversion, ruled by his belly, balls and bowels. In the play *Twelfth Night*, the aptly named Sir Toby Belch is a glutton and a drunk with an inappropriate sexual appetite, ultimately marrying the playful chambermaid Maria (one of Shakespeare's *very* few mixed-class pairings) in gratitude for her assistance pranking a local Puritan.

> *The devil a Puritan that he is, or anything constantly but a time-pleaser; an affection'd ass that cons state without book and utters it by great swarths; the best persuaded of himself, so cramm'd, as he thinks, with excellencies that it is his grounds of faith that all that look on him love him; and on that vice in him will my revenge find notable cause to work.* (TN II.iii)

The Puritan in question, Malvolio (a name that means "malicious intent") is introduced as an enemy of festivity. Sir Toby jabs, *"Dost thou think, because thou art virtuous, there shall be no more cakes and ale?"* (TN II.iii) And thus with the chambermaid and court jester he plans a practical joke, to forge a love-letter encouraging the grim Puritan to criss-cross his sock garters, wear yellow and smile all the time. This uncharacteristic behavior, which Olivia calls *"Midsummer madness,"* eventually lands Malvolio in a darkened cellar (the Elizabethan method of treating insanity) from which he finally emerges at the end, re-dedicated to gloomy Puritan malevolence.[70]

The Master of Ceremonies in the play is Feste, the court jester who entertains drunkards with ballads. During Malvolio's confinement, the clown dons the disguise of a priest to convince the Puritan that he's gone mad. And into the middle of this muddle fall a pair of shipwrecked twins – Viola who disguises herself as a man, and her brother Sebastian who shows up at the end to marry the woman Viola accidentally wooed.

The plot of *Twelfth Night* is fragile and tedious like a model Eiffel-Tower built with toothpicks (I had to see this play numerous times just to figure out, finally, that I just don't care). But if we watched the whole thing on fast-forward, the swirl of drunken practical jokes and mistaken identities would make a good composite of Twelfth Night festivity: a woman becomes a man, a Puritan becomes a clown, a clown becomes a priest, a chambermaid becomes a countess, three pairs get married and the scolding Puritan vows revenge.

Linda Woodbridge points out that "Shakespeare heavily favors spring: he never refers to September, October, or November, and only once to February and twice to January, July, and August; but he refers ten times to March, eighteen to April, twenty-two to May, and four to June. The only nonspring month stressed is December; and six of seven references stress its cold barrenness, contrasted with spring or summer."[71]

Autumn with its *"foul and fair"* weather was marked by Samhain, the English day of the dead, observed with necromancy, divination, and considerations of mortality (since not every villager would survive till spring). Although Shakespeare never mentions October by name, the season seems a natural setting for his masterpiece of the macabre, *Macbeth*, in which he resurrects a long-dead pagan king haunted by ghosts and harried by witches.

Winter was a dark and gloomy season for Shakespeare, who lived before the advent of electric lights and heating. He does not refer to any festivity of ringing in the New Year, and his few references to Christmas stress grim survival, not bright renewal. He does seem to have had a fondness for the carnivalesque Twelfth Night, but his play *Twelfth Night* relocates those festivities into spring so that some of the action can take place outdoors. Winter was a huddled, bracing time of morbid musings, awaiting the resurrection of festive fertility in spring.

Afterlife and Ghosts

Funerals

CYMBELINE

All things that we ordained festival
Turn from their office to black funeral:
Our instruments to melancholy bells,
Our wedding cheer to a sad burial feast;
Our solemn hymns to sullen dirges change;
Our bridal flowers serve for a buried corpse,
And all things change them to the contrary. (R&J IV.iv)

Funerals can obviously happen at any time of year, but in terms of this study it makes sense to explore burial customs as we enter into the wintery topics of ghosts and the afterlife.

Shakespeare's most famous funeral scene must be that of Ophelia in *Hamlet*, but it's not indicative of common custom. Ophelia's funeral is a mess, with her brother Laertes picking a fight with the priest, Hamlet leaping into the grave, then picking a fight the Laertes, all while we in the audience digest the news that the grave's former occupant (the clown Yorick) is being evicted and people are toying with his skull. The whole scene is like some ghastly carnival, climaxing in Hamlet and Laertes agreeing to duel over who has a greater claim to the love of this waterlogged cadaver.

Shakespeare gives us a calmer and more common funeral in *Cymbeline*, when the brothers Guiderius and Arviragus must bury a young man they've met (actually a princess in disguise, their unknown sister, who's not really dead but been semi-poisoned by her evil step-mother... It's complicated). I've abbreviated this scene to focus on the mechanics of a funeral. Decorating a body with flowers was symbolic of death-and-resurrection, since flowers that seem to die in winter rise again in spring. Laying the body facing east came from ancient flat earth beliefs about the sun dying in the west to be reborn in the east, and thus a body was to be laid in place to witness the rebirth of the sun. Christianity continued this old custom, with the idea that the "son" would someday rise again in the east and dead believers should be positioned to see this on resurrection day.

This funeral in *Cymbeline* would have been conducted mostly in song. One of the brothers will discourage the other from giving a long speech because singing was considered to be more appropriate. And the content of the song will be a magic spell to protect the body from any disturbance by fairies, witches, ghosts or necromancers (conjurers who interrogate the dead, here called exorcisers):

> GUIDERIUS. *Why, he but sleeps.*
> *If he be gone he'll make his grave a bed;*
> *with female fairies will his tomb be haunted,*
> *And worms will not come to thee.*
> ARVIRAGUS. *With fairest flowers,*
> *Whilst summer lasts and I live here, Fidele,*
> *I'll sweeten thy sad grave...*
> GUIDERIUS. *Prithee have done,*
> *And do not play in wench-like words with that*
> *Which is so serious. Let us bury him,*
> *And not protract with admiration what*
> *Is now due debt. To th' grave.*
> *...We must lay his head to th' East;*
> *My father hath a reason for't.*
> [SONG]
> GUIDERIUS. *Fear no more the heat o' th' sun*
> *Nor the furious winter's rages;*
> *Thou thy worldly task hast done,*

Home art gone, and ta'en thy wages.
Golden lads and girls all must,
As chimney-sweepers, come to dust.
ARVIRAGUS. Fear no more the frown o' th' great;
Thou art past the tyrant's stroke.
Care no more to clothe and eat;
To thee the reed is as the oak.
The sceptre, learning, physic, must
All follow this and come to dust.
GUIDERIUS. Fear no more the lightning flash,
ARVIRAGUS. Nor th' all-dreaded thunder-stone;
GUIDERIUS. Fear not slander, censure rash;
ARVIRAGUS. Thou hast finish'd joy and moan.
BOTH. All lovers young, all lovers must
Consign to thee and come to dust.
GUIDERIUS. No exorciser harm thee!
ARVIRAGUS. Nor no witchcraft charm thee!
GUIDERIUS. Ghost unlaid forbear thee!
ARVIRAGUS. Nothing ill come near thee!
BOTH. Quiet consummation have,
And renowned be thy grave!
[End of singing]
GUIDERIUS. We have done our obsequies. Come, lay him down.
BELARIUS. Here's a few flowers; but 'bout midnight, more.
The herbs that have on them cold dew o' th' night
Are strewings fit'st for graves. Upon their faces.
You were as flow'rs, now wither'd. Even so
These herblets shall which we upon you strew.
Come on, away. Apart upon our knees.
The ground that gave them first has them again.
Their pleasures here are past, so is their pain. (CYM IV.ii)

Purgatory
HAMLET | KING LEAR

Shakespeare has a few nice lines about the afterlife, like Horatio's prayer for dead Hamlet: *"And flights of angels sing thee to thy rest."* (HAM V.ii) But on the whole, the view of death is grim and dismal. In *Measure for Measure*, a prisoner awaiting execution speaks of what he expects:

> *Death is a fearful thing...*
> *Ay, but to die, and go we know not where;*
> *To lie in cold obstruction, and to rot;*
> *This sensible warm motion to become*
> *A kneaded clod; and the delighted spirit*
> *To bathe in fiery floods or to reside*
> *In thrilling region of thick-ribbed ice;*
> *To be imprison'd in the viewless winds,*
> *And blown with restless violence round about*
> *The pendent world; or to be worse than worst*
> *Of those that lawless and incertain thought*
> *Imagine howling- 'tis too horrible.*
> *The weariest and most loathed worldly life*
> *That age, ache, penury, and imprisonment,*
> *Can lay on nature is a paradise*
> *To what we fear of death.* (MFM III.ii)

And the ghost of King Hamlet, as an eyewitness, can only offer a few ghastly details:

> *My hour is almost come,*
> *When I to sulph'rous and tormenting flames*
> *Must render up myself...*
> *I am thy father's spirit,*
> *Doom'd for a certain term to walk the night,*
> *And for the day confin'd to fast in fires,*
> *Till the foul crimes done in my days of nature*
> *Are burnt and purg'd away. But that I am forbid*

To tell the secrets of my prison-house,
I could a tale unfold whose lightest word
Would harrow up thy soul; freeze thy young blood,
Make thy two eyes like stars start from their spheres,
Thy knotted and combined locks to part,
And each particular hair to stand on end
Like quills upon the fretful porcupine.
But this eternal blazon must not be
To ears of flesh and blood. (HAM I.v)

The key word here is *"purg'd."* The dead king is imprisoned in a place where his soul is being purged/cleansed through torment. He is in Purgatory.

Purgatory was a Roman addition to Christianity, stemming from a belief that no human could really be righteous enough to go straight to heaven, and yet small sins and omissions would not necessarily mean an eternity in Hell (if people believe they'll be damned for small sins, then in frustration they may go ahead with bigger ones). And so the Roman Church established that after death, basically-decent Christians could serve a brief sentence for minor sins, work off their debt and get to paradise, even if it took centuries. Rome then added that giving money to the church (on one's own behalf or as a gift-certificate for someone else) could decrease one's Purgatory sentence and paying a priest to hear a final confession could help as well.[72]

The ghost of king Hamlet later clarifies that, worse than just being murdered, he was:

Cut off even in the blossoms of my sin...
No reckoning made, but sent to my account
With all my imperfections on my head. (HAM I.v)

Because he never had a chance to offer a final confession, the sins of his life were not absolved by a priest. Hamlet will later express the same belief, when he sneaks up on Claudius and almost kills him, but hears his uncle confessing his sins.

HAMLET. Now might I do it pat, now he is praying.
And now I'll do't. And so he goes to heaven;
And so am I reveng'd. That would be scann'd:

A villain kills my father, and for that
I, his sole son, do this same villain send
To heaven. O, this is hire and salary, not revenge...
To take him in the purging of his soul,
When he is fit and season'd for his passage? No...
When he is drunk asleep; or in his rage,
Or in th'incestuous pleasure of his bed,
At gaming, swearing; or about some act
That has no relish of salvation in't,
Then trip him, that his heels may kick at heaven,
And that his soul may be as damn'd and black
As hell, whereto it goes. (HAM III.iii)

So Hamlet leaves (ironically, Claudius then admits his prayer was empty). And although Hamlet does succeed in killing his uncle in the act of some wicked deeds, Hamlet himself never makes a religious confession, and the play gives no hint that King Hamlet's ghost will benefit from this revenge. After all that effort and bloodshed, the ghost doesn't even show up to say "Thank ye."[73]

Shakespeare was a lapsed Catholic writing for an audience mostly composed of lapsed Catholics, and so it's no surprise that he should present the afterlife in this way. But he also managed to craftily weave the doctrine of Purgatory into some of his other plays and accomplish this so subtly that it could easily be missed.

Like the source play that inspired it, King Lear begins as a comedy (a silly fairy tale king banishes his loving daughter, is tormented by wicked sisters, the penniless princess marries a prince, they live happily ever after) but in Shakespeare's hands this pleasant Pastoral mutates into a Purgatory.

In the opening scene, King Lear symbolically dies by giving up his rule and banishing Cordelia, the daughter who loves him. He then banishes himself, alienating his two heiresses, and spends most of the play wandering in the wilderness, the no-where between communities. There he is tormented, and his refusal to weep causes the skies to open.[74] His loyal and likewise banished friend Kent speaks of this ungodly weather as supernatural, beyond human capacity to bear:

Alas, sir, are you here? Things that love night
Love not such nights as these; the wrathful skies

Gallow the very wanderers of the dark,
And make them keep their caves. Since I was man,
Such sheets of fire, such bursts of horrid thunder,
Such groans of roaring wind and rain I never
Remember to have heard. Man's nature cannot carry
Th'affliction, nor the fear. (KL III.ii)

Lear is greatly relieved when he is apprehended and imprisoned. After all his mad bluster against the winds and weather, the prospect of a man-made dungeon is calming, it makes more sense to him than the howling void, the limbo between the kingdoms. And here he can be reunited with what's best about him: Cordelia.

Come, let's away to prison:
We two alone will sing like birds i' the cage:
When thou dost ask me blessing I'll kneel down
And ask of thee forgiveness. So we'll live,
And pray, and sing, and tell old tales, and laugh
At gilded butterflies. (KL V.iii)

Cordelia is released from Purgatory first, into death, and her release into eternity finally enables Lear to weep, which releases him into death as well. He dies of happiness.

The Penal Colony

TEMPEST

The Tempest is at once Shakespeare's most metaphorical depiction of Purgatory *and* his most literal. The story begins with a nightmarish storm: sea and sky recombine into primordial chaos infested with demonic phantasms, a man on the ship cries out, *"Hell is empty and all the devils are here!"*[75] Shipwrecked survivors wash up on the shore like the Biblical Jonah, and yet the island itself is like the belly of a whale.

Every character on this penal colony island is banished: Prospero and Miranda from Milan, Ariel from liberty, Caliban from his inheritance, the voyagers from their ship, their comrades, and reality. And each group of travelers believes that all other passengers are dead. The play takes place nowhere—an island of indeterminate size, shape, and climate.[76] Each character sees a different landscape, depending on their own temperament. The honest Gonzalo sees *"lush and lusty"* greenery while the others see barrenness. Another unsettled and unsettling dimension of the play is time (the Latin *tempestas* refers to both storm and time). At the end we are told that only three hours have gone by, and this may indeed be true for the audience, and for show's on stage director-producer-designer Prospero, but the king and his retainers seem to have been there for two days. Each character's sentence is relative to their own transgressions.[77]

The longest and worst of Prospero's punishments are reserved for his brother, who usurped him as Duke of Milan, and the king of Naples who allowed it to happen (and whose own brother plans to kill and replace him). They wander lost and haunted in a desolate wasteland for an indeterminate period. At the midpoint, Prospero taunts them with a banquet:

> *Solemn and strange music; and PROSPERO on the top, invisible.*
> *Enter several strange SHAPES, bringing in a banquet; and dance*
> *about it with gentle actions of salutations; and inviting the KING,*
> *etc., to eat, they depart.* (TEM III.iii)

Then, after the king and his courtiers express their sense of entitlement and comment on how they'll enjoy this feast,

> *Thunder and lightning. Enter ARIEL, like a harpy; claps his wings*
> *upon the table; and, with a quaint device, the banquet vanishes.*
> (TEM III.iii)

Ariel is called a harpy here, but sounds Satanic:

> *You are three men of sin... I and my fellows*
> *Are ministers of Fate...and do pronounce...*
> *Ling'ring perdition, worse than any death*
> *Can be at once, shall step by step attend*
> *You and your ways; whose wraths to guard you from —*
> *Which here, in this most desolate isle, else falls*

Upon your heads – is nothing but heart's sorrow,
And clear life ensuing. (TEM III.iii)

In this speech we see *"sin"* deserving *"ling'ring perdition"* in a *"lower world"* in order to purify them for a *"clear life."* And they do indeed clean up their act.

In Prospero's climactic monologue, he claims to have raised the dead:

Graves at my command
Have wak'd their sleepers, op'd, and let 'em forth,
By my so potent art. (TEM V.i)

Commentators have asked why we don't get to see this act as part of the play, but arguably we do. The text protests too much that no one was harmed or killed in the storm, but the story makes far more sense if we accept that the voyagers all died, did various penances to purify themselves, and were restored to life.

Then Prospero's speech continues with a longing for heavenly music, his own personal release from the purgatory of vengefulness, and he acknowledges that it will cost him his magical power over life and death (he must bury his implements in land and sea):

But this rough magic
I here abjure; and, when I have requir'd
Some heavenly music – which even now I do –
To work mine end upon their senses that
This airy charm is for, I'll break my staff,
Bury it certain fathoms in the earth,
And deeper than did ever plummet sound
I'll drown my book. (TEM V.i)

Prospero speaks of return to the earthly Milan, but not with any positivity: it's bland in comparison with his island of illusions, and he says every third thought will be of his death.

Prospero then returns for a final speech to the audience (the unseen watcher and judge), praying for release. Northrop Frye comments that the tone echoes The Lord's Prayer.[78] It also bears a certain rhythmic relation to "Now I Lay Me Down to Sleep" (composed a century later in 1711, but still a fascinating coincidence).

> *Now my charms are all o'erthrown,*
> *And what strength I have's mine own,*
> *Which is most faint. Now 'tis true,*
> *I must be here confin'd by you,*
> *Or sent to Naples. Let me not,*
> *Since I have my dukedom got,*
> *And pardon'd the deceiver, dwell*
> *In this bare island by your spell;*
> *But release me from my bands*
> *With the help of your good hands...*
> *And my ending is despair*
> *Unless I be reliev'd by prayer,*
> *Which pierces so that it assaults*
> *Mercy itself, and frees all faults.*
> *As you from crimes would pardon'd be,*
> *Let your indulgence set me free.* (TEM Epilogue)

This coda is filled with Catholic doctrine: that the joining of hands (applause yes, but also in prayer) will be the *"indulgence"* (a coupon to decrease a loved one's term in Purgatory) that will pardon sins and release the sinner.[79] *The Tempest* is a worthy title for the play, not only for the storm that strands the characters in Prospero's freak show revenge-carnival, but also for the personal cyclone each character must weather. And yet Shakespeare could have called this one *Purgatorio.*

Ghost-Lore
WINTER'S TALE

> *HERMIONE. Pray you sit by us,*
> *And tell's a tale...*
> *MAMILLIUS. A sad tale's best for winter. I have one*

Of sprites and goblins.
HERMIONE. Let's have that, good sir.
Come on, sit down; come on, and do your best
To fright me with your sprites; you're pow'rfull at it.
MAMILLIUS. There was a man...
Dwelt by a churchyard – I will tell it softly;
Yond crickets shall not hear it.
HERMIONE. Come on then,
And give't me in mine ear. (WT II.i)

This warm scene of a mother requesting a ghost story from her young son is interrupted by the entrance of King Leontes, whose mad jealousy kills them both. But here in this brief exchange we see the familiar image of sharing ghost stories as family entertainment. Whether or not these characters believe in these sprites we do not know, but later in the story there will be a horrific sighting of Hermione's ghost.

Long winter nights were a natural time for supernatural tales of sprites (which could mean either spirits/ghosts or fairies) and goblins. These were the dark days before electric light, central heating or modern insulation, when huddling close together by the household fireplace could literally be a matter of life and death. And in this setting, as the old year died and the new was born, women would tell and retell stories about transition: fairy tales (about children becoming adults) and ghost stories (about life and death). These fireside tales tended to be multi-layered, appealing to children and adults on different levels. "Little Red Riding Hood" is an easy example, a story about caution and obedience, but also about sexual predation. And while our modern children's fairy-tale industry focuses primarily on the wish-fulfillment, kitchen-to-castle, rags-to-riches side, old oral fairy tales tended to be darker, delving into fears and anxieties, peeking into shadows of that realm that we now call the unconscious.

The ghost story scene of *Winter's Tale* contains what at first seems an inversion: a boy telling a ghost story to his mother. Then this turns out to foreshadow the boy's approaching death, and the tale is significantly interrupted by his father Leontes, who will be the cause of it. But the boy's spoken prologue, a man who lived by a graveyard will encounter sprites and goblins, tells us enough: the boundary between death and life will be crossed, and that's a fitting tale for winter.

Ghost lore seems to be universal—the question of whether our consciousness continues after death seems to be as old as human consciousness itself. And the question of whether we can continue to play a role in human affairs has had a tremendous variety of responses from different cultures: can we still guide those we love? Get back at those we hate? Enjoy a nice night-time stroll? Shakespeare's plays are filled with night-walking spirits. The fairy Puck warns Oberon at daybreak:

> *My fairy lord, this must be done with haste,*
> *For night's swift dragons cut the clouds full fast,*
> *And yonder shines Aurora's harbinger;*
> *At whose approach, ghosts, wandering here and there,*
> *Troop home to churchyards. Damned spirits all,*
> *That in crossways and floods have burial,*[80]
> *Already to their wormy beds are gone.*
> *For fear lest day should look their shames upon,*
> *They wilfully themselves exile from light,*
> *And must for aye consort with black-browed night.* (MND III.ii)

Shakespeare inherited the tradition of the ghost as nemesis from Roman theater, a manifestation of a victim haunting a murderer for vengeance. On stage these tended to be stiff and either silent or repetitive. Shakespeare's first ghosts speak, as in *Richard III*, but then he writes silent ghosts for nearly a decade before giving Caesar's ghost a few lines, King Hamlet a whole meaty scene, and one line each to three phantoms in *Macbeth*.

During Shakespeare's lifetime, there was a cultural debate going on about the nature of "ghosts." In old, pre-Christian pagan times, it was widely believed that spirits of the dead would remain to watch over living relatives. With the arrival of Christianity, this was gradually adjusted to the belief that good people departed for Heaven, while shades of murder victims, suicides and executed criminals were cursed to wander the earth after death. This fit well with the developing Roman Catholic doctrine of Purgatory, a sort of debtor's prison for souls that had not been sufficiently purified through expensive Catholic penances.[81]

Shakespeare lived and wrote during the early years of the Protestant Reformation, which rejected Purgatory as a sort of hostage/extortion racket, and insisted that "ghosts" were just devils who could assume familiar shapes of dead loved ones to fool believers into committing rash deeds. To make this more confusing, there seems also to have been a counter-belief that angels could also assume familiar forms to steer believers correctly. Shakespeare's plays contain examples of all these forms of ghosts: Greek nemeses, unredeemed victims, and mischievous fiends in disguise. Hamlet in particular will debate with himself at length about which of these he has seen.

Nemesis
Titus | Romeo and Juliet | Julius Caesar | Macbeth | Winter's Tale

Shakespeare's *Richard III* is a long bloody series of murders by which the hunchback Richard joyfully gains and briefly keeps the throne of England. It's also Shakespeare's second longest play (just a bit shorter than *Hamlet*). And so to heighten the drama as it builds to climax, we see Richard on the night before his final battle visited in series by the ghosts of his victims–almost everyone in the play. They proceed like a death-masque parade, each cursing Richard to *"despair and die,"* and each blessing Henry the Earl of Richmond to kill him.

> *The lights burn blue. It is now dead midnight.*
> *Cold fearful drops stand on my trembling flesh.*
> *What do I fear? Myself? There's none else by.*
> *Richard loves Richard; that is, I am I...*
> *My conscience hath a thousand several tongues,*
> *And every tongue brings in a several tale,*
> *And every tale condemns me for a villain...*
> *Methought the souls of all that I had murder'd*
> *Came to my tent, and every one did threat*
> *To-morrow's vengeance on the head of Richard.* (R3 V.iii)

Richard, perhaps Shakespeare's most gleeful and cartoonish villain, pretty much takes this in stride. He already knows he's bad, and never expected to live forever.

Another of Shakespeare's earliest blockbusters was *Titus Andronicus*, a horrific atrocity show about a Roman general who is tragically rigid in politics and religion. And his strict formalism ironically throws all of Rome into a chaos of nightmarish debauchery and barbarity. S. Clark Hulse calculated that this tragedy contains "14 killings, 9 of them on stage, 6 severed members, 1 rape (or 2 or 3, depending on how you count), 1 live burial, 1 case of insanity, and 1 of cannibalism—an average of 5.2 atrocities per act, or one for every 97 lines."[82] It is also, at times, quite funny.

The play opens with the battle-weary general returning from a decade at war with the Goths. He brings corpses of his sons slain in battle, and also four prisoners: the Goth queen Tamora and her three sons.

> *TITUS. [to himself] Titus, unkind, and careless of thine own,*
> *Why suffer'st thou thy sons, unburied yet,*
> *To hover on the dreadful shore of Styx?*
> *Make way to lay them by their brethren...*
> *LUCIUS. Give us the proudest prisoner of the Goths,*
> *That we may hew his limbs, and on a pile*
> *Ad manes fratrum [to brothers' spirits] sacrifice his flesh*
> *Before this earthy prison of their bones,*
> *That so the shadows be not unappeas'd,*
> *Nor we disturb'd with prodigies on earth...*
> *TITUS. Religiously they ask a sacrifice.*
> *To this your son is mark'd, and die he must*
> *T'appease their groaning shadows that are gone.* (TA I.i)

Despite the Goth queen's plea for her eldest son's life, Titus has him sacrificed for vengeance, so that his dead sons will not become vengeful nemesis-ghosts. He does this according to Roman religious belief, not suspecting that the Goth queen's vendetta will initiate a cycle of violence eventually killing just about everyone. But the play ends happily enough, with Titus making the Goth queen eat her sons' testicles. (Appetite-spoiler alert.)

Romeo and Juliet contains the same belief in spirits of the slain demanding sacrifice. After Juliet's cousin has killed Romeo's friend, Romeo demands a duel, saying:

Mercutio's soul
Is but a little way above our heads,
Staying for thine to keep him company.
Either thou or I, or both, must go with him. (R&J III.i)

Because of the way that Mercutio died (Romeo restrained him and Tybalt stabbed him) it's unclear which of them is responsible for his death. It's possible that Romeo's cry of *"thou or I, or both, must go with him"* is a summons for Mercutio's ghost to adjudicate who should bear the responsibility. Juliet in turn believes that the ghost of Tybalt will haunt Romeo or her or both. She fears that after semi-poisoning herself she'll awaken in the family crypt:

As in a vault, an ancient receptacle...
Where bloody Tybalt, yet but green in earth,
Lies festering in his shroud; where, as they say,
At some hours in the night spirits resort—
[With] shrieks like mandrakes torn out of the earth,
That living mortals, hearing them, run mad.
O, if I wake, shall I not be distraught,
Environed with all these hideous fears,
And madly play with my forefathers' joints?
And pluck the mangled Tybalt from his shroud?
And, in this rage, with some great kinsman's bone,
As with a club, dash out my desperate brains?
O look, methinks I see my cousin's ghost
Seeking out Romeo that did spit his body
Upon a rapier's point. Stay, Tybalt, stay!
Romeo, Romeo, Romeo, here's drink! I drink to thee. (R&J IV.iii)

Caesar's ghost is one of many apparitions haunting Shakespeare's *Julius Caesar*. Before Caesar's assassination, two characters report that graves are opening and angry spirits are possessing people and animals, waging battles in the air. The first report comes from the conspirator Cassius:

See the strange impatience of the Heavens:
But if you would consider the true cause

Why all these fires, why all these gliding ghosts,
Why birds and beasts, from quality and kind;
Why old men, fools, and children calculate,...
Heaven hath infus'd them with these spirits
To make them instruments of fear and warning
Unto some monstrous state...this dreadful night,
That thunders, lightens, opens graves, and roars,
As doth the lion in the Capitol. (JC I.iii)

The second report is Caesar's wife Calphurnia, warning her husband:

A lioness hath whelped in the streets,
And graves have yawn'd, and yielded up their dead;
Fierce fiery warriors fight upon the clouds
In ranks and squadrons and right form of war,
Which drizzled blood upon the Capitol;
The noise of battle hurtled in the air,
Horses did neigh, and dying men did groan,
And ghosts did shriek and squeal about the streets. (JC II.ii)

Then, before the final battle, Cassius delivers the Shakespeare-ism, *"Our army lies, ready to give up the ghost."* (JC V.i)

With all this going on, the actual appearance of "Great Caesar's Ghost" is a bit anticlimactic. As Brutus prepares the night before a battle, his candlelight turns blue.

BRUTUS. How ill this taper burns! Ha! who comes here?
I think it is the weakness of mine eyes
That shapes this monstrous apparition.
It comes upon me. Art thou anything?
Art thou some god, some angel, or some devil,
That mak'st my blood cold and my hair to stare?
Speak to me what thou art.
GHOST. Thy evil spirit, Brutus.
BRUTUS. Why com'st thou?
GHOST. To tell thee thou shalt see me at Philippi...
BRUTUS. Why, I will see thee at Philippi then. (Ghost vanishes.)

Now I have taken heart, thou vanishest.
Ill spirit, I would hold more talk with thee. (JC IV.iii)

He pursues and asks if others have seen the ghost but it is gone. Shakespeare copied this exchange almost word-for-word from first century Roman historical novelist Plutarch's *Life of Brutus*. Plutarch does not identify this as the ghost of Caesar himself, but as a generic nemesis, "thy evil spirit," and Shakespeare preserves this ambiguity. In this scene, Brutus shows no emotional attachment to this ghost and doesn't even seem that afraid of it.

Only later does Brutus seem to figure out that the ghost he saw was specifically Julius Caesar: "*The ghost of Caesar hath appear'd to me / ...I know my hour is come.*" (JC V.v)

And his last words before suicidally leaping on his own sword acknowledge that the emperor cannot rest until he's dead: "*Caesar, now be still / I kill'd not thee with half so good a will.*" (JC V.v)

The ghost in *Hamlet* is silent in its first appearance (to some random guys, not the killer). It appears just after midnight, and then vanishes when the rooster crows a few minutes later. Either Shakespeare believed Scandinavian nights were very short, or perhaps intended that this prologue scene be seven hours long. The philosophy student Horatio explains:

> *I have heard*
> *The cock, that is the trumpet to the morn,*
> *Doth with his lofty and shrill-sounding throat*
> *Awake the god of day; and at his warning,*
> *Whether in sea or fire, in earth or air,*
> *Th'extravagant and erring spirit hies* [hurries]
> *To his confine.* (HAM I.i)

He then reports a folk-belief that roosters crow all night on Christmas Eve so that ghosts will not come wandering. The speaking role of King Hamlet's ghost will be explored in the next section.

Macbeth has numerous phantom apparitions, including a silent spectre in the form of Banquo. Before sending his friend off to die, Macbeth absent-mindedly commands him to attend the coronation banquet: "*fail not our feast,*" and Banquo answers "*My lord, I will not.*" (MAC III.i) And then his ghost does indeed honor the invitation, spoiling Macbeth's victory party by sitting in the king's own chair (reminding us of the Weird Sisters' prophecy that Banquo's offspring will have the throne).

> *MACBETH. If charnel houses and our graves must send*
> *Those that we bury back, our monuments*
> *Shall be the maws of kites... The time has been,*
> *That, when the brains were out, the man would die,*
> *And there an end; but now they rise again...*
> *And push us from our stools. This is more strange*
> *Than such a murther is...* (MAC III.iv)

But then Macbeth dismisses the possibility that this is the spirit of Banquo in particular, and addresses it as a generic nemesis who's assumed Banquo's form:

> *Approach thou like the rugged Russian bear,*
> *The arm'd rhinoceros, or the Hyrcan tiger;*
> *Take any shape but that, and my firm nerves*
> *Shall never tremble. Or be alive again,*
> *And dare me to the desert with thy sword.*
> *Hence, horrible shadow! ...Unreal mockery, hence!* (MAC III.iv)

Shakespeare saves his most terrifying ghost for last. In *The Winter's Tale*, the insanely jealous King Leontes orders his pregnant wife be thrown in prison, then commands that their newborn baby be abandoned in the wilderness. The queen collapses on-stage; she is dragged off and declared dead. A courtier named Antigonus is charged with dumping the infant on a far-away shore, and during a horrific tempest at sea, queen Hermione's ghost appears to him.

> *ANTIGONUS. I have heard, but not believ'd, the spirits o' th' dead*
> *May walk again. If such thing be, thy mother*
> *Appear'd to me last night; for ne'er was dream*
> *So like a waking. To me comes a creature,*
> *Sometimes her head on one side some another –*
> *I never saw a vessel of like sorrow,*
> *So fill'd and so becoming; in pure white robes,*

Like very sanctity, she did approach
My cabin where I lay; thrice bow'd before me;
And, gasping to begin some speech, her eyes
Became two spouts; the fury spent, anon
Did this break from her: 'Good Antigonus,
Since fate, against thy better disposition,
Hath made thy person for the thrower-out
Of my poor babe, according to thine oath,
Places remote enough are in Bohemia,
There weep, and leave it crying; and, for the babe
Is counted lost for ever, Perdita
I prithee call't. For this ungentle business,
Put on thee by my lord, thou ne'er shalt see
Thy wife Paulina more.' so, with shrieks,
She melted into air. (WT III.iii)

Antigonus leaves the child in a basket and then is eaten by a bear (perhaps a jab at Elizabethan theater's entertainment market competitor, bear-baiting). In the final resolution scene when all this ghastly mess gets sorted out and Hermione returns, Shakespeare half-heartedly hints that she was alive all along, hidden away for sixteen years. But the vivid apparition of this ghost testifies that Hermione was dead and is later resurrected.

King Hamlet

HAMLET

King Hamlet is Shakespeare's most famous ghost, and deservedly so. Here we see a major leap forward in ghost lore.[83] Legend has it William Shakespeare played this ghost himself early in his acting career (this may have been a mysterious Thomas Kyd script that vanished without a trace, but was more likely Shakespeare's own first draft), and the ghost stiffly bellowed "Hamlet! Revenge!" Then for about a decade people drunkenly jostled poor William in pubs, shouting "Hamlet! Revenge!" So he returned to the role with a vengeance, as both author and actor, conjuring his most nuanced spectre.[84]

Even in the earlier play, the ghost of King Hamlet was unique in that he did not haunt his murderer, but only spoke to his chosen avenger. And in a bizarre twist, this Viking warrior's son is a theater-going bookworm, a doubly ironic beat poet hipster, a Renaissance man-boy trapped in a medieval blood feud. The warrior-king must have been turning in his grave, tormented by this sarcastic prince's utter refusal to be Machiavellian—he doesn't care enough about the prize (hillbilly Elsinore) to play to win (which would entail *becoming* Claudius and turning Ophelia into Gertrude).

Hamlet's famous indecision is largely a vacillation between the old Pagan/Catholic belief in souls crying out for vengeance/release, and the new Protestant belief in devilish fiends taking familiar forms to trick believers. This debate within the play begins as soon as the apparition appears.

The first witnesses follow the Protestant assumption that this is *not* the particular ghost of King Hamlet, but some spirit that has chosen to look like him:

> BARNARDO. *In the same figure,* like *the King that's dead*
> *...Looks it not* like *the King? Mark it, Horatio.*
> HORATIO. *Most* like. ...*What art thou that usurp'st this time of night,*
> *Together with that fair and warlike* form
> *In which the majesty of buried Denmark*
> *Did sometimes march? By heaven I charge thee speak.*
> (HAM I.i, emphasis added)

There's no way he would have spoken to *King* Hamlet in this manner. Later when they bring prince Hamlet to see this apparition, he too initially imagines it to be an angel or devil in his father's shape, then makes a subtle transition to the Catholic belief that this *is* his father:

> HAMLET. *Be thou a spirit of health* [healed/saved] *or goblin damn'd,*
> *Bring with thee airs from heaven or blasts from hell,*
> *Be thy intents wicked or charitable,*
> *Thou com'st in such a questionable shape*
> *That I will speak to thee. I'll call thee Hamlet,*
> *King, father, royal Dane. O, answer me!* (HAM I.iv)

His friend once more attempts to pull Hamlet back to Protestantism:

> *HORATIO. What if it tempt you toward the flood, my lord,*
> *Or to the dreadful summit of the cliff*
> *beetles o'er his base into the sea,*
> *And there assume some other horrible form|*
> *Which might deprive your sovereignty of reason,*
> *And draw you into madness?* (HAM I.iv)

But Hamlet follows the ghost to a remote place where it clearly says *"I am thy father's spirit,"* and proceeds to demonstrate this with intimate details, including the embarrassing admission that his wife cheated on him. *"It is an honest ghost, that let me tell you,"* mutters the too-much-information scarred prince afterward. And so Hamlet is all set for revenge...until he over-thinks it.

> *HAMLET. The spirit that I have seen*
> *May be the devil, and the devil hath power*
> *T'assume a pleasing shape, yea, and perhaps*
> *Out of my weakness and my melancholy,*
> *As he is very potent with such spirits,*
> *Abuses me to damn me. I'll have grounds*
> *More relative than this. The play's the thing*
> *Wherein I'll catch the conscience of the King.* (HAM II.ii)

Hamlet employs his theatricality (his greatest power–he practically directs the whole play from on stage). And once King Claudius has revealed his guilt during the players' performance, Hamlet is finally satisfied: *"I'll take the ghost's word for a thousand pound."* Pounds of what, we don't know, since the Pound was not Danish currency. He finds Claudius praying and almost kills him, but then his Roman Catholicism stops him: if he kills Claudius after a confession, his uncle will go straight to Heaven, and Hamlet resolves that his uncle must go to Hell, where he intends to follow and continue tormenting Claudius for all eternity. Then in a dark comic twist, after Hamlet slinks away, Claudius reveals that his confession was empty.

Prince Hamlet is tragically Roman Catholic in his belief that his father is in Purgatory and his mother is a virgin. He studied in Wittenberg 500 years too early to meet Martin Luther (although he does make an obscure joke about the Diet of Worms). And so the bodies pile up for another three acts. French philosopher Voltaire summarizes:

> It is a coarse and barbarous piece, which would not be tolerated by the lowest rabble of France and Italy. In it Hamlet becomes mad in the second act, his mistress becomes mad in the third; the prince kills the father of his mistress under pretense of killing a rat, and the heroine throws herself into the river... Grave-diggers indulge in quibbles worthy of themselves, while holding in their hands the skulls of the dead. Prince Hamlet replies to their abominable vulgarities by stuff not less disgusting. During this time one of the actors makes the conquest of Poland. Hamlet, his mother, and his stepfather drink together on the stage. They sing at the table, they quarrel, they beat one another, they kill one another. One would suppose this work to be the fruit of the imagination of a drunken savage.[85]

The Ghost of King Hamlet is impressive in early scenes, but the role takes on its greatest depth in his final appearance: as Hamlet harangues his mother about her sex life, the Ghost reappears to sharpen his son's focus and demand tenderness for his widow. We've seen King Hamlet in his battle armor giving militaristic marching orders, but now we see an endearing family snapshot (so rare in Shakespeare!), and this is the enduring originality of this stage-Ghost. "Shakespeare offers us the warrior king, the gracious father, and the husband who bears with him to the abode of spirits a love for a faithless wife."[86]

The Curse of "The Scottish Play"

MACBETH

The grotesque Halloween atrocity-carnival *Macbeth* contains numerous ghost sightings in various forms, including a floating dagger, three invisible wraiths entering at the gate, the murdered Banquo, an *"armed head,"*[87] two babies (*"bloody child"* and *"child crowned with a tree in his hand"*), a parade of eight future kings, and phantom blood on Lady Macbeth's hands. The play is multi-dimensional; while we watch the Macbeths, they witness these bloody pageants.

Upon hearing of his wife's death, Macbeth himself concludes that *"Life's but a walking shadow,"* which reminds us of yet another dimension of this piece: the play is, itself, a ghostly apparition, a phantom-masque of long-dead personalities being conjured to possess the bodies of performers on a stage. There's a theatrical superstition against calling this play by its name during production, because "the Scottish Play" is supposed to be cursed. I would dismiss this, but after researching the historical Macbeths, I can't help but wonder if their ghosts do haunt this play, seeking revenge for how badly they've been misrepresented.

The historical Macbeth killed Duncan fair-and-square in battle, and as nephew to former king Malcolm II, had a legitimate claim to the throne. His wife, Gruoch,[88] was granddaughter to a prior Scottish king, Kenneth IV, who'd been slain and usurped by Duncan's grandfather, so she had a justified familial vendetta to take the throne *back*. Macbeth reigned from 1040-1057 (which means he may have known the historical Hamlet's father) and did apparently become paranoid during the last seven years—understandably so, considering the bloody history of royal successions. He did die by violence and was succeeded by a stepson who reigned for less than a year before being assassinated and succeeded by Malcolm III.

The real indignity here is that Shakespeare built the play to please King James, descended from the historical Banquo and obsessed with witches. There was indeed some report of the Celtic Macbeth consorting with "weird sisters." But seeking a more shocking succession, the sensationalist Shakespeare found another story in Holinshed's *Chronicles*, of a Donwald whose wife convinced him to murder their house guest King Duff. Isaac Asimov comments, "Shakespeare transplanted the deed bodily from Donwald to Macbeth, saddling the latter forever with a crime he probably would never have dreamed of committing. What's more, he made Lady Macbeth bear the blame of Lady Donwald through all the centuries. It is indeed a fearful example of the power of the pen to alter the truth itself if it is wielded with sufficient genius."[89]

So it would be no surprise if these unjustly slandered spirits were to work mischief against theatrical companies for profiting by this libel. Or maybe the Donwalds haunt the show for stealing credit for their rash and bloody deeds. Who knows what spirits are invoked when they hear the name "Macbeth?"

Spring Festivals

Valentine's Day | Lupercalia
HAMLET | JULIUS CAESAR

OPHELIA. (Sings.)
Tomorrow is Saint Valentine's day,
All in the morning betime,
And I a maid at your window,
To be your Valentine.
Then up he rose and donn'd his clothes,
And dupp'd the chamber door,
Let in the maid, that out a maid
Never departed more....
　　　By Gis and by Saint Charity,
　　　Alack, and fie for shame!
　　　Young men will do't if they come to't;
　　　By Cock, they are to blame.
Quoth she, before you tumbled me,
You promis'd me to wed.
[He replied] So would I ha' done, by yonder sun,
[if] thou hadst not come to my bed. (HAM IV.v)

The maddened Ophelia's Valentine ballad concerns an old folk-belief that the first two unmarried people to see each other on that day would later be married, and thus the maiden positions herself outside this bachelor's window in the morning. However, this forward maiden learns the hard lesson that, in seducing this man, she has made herself ineligible for marriage. Whether or not this song reflects Ophelia's own breakup with Hamlet we do not know.

Superstitions about divining future marriages are related to an old belief that birds choose their mates on this day. In *Midsummer Night's Dream*, Theseus refers to this when he finds two couples sleeping at the edge of the forest: "*Good-morrow, friends. Saint Valentine is past; / Begin these wood-birds but to couple now?*" (MND IV.i) This was also a day for married couples to celebrate that their marriage had survived another winter cooped up together with dwindling supplies of food.

St. Valentine's Day is older than Saint Valentine (a celibate priest who would, doubtless, resent being associated with any licentious revelry). It originated as the Roman fertility holiday Lupercalia—celebration of the she-wolf. This was a special day when a goat and dog were sacrificed and flayed, then "many of the noble youths and of the magistrates run up and down through the city naked, for sport and laughter striking those they meet with shaggy thongs. And many women of rank also purposely get in their way, and like children at school present their hands to be struck, believing that the pregnant will thus be helped in delivery, and the barren to pregnancy."[90] Shakespeare's *Julius Caesar* begins on this day, with Caesar instructing his barren wife Calphurnia to:

> *Stand you directly in Antonius' way,*
> *When he doth run his course...*
> *Forget not in your speed, Antonius,*
> *To touch Calphurnia; for our elders say,*
> *The barren, touched in this holy chase,*
> *Shake off their sterile curse...*
> *Set on; and leave no ceremony out.* (JC I.ii)

"Love"

LOVE'S LABOUR'S LOST | ROMEO AND JULIET

PHEBE. Good shepherd, tell this youth what 'tis to love.
SILVIUS. It is to be all made of sighs and tears...
It is to be all made of faith and service...
It is to be all made of fantasy,
All made of passion, and all made of wishes,
All adoration, duty, and observance,
All humbleness, all patience, and impatience,
All purity, all trial, all obedience. (AYL V.ii)

CLOWN [sings] What is love? 'Tis not hereafter;
Present mirth hath present laughter;
What's to come is still unsure.
In delay there lies no plenty,
Then come kiss me, sweet and twenty;
Youth's a stuff will not endure. (TN II.iii)

The most mysterious magic in Shakespeare is "love." Sex is natural, but Shakespeare's immaculate "love" is supernatural, associated with pagan deities like Cupid and Hymen (apparently the anatomical hymen is named after the Greek god of marriage ceremonies).

BEROWNE: This wimpled, whining, purblind, wayward boy,
This senior-junior, giant-dwarf, Dan Cupid;
Regent of love-rhymes, lord of folded arms,
Th' anointed sovereign of sighs and groans,
Liege of all loiterers and malcontents,
Dread prince of plackets, king of codpieces,
Sole imperator, and great general
Of trotting paritors. O my little heart!
And I to be a corporal of his field,
And wear his colours like a tumbler's hoop! (LLL III.i)[91]

Shakespeare's "love" can cause a monomaniacal focus on one person, and yet the target of this obsession is generally random and interchangeable. Romeo when we first meet him is totally in "love" with Rosaline, and then he's totally in "love" with Juliet. We in the audience accept this with a vague distaste–Shakespeare never shows us this Rosaline so we can't form an opinion (if she's like the resourceful Rosalind in *As You Like It* he was a fool to give her up, but if she's like the sadistic Rosaline in *Love's Labour's Lost* he probably did the right thing). Yet we accept the abandonment of this Rosaline because obviously her name is not in the title. Friar Lawrence comments:

> *Is Rosaline, that thou didst love so dear,*
> *So soon forsaken? Young men's love then lies*
> *Not truly in their hearts, but in their eyes.* (R&J II.iii)

And grown-ups among us may recall Pete Postlethwaite in the 1996 film glancing down at his crotch before saying *"eyes."* But Shakespeare seems to have meant this in earnest.

At around the same time Shakespeare wrote *Romeo and Juliet*, he was also writing *A Midsummer Night's Dream*, in which the mischievous fairy Puck finds some of Cupid's love juice on a flower called *"love-in-idleness"* and uses it to swap couples around by dabbing their eyes. In the structure of the play, the two young men are evenly matched (and they must be, or else we would be sad for one of the brides in the end). Helena and Hermia are also evenly matched, and the story shuffles these lovers' affections like playing cards. Shakespeare pokes fun at this by *showing* the audience how Lysander's love can be transferred willy-nilly, and then giving Lysander a speech about how he has made a logical, rational choice:

> *The will of man is by his* reason *sway'd*
> *And* reason *says you are the worthier maid.*
> *Things growing are not ripe until their season;*
> *So I, being young, till now ripe not to* reason;
> *And touching now the point of human skill,*
> Reason *becomes the marshal to my will.* (MND II.ii, emphasis added)

Lysander gives clever justifications, but he has been possessed by a totally irrational force. In an even more bizarre twist, Shakespeare wrote two plays in which a woman's love can be instantly transferred from a cross-dressed woman to a man, *As You Like It* and *Twelfth Night*.

"Love at first sight" is a common convention in Shakespeare's plays:

> *Did my heart love till now? Forswear it, sight!*
> *For I ne'er saw true beauty till this night.* (R&J I.v)

> *Sweet mistress – what your name is else, I know not...*
> *Are you a god? Would you create me new?*
> *Transform me then, and to your power I'll yield.* (COE III.ii)

Women are not immune to this contagion:

> *Even so quickly may one catch the plague?*
> *Methinks I feel this youth's perfections*
> *With an invisible and subtle stealth*
> *To creep in at mine eyes. Well, let it be.* (TN I.v)

But they're a little bit less susceptible, as we find at the end of *Love's Labour's Lost* when the Princess says that even a full two days of wooing is: "*a time, methinks, too short / To make a world-without-end bargain in.*" (LLL V.ii)

The notion that someone's character (and particularly how trustworthy they are) can be read in their eyes or face is called "physiognomy," a magical form of fortune-telling on par with palm-reading or poking through animal entrails to predict the future. It is nonetheless a superstition that all of Shakespeare's lovers have in common—a dramatist's tool to move the story forward. Yes, we in the audience are more satisfied by a hard-won zesty love like Beatrice and Benedick in *Much Ado*, but we'll generally accept a bland love-at-first-sight like Miranda and Ferdinand in *The Tempest*.

The superstition of physiognomy is still alive and well. We can tell by the tired cliché of warnings against it, like "beauty is only skin-deep" or "don't judge a book by its cover." Nobody would have to say that unless we retained a belief that a person's looks were still an indicator of their loyalty.

While Shakespeare's men are more likely to find love by sight, his women find love by *sound*. They express their attraction in nimble wordplay, and the desired male struggles to keep up:

BEROWNE. Your wit's too hot, it speeds too fast, 'twill tire
ROSALINE. Not till it leave the rider in the mire. (LLL II.ii)

Verbal dueling is Shakespeare's poetic form of foreplay, like fencing, with alternate lunges and thrusts as they try to penetrate each other. It was a popular and entertaining game: he says ten words or so, she picks one word, wraps it in nine words of a different context and throws it back, then he picks one of those words, wraps it up, etc. Punning, the poetic-alchemical metamorphosis of words, is Shakespeare's favorite device for expressing the magic of sexual chemistry (we can't miss the sexual undertones of agility, improvisation and fertile imagination). In *Much Ado*, Claudio and Hero *see* each other and their love is boring and fragile. Meanwhile Beatrice and Benedick conduct their *"merry war"* of wit, sometimes publicly and sometimes in masks, and it is at once sublime *and* animal.

In Shakespeare's time this was called a "flyting contest," an appropriate title for the verbal equivalent of a bird mating dance. We in the audience know this will make for a spicy sex-life and (subliminally we suspect) vivacious offspring, maybe even some balance of domestic power. Shakespeare's most compelling courtships–Rosalind and Orlando, Kate and Petruchio, Juliet and Romeo, Rosaline and Berowne–all have this verbal foreplay in common.

Shakespeare's "love" is sometimes a rebellion against patriarchal marriage, which was often a byproduct of a property deal between two men, as Juliet's father rails:

> *And you be mine, I'll give you to my friend;*
> *And [if] you be not, hang, beg, starve, die in the streets...*
> *Nor what is mine shall never do thee good.* (R&J III.v),

or in *A Midsummer Night's Dream* where Hermia's father chooses Demetrius, but her sweetheart Lysander says:

> *You have her father's love, Demetrius;*
> *Let me have Hermia's. Do you marry him.* (MND I.i)

In these plays, the word *"consent"* means one man accepting another as a son-in-law, regardless of a preteen girl's feelings. And Shakespeare's suitors are generally pretty open about having an eye on the inheritance. There's a fascinating pattern where a stricken lover's first question is "what's her name?" quickly followed by, "and is she her wealthy father's only heir?" Like in the old Zombies song, "What's your name? Who's your daddy? Is he rich like me?" Petruchio in *Taming of the Shrew* is right up front about it: "*I come to wive it wealthily,*" or, how much will you pay me to take this girl off your hands? Other examples include Romeo, Claudio, Bassiano, all the guys in *Love's Labour's Lost*, etc. Often the most laughable thing about the comic ending is that an intelligent woman settles for a gold-digging gigolo. I guess we're supposed to be happy that the children of these marriages might inherit their mothers' intelligence and their fathers' financial ambitions.

Shakespearean chastity is a father's property. In *The Tempest*, Miranda's "*virgin knot*" is Prospero's prized possession, his ticket off the island. He's protective of it and shrewdly deals it to win his future grandson the crown of Naples. In *Much Ado*, Leonato is tricked into believing his daughter Hero has surrendered her (really *his*) virginity, and wishes she were dead or had never been born.

William Shakespeare, father of two daughters and "father" of all his characters, is likewise highly protective of his maidens' virginity, which he safeguards through all sorts of complex plot devices. In his romances, a maiden's chastity is "*the prize*" a male character must win through a good deal of chivalrous Holy Grail-quest testing.[92] Then at play's end, once the couples had scampered off and it came to the biological business of baby-making, Shakespeare was done with them. Like a good "father," he did generally provide them with an inheritance to cover expenses, but he didn't keep in touch.

> *Men are April when they woo, December when they wed: maids are May when they are maids, but the sky changes when they are wives.*
> (AYL IV.i)

> *Wooing, wedding, and repenting is as a Scotch jig, a measure, and a cinquepace: the first suit is hot and hasty, like a Scotch jig, and full as fantastical; the wedding, mannerly modest, as a measure, full of state and ancientry; and then comes Repentance, and with his bad legs, falls into the cinquepace faster and faster, till he sink into his grave.*
> (MAAN II.i)

There's an old truism that Shakespearean comedy ends in marriages because that is where Shakespearean tragedy begins. It can even happen half-way through the play.

Romeo and Juliet are often considered Shakespeare's greatest expression of "love," but a closer look reveals their marriage is dysfunctional: they don't communicate effectively, cannot handle problems as a team, and thus the couple is tragically doomed (more than either one individually, the combination of these teeny-boppers is the tragic hero of the play). The Macbeths had a stronger marriage than this. Antony and Cleopatra had an incredible love for *themselves*, but they had a hard time communicating with one another. However painful it may be to admit, when it comes to communication, cooperation and sexual chemistry, Hamlet's mother and stepfather were a really good couple, tragically doomed by the brat from her previous marriage. But Shakespeare's match-making masterpiece must be Beatrice and Benedick in *Much Ado*—she's upfront that she will eventually cheat on him and probably eat him too, but you know they'll have a great time till then.

At the mid-point of his career, Shakespeare's "love" rotted from the inside, became rancid, perhaps related to the putrification of his own sexuality by venereal disease. The sickness of his authorial "love" reared its ugly head early on, in the noxiously sleazy *Two Gentlemen of Verona*. Shakespeare tried to laugh his sickness away in *The Merry Wives of Windsor*, kill it in *Hamlet*, and justify it in *Troilus and Cressida*. But from *All's Well* on, the disease takes hold of his heroes, poisoning them with disgusted lust and bloodthirsty jealousy. In *Measure for Measure, Othello, King Lear, the Winter's Tale* and others (the "comedies" that are un-funny and deservedly un-famous) love is generally a sordid, gangrenous disease. Iago in *Othello* is its clearest manifestation—a demonic imp or incubus, infecting the husband's brain. Later, King Leontes in *The Winter's Tale* will have an internal Iago. Shakespeare's pure "love" blossoms again with Perdita in *The Winter's Tale* and gets a last gasp in *The Tempest*, but we may notice that "*perfect*" Miranda speaks very little, and her father Prospero is immediately anxious that even within moments of meeting her, the princely suitor will grow disillusioned.

Weddings

TWELFTH NIGHT | TAMING OF THE SHREW

Wedding ceremonies are rituals of unity and continuity. Unity in the sense of combining two families, and continuity in terms of giving relatives a chance to approve a partnership and its influence on the community's future (in Shakespeare's time this meant procreating and raising the next generation). Whether a wedding ritual falls into the category of "supernatural" is debatable–love can be considered supernatural, sex is natural, but in the early 1600s, aristocratic matchmaking was a real estate deal. And in the poorer classes, a wife was a necessary piece of farming equipment, needed to thresh grain, churn butter, mend clothes, and pop out little unpaid laborers.

"The man shall have his mare," Puck says in *Midsummer Night's Dream*. While this might strike us as a strange image of marriage, "mare" and "marriage" do seem to be linguistically related.[93] A man on his wedding day is still called a "groom," meaning someone who trains a horse, and the word "bridal" bears a suspicious resemblance to "bridle," meaning straps around a horse's head used to lead it around. Although the English word "bride" might descend from the German "brew," to make soup, or perhaps be related to the Irish fertility goddess Brigid and "breed," I don't see any etymology that's very empowering. The word "husband" means an overseer of seeding, as in crop-planting or "animal husbandry," while "wife" is just an old word for woman. Hence couples are pronounced "man and wife."

In Shakespeare's plays, the big wedding ceremony generally takes place after the play is over – they're difficult to stage, dull, and legalistic. But his plays contain numerous betrothal rituals, what we today would call getting engaged. In Shakespeare's time, a couple could be considered married if they'd exchanged vows, rings, and a kiss in front of a witness, generally a cleric. The big public wedding would then be performed on some Sunday when the father-of-the-bride and the groom had made arrangements for it. This betrothal made it basically alright to get conjugal, but it was still problematic for the bride to be in her second trimester during the public unveiling. William Shakespeare's firstborn daughter was baptized six months after his wedding and he never got over the scandal. And this situation of a bride getting noticeably pregnant between betrothal and wedding brings down a death-sentence on the groom in the Puritanical dystopia of *Measure for Measure.*

Romeo and Juliet elope privately in Friar Laurence's cell, with the intention of doing a big Capulet-Montague wedding in the near future. It doesn't quite work out that way, but the intention was there. *Much Ado About Nothing* contains two of these small ceremonies, the first of which is interrupted by objections (and if someone closely involved with the wedding was going to object, it was better to handle this within a smaller group of people than in a big public church service). But even after Claudio and Hero have completed their vows before a priest in the final scene, they *still* need to get to a church and make it publicly official. The technical procedure of an engagement ceremony is described in *Twelfth Night:*

> *Now go with me and with this holy man*
> *Into the chantry by; there, before him*
> *And underneath that consecrated roof,*
> *Plight me the full assurance of your faith...*
> *Whiles you are willing it shall come to note,*
> *What time we will our celebration keep*
> *According to my birth. What do you say?* (TN V.i)

The priest later confirms that this has taken place:

> *A contract of eternal bond of love,*
> *Confirm'd by mutual joinder of your hands,*
> *Attested by the holy close of lips,*
> *Strength'ned by interchangement of your rings;*
> *And all the ceremony of this compact*
> *Seal'd in my function, by my testimony.* (TN V.i)

The "joinder" of hands may refer to the couple's clasped hands being wrapped in a rope or stole (the origin of the expression "tying the knot"), the kiss and the exchange of rings make it official, and Olivia adds that a larger ceremony *"according to my* [countess] *birth"* will follow. The good news is that all her male relatives are dead, so there will be no strife about her choosing a husband. The questionable news is, she's marrying someone she's never met, having mistaken Sebastian for his twin sister who's been going about dressed as a man.

Prospero in *The Tempest* stands in for both the bride's father and the monk, producing an elaborate mirage to celebrate the betrothal of Miranda and Ferdinand, but sternly warning them not to get physical before it's been officiated in a church:

> *Then, as my gift, and thine own acquisition*
> *Wort'hily purchas'd, take my daughter. But*
> *If thou dost break her virgin-knot before*
> *All sanctimonious ceremonies may*
> *With full and holy rite be minist'red...*
> *Sour-ey'd disdain, and discord, shall bestrew*
> *The union of your bed with weeds so loathly*
> *That you shall hate it both.* (TEM IV.i)

This curse of noxious weeds on the bridal bed is a reversal of the usual custom of strewing the marriage bed with flowers, as we see when Hamlet's mother regrets that she did not get to deck (decorate) Ophelia's bridal bed.

In certain festival times like Mayday, vows could be made more lightly in front of a less distinguished witness. "Friar Tuck," accomplice to the Mayday hero Robin Hood, seems to have originated as a sort of clown-priest to bless "mad-merry-marriages" (a term that could mean impulsive holiday coupling, *or* a chance for young rural teens to evade parental brokerage). Touchstone, the clown in *As You Like It*, intentionally seeks out a fake friar to witness and bless a Mayday marriage to the lusty wench Audrey, reasoning that he can fulfill his desires and then weasel out of a real wedding. But the melancholy philosopher Jaques talks him out of this plan, and Touchstone decides to go through with the real deal:

> *Come, sweet Audrey;*
> *We must be married or we must live in bawdry.* (AYL III.iii)

During the sheep-shearing festivities of *The Winter's Tale*, the young prince proposes to a shepherdess, and for witnesses he chooses her father, and some other random old guy:

O, hear me breathe my life
Before this ancient sir, whom, it should seem,
Hath sometime lov'd. I take thy hand - this hand...
Do, and be witness to't. (WT IV.iv)

In a festive mood, he seems to think this old man will stand in for Friar Tuck, but it turns out to be his royal father in disguise. Revealing himself, the king does not contend that his son's vows were illegitimate, but rather commands: *"Mark your divorce, young sir."*

Taming of the Shrew shows an oddly tidy engagement ceremony, except that the bride has mixed feelings (and we may note she's silenced during this transaction). But Kate does join hands with Petruchio, it's witnessed by her father and a couple other guys, and then Petruchio calls Baptista his father and Kate his wife:

> PETRUCHIO. *Give me thy hand, Kate; I will unto Venice,*
> *To buy apparel 'gainst the wedding-day.*
> *Provide the feast, father, and bid the guests;*
> *I will be sure my Katherine shall be fine.*
> BAPTISTA. *I know not what to say; but give me your hands.*
> *God send you joy, Petruchio! 'Tis a match.*
> GREMIO, TRANIO. *Amen, say we; we will be witnesses.*
> PETRUCHIO. *Father, and wife, and gentlemen, adieu.*
> *I will to Venice; Sunday comes apace;*
> *We will have rings and things, and fine array;*
> *And kiss me, Kate; we will be married o' Sunday.* (TOS II.ii)

Following this engagement, the church wedding must be arranged for a Sunday, the father of the bride will handle invitations and provide the reception, and the groom is off to prepare his home and get some wedding clothes. The official ceremony is done offstage (for budget purposes) but Petruchio shows up in a clown costume, it is reported that he humiliates the priest, and then he drags Kate away before their reception can begin.

Petruchio is an obnoxious groom, but apparently spares Kate a crueler fate reserved for women who refused to marry. She has complained that if her younger sister got married first: *"I must dance bare-foot on her wedding-day, and, for your love to her, lead apes in hell."* (TOS II.i)

This sounds bizarre, but Beatrice in *Much Ado About Nothing* shares the same concern about apes, so it must have been fairly common.[94] Scholarly theories include the possibility that women who refused to have children would be doomed to an eternity of primate childcare, *or* perhaps that women who had led suitors on and made fools of them would be forever chased by semi-human pursuers.

Shakespearean weddings do contain a certain element of supernatural metamorphosis in terms of a change of familial identity. In modern times, with relatives geographically spread out, we get a good deal of choice about how close we want to get with our in-laws. But in Shakespeare's time, a bride or groom really *became* a child of their in-laws. The father-of-the-bride gains a son, and we immediately see this linguistic transformation in the way they address each other. When Hamlet's mother re-marries, Claudius *becomes* Hamlet's father (and, Hamlet jokes, Claudius becomes his mother as well, since they're one flesh).

There is also a possibility that marriage can change a person's social status (like the fairy-tale ideal of a kitchen maid transformed to a princess) but this is *very* rare in Shakespeare. He could be wildly imaginative and poetic about love but was pretty rigid about class-mixing. In *Winter's Tale*, the shepherdess selected by the prince turns out to be a true princess by birth. But this does lead to a comical moment, since the shepherds that adopted her are suddenly transformed into noblemen, symbolically re-born as gentlemen:

> CLOWN. *See you these clothes? ...Try whether I am not now a*
> *gentleman born... And have been so any time these four hours.*
> SHEPHERD. *And so have I, boy.*
> CLOWN. *So you have; but I was a gentleman born before my father;*
> *for the King's son took me by the hand and call'd me brother; and*
> *then the two kings call'd my father brother; and then the Prince, my*
> *brother, and the Princess, my sister, call'd my father father. And so we*
> *wept; and there was the first gentleman-like tears that ever we shed.*
> (WT V.ii)

Shrovetide

HENRY IV | MERCHANT OF VENICE

Shrovetide took its name from "shrive," meaning to deprive oneself as a penance, which in Lent could mean giving up meat and various forms of merriment until Easter. So the days leading up to Ash Wednesday were a festive time to use up the last of the stored meats of winter, especially on Fat Tuesday, better known by its French name *Mardi Gras*. A masque from 1638 shows Christmas and Shrovetide in a merry rivalry:

> SHROVETIDE. I say Christmas you are past date, you are out of the Almanac. Resign, resign. Let the oven give place to the frying pan, and minced pies yield superiority to pancakes and fritters.
> CHRISTMAS. Resign to thee! I that am the King of good cheer and feasting, though I come but once a year to reign over baked, boiled, roast, and plum-porridge, will have being in despite of thy lard-ship... I'll have Lent choke thee with a red herring.
> SHROVETIDE. I'll arm myself for that. In three days I can victual [supply with food] my garrison for seven weeks.[95]

Shrovetide's representative here argues that three days of feasting can prepare people for seven weeks of fasting. He refers to pancakes fried in the last of the winter lard, hence Father Christmas calls the Shrovetide fool "Thy lardship."

A fool in *All's Well* says nothing is more natural than *"a pancake for Shrove-Tuesday."* (AWTEW II.ii) A contemporary satirist described these flap-jacks in more sinister terms: "By that time that the clock strikes eleven, which (by the help of a knavish sexton) is commonly before nine, then there is a bell rung, called the Pancake-bell, the sound whereof makes thousands of people distracted, and forgetful either of manners or of humanity; then there is a thing called wheaten flour, which the sulphury Necromantic cooks do mingle with water, eggs, spice and other tragical, magical, enchantments, and then they put it by little and little into a frying-pan of boiling suet, where it makes a confused dismal hissing (like the Lemean snakes in the reeds of Acheron, Styx or Phlegeton) until at last, by the skill of the cooks it is transformed into the form of a Flap-Jack, which in our translation is called a Pancake, which ominous incantation the ignorant people do devour very greedily."[96]

Very much like Twelfth Night, Shrovetide was presided over by a Lord of Misrule with many mock-lordly titles: "But now stand off, give roome I say: for here must enter that waddling, stradling, bursten-gutted *Carnifex* of all Christendome; vulgarly entitled *Shrove-Tuesday*, but more pertinently, sole-monarch of the Mouth, high Steward to the Stomack, chiefe Ganimede to the Guts, prime Peere of the Pullets, first Favourite to the Frying pans, greatest Bashaw to the Batter-bowles, Protector of the pan-cakes, First Founder of the Fritters, Baron of Bacon flitch, Earle of Egg-baskets, and in the least and last place, lower Warden of the Stinke-ports."[97] Here we find numerous references to gluttony, digestion and defecation (mouth-stomach-intestines-bowels). Flatulence was also encouraged as a form of festive musical accompaniment, as François Laroque notes, "At festival time bodies became bagpipes."[98]

Shakespeare's most beloved Lord of Misrule was Falstaff, Prince Hal's overweight drinking buddy in *Henry IV*. Pretending to be his father in a barroom pageant, Hal bestows a string of epithets on his friend:

> *That trunk of humours, that bolting-hutch of beastliness, that swollen parcel of dropsies, that huge bombard of sack, that roasted Manningtree ox with the pudding in his belly, that reverend Vice, that grey Iniquity, that father ruffian, that vanity in years.* (1H4 II.iv)

Shakespeare inserts a drunken Shrovetide song into the second part of *Henry IV*:

> *Do nothing but eat and make good cheer,*
> *And praise God for the merry year;*
> *When flesh is cheap and females dear,*
> *And lusty lads roam here and there,*
> *So merrily, / And ever among so merrily.*
> *...Be merry, be merry, my wife has all;*
> *For women are shrews, both short and tall;*
> *'Tis merry in hall when beards wag an;*
> *And welcome merry Shrove-tide.*
> *Be merry, be merry.*

> *...A cup of wine that's brisk and fine,*
> *And drink unto the leman [lover] mine;*
> *And a merry heart lives long-a.*
> *...Fill the cup, and let it come,*
> *I'll pledge you a mile to th' bottom.* (2H4 V.iii)

Shrove Tuesday seems to the carnival backdrop of *Merchant of Venice*. Shylock the moneylender feels compelled to wade through the riotous festivity, and his servant comments on an ill omen:

> *I will not say you shall see a masque, but if you do, then it was not*
> *for nothing that my nose fell a-bleeding on Black Monday last at six*
> *o'clock i' th' morning, falling out that year on Ash Wednesday was four*
> *year, in th' afternoon.* (MOV II.v*)*

Shylock nonetheless goes out, but orders his daughter to seal the house tightly against this contagious merriment:

> *What, are there masques? Hear you me, Jessica:*
> *Lock up my doors, and when you hear the drum,*
> *And the vile squealing of the wry-neck'd fife,*
> *Clamber not you up to the casements then,*
> *Nor thrust your head into the public street*
> *To gaze on Christian fools with varnish'd faces;*
> *But stop my house's ears - I mean my casements;*
> *Let not the sound of shallow fopp'ry enter*
> *My sober house.* (MOV II.v)

Little does he suspect that his daughter already plots to escape and elope, absconding with a good deal of his wealth. The masque theme of the play continues with multiple disguises, culminating in many cruel practical jokes to humiliate the man who hates festivity. Ultimately, Shylock will be shorn of his wealth, livelihood, daughter, and even his religion, condemned to an eternal Lent.

Drunken gangs of London schoolboys and apprentices would rove urban streets in a sort of vigilante crusade against theatres and brothels, which were expected to close for Lent. First the theatres were besieged, actors were forced to perform favorite scenes from that year's hit plays, then "they were forc'd to undresse and put off their Tragick habits, and conclude the day with the merry milk-maides." If they refused, the theatre would be torn to pieces. Next the "Bawdy-houses" would be surrounded and threatened to shutter till Easter. And last, the arenas "where the poor Beares must conclude the riot, and fight twenty dogs at a time beside the Butchers, which sometimes fell into the service; this performed, and the Horse and Jack-an-Apes for a jigge, they had sport enough that day for nothing."[99] This would give peasants something to look forward to on Easter, when the dens of vice would rise again, and they could celebrate the resurrection by returning to theatres, brothels and bear-baiting.

Though there was a temporary halt to animal-fights (which rivaled the theatre as popular entertainment), Shrovetide games still involved cruelty to animals, especially roosters. Apparently, the custom of giving up eggs for Lent resulted in a general resentment of poultry. Cock fights were common all year round, but Shrovetide featured a more extreme version where a wounded or crippled contender would be tied to a stick and forced to stay in the match until death. And to this was added "Cock-Threshing," in which a rooster would be bound and ritually bludgeoned or buried up to its neck and pelted with stones or root vegetables. Shakespeare refers to this ghastly tradition in *The Merry Wives of Windsor*, when a young maiden pleads: "*Good mother, do not marry me to yond fool... Alas, I had rather be set quick i' th' earth. And bowl'd to death with turnips.*" (MWW III.iv)[100]

After a morning of rooster-killing, the locals would spend the afternoon playing at that other time-honored cock fight called "Football." Whether this was more like European or American "Football" is unclear, it may have had no rules at all except somehow to move a ball some distance, which could be a few hundred yards or the miles between two rival towns. Competing teams could be up to a thousand players each, comprised of whole villages, or competitive guilds, or bachelors versus married men (the Scottish town of Inverness inverted this, with married versus unmarried women, and unsurprisingly the wives always won).[101]

A squire in 1602 compared the ball to "an infernal spirit, for whosoever catcheth it fareth straightways like a madman, struggling and fighting with those that go about to hold him."[102] It's fascinating here that he says the *ball* possesses the *player*, which may connect back to the legend that the original ball was the head of an enemy taken in battle. The ball in Shakespeare's time was an inflated bull-bladder wrapped in leather. A manservant in *Comedy of Errors* complains that his master and mistress keep kicking him back and forth with their contradictory commands:

> *Am I so round with you as you with me,*
> *That like a football you do spurn me thus?*
> *You spurn me hence, and he will spurn me hither.*
> *If I last in this service, you must case me in leather.* (COE II.i)

The object of the game was not so much to score, as to vent some pre-Lenten frustration, and settle personal grudges from the preceding year. An eyewitness in 1583 reports:

> "For as concerning football playing, I protest unto you it
> may rather be called a freendly kinde of fight, than a play or
> recreation; A bloody and murthering practise, than a felowly
> sporte or pastime. For dooth not every one lye in waight for his
> adversarie, seeking to overthrowe him & to picke him on his
> nose, though it be uppon hard stones? In ditch or dale, in valley
> or hil, or what place soever it be, hee careth not, so he have
> him down... By this meanes, sometimes their necks are broken,
> sometimes their backs, sometime their legs, sometime their
> armes; sometime one part thrust out of joynt, sometime an other;
> sometime the noses gush out with blood, sometime their eies
> start out; and sometimes hurt in one place, sometimes in another.
> But whosoever escapeth away the best, goeth not scotfree, but is
> either sore wounded, craised, and brused, so as he dyeth of it, or
> els scapeth very hardly." [sic][103]

It's this general disorganized brutality that causes King Lear's friend to call Goneril's henchman a *"base football player."* (KL I.iv)

After this long day of rioting, violence and abuse, the evening festivity could be yet another eruption of toxic masculinity: the parade pageant known as Skimmington.

The Cuckold

WINTER'S TALE

When daisies pied and violets blue
And lady-smocks all silver-white
And cuckoo-buds of yellow hue
Do paint the meadows with delight,
The cuckoo then on every tree
Mocks married men, for thus sings he:
'Cuckoo;
Cuckoo, cuckoo' - O word of fear,
Unpleasing to a married ear!
When shepherds pipe on oaten straws,
And merry larks are ploughmen's clocks;
When turtles tread, and rooks and daws,
And maidens bleach their summer smocks;
The cuckoo then on every tree
Mocks married men, for thus sings he:
'Cuckoo;
Cuckoo, cuckoo' - O word of fear,
Unpleasing to a married ear! (LLL V.ii)

William Shakespeare might be the greatest writer of all time or whatever, but he was also highly idiosyncratic, and his writings contain a disturbing neurosis of masculine insecurity. Women who "wear the pants" in his plays must be punished either by death (Cleopatra, Lady Macbeth) or marriage to a clod (Rosalind in *As You Like It*, Helena in *All's Well*). And Shakespeare was cuckoo about "Cuckoldry." The word seems to originate with the cuckoo who lays eggs in the nest of another bird, fooling it into feeding a young cuckoo. As Lear's Fool says: "*The hedge-sparrow fed the cuckoo so long that it's had it head bit off by it young.*" [sic] (KL I.iv)

Romans referred to a man who impregnates his neighbor's wife as a cuckoo, and somehow as the slang term traveled northward it got switched to the cheated husband and the bird's name became synonymous with idiot. In another twist of transmission, northern Europeans transformed the bird to a buck or stag, and the cuckold became identifiable by his antlers. It's from this we get the modern expression for someone who is sexually unfulfilled: "horny."

Recent scientific research has produced a theory that human males do not make eggs (apparently male cuckoos don't either), and so this whole concept of a man laying eggs in another man's nest has been called into question. But defying all our desire to make Shakespeare an honorary modern, he remains steadfastly medieval about paternity. His plays express a belief that the female contribution to reproduction was a blank generic form that would then receive all specifics from the male seed. We see this in *A Midsummer Night's Dream*, where the duke commands a girl to accept her father's choice of a husband:

> *To you your father should be as a god*
> *One that compos'd your beauties; yea, and one*
> *To whom you are but as a form in wax,*
> *By him imprinted.* (MND I.i)

Similarly Leontes in *Winter's Tale* tells a young man, "*Your mother was most true to wedlock, Prince; For she did print your royal father off, Conceiving you* [in] *Your father's image.*" (WT V.i) In *Measure for Measure*, the Puritan Angelo condemns illegitimate begetters who "*coin in heaven's image in stamps that are forbid*" and calls bastards "*false*" or fake people. (MFM II.iv) And so in Shakespeare's world, the metaphor of a man laying an egg in another man's nest is appropriate: a man copies himself by means of a woman, and thereby the offspring of one man can inherit the property of another.

For all their fancy poetry, Shakespeare's male characters are generally very transactional about "love" and reproduction. They often equate women with farm-land to be seeded, and marriages arranged by fathers are really economic property/title transfers with a maiden thrown in.[104] "*Gentlemen, now I play a merchant's part,*" says Baptista, auctioning his daughter in *Taming of the Shrew*. (TOS II.i) Perhaps Kate would have been less shrewish if her father wasn't into human trafficking. Shakespeare's young wooers, from the dreamy Romeo to the dreary Claudio, will hastily ascertain whether the young virgin is her father's only heir. They almost always are, and most of these maidens have no mother to hamper the deal with nit-picky questions like "*What say you? Can you like the gentleman?*" (R&J I.iii)

An old saying goes, "marriage without love leads to love without marriage." Would Juliet have cheated on Paris if she'd been forced to marry him? We'll never know. Or for that matter, whether Romeo could have been faithful to Juliet–he was a bit flighty. When a prince proposes to the high-spirited Beatrice in *Much Ado*, she genially says she'd cheat on him, and finally marries Benedick who accepts that she'll be unfaithful.[105] But Beatrice is an exception: in Shakespeare's world generally, cheating is not something a wife does punish to her husband, but something one man does to shame another, and the woman is not so much an accomplice as a weapon. Nothing Desdemona says can convince Othello she's faithful, once he's convinced that Cassio would betray him. The same is true of all Shakespeare's insecure jealous husbands, Mr. Ford in *Merry Wives*, Leontes in *Winter's Tale* and Posthumous Leonatus in *Cymbeline*. But Shakespeare almost always protects his male characters from cuckoldry (the rare exceptions are Albany in *King Lear*, Henry VI, Saturninus in *Titus Andronicus*, and one other guy I can't remember right now, a minor character).

The jealous king Leontes in *Winter's Tale* actually pauses the show to leer out into the audience:

> *There have been,*
> *Or I am much deceiv'd, cuckolds ere now;*
> *And many a man there is, even at this present,*
> *Now while I speak this, holds his wife by th' arm*
> *That little thinks she has been sluic'd in's absence,*
> *And his pond fish'd by his next neighbour, by*
> *Sir Smile, his neighbour. Nay, there's comfort in't,*
> *Whiles other men have gates and those gates open'd,*
> *As mine, against their will. Should all despair*
> *That hath revolted wives, the tenth of mankind*
> *Would hang themselves.* (WT I.ii)

In a bizarre twist, the word is back in fashion, "Cuck," internet slang for a man who gets his jollies by watching his wife have sex with someone else. Some may see this in Oberon enchanting his wife Titania to fall in love with the ass-headed Bottom in *A Midsummer Night's Dream*, but her *"doting"* seems to be more maternal than sexual.

Skimmington

OTHELLO | HAMLET | MERRY WIVES OF WINDSOR

In Shakespeare's time there was a folk ritual called Skimmington or *Charivaris* designed to publicly shame henpecked husbands and/or older men who married younger women. This often took the form of a noisy public parade arranged by the local bachelors, who felt threatened by the prospect of being ruled (and cuckolded) by their future wives, and resentful that some of the village's most fertile maidens were being claimed by sterile widowers. They would form a sort of merry lynch mob and abduct the offending husband, or his next-door neighbor, and drag him out while playing a mock fanfare of clanging pots and pans.

William Hogarth's 1663 drawing "Hudibras Encounters Skimmington" depicts the victim being paraded through town backward on a donkey, forced to spin wool around a phallic distaff while a man in drag rides ahead of him, striking him with a skimming ladle, which gives the ritual its name. Their herald, called "the scourge of marriage," accompanies them holding a woman's smock like a banner, hung from a staff crowned by horns. An old song accompanying this image goes:

> When wives their sexes shift, like hares,
> And ride their husbands, like night-mares...
> For when Men by their Wives are Cow'd,
> Their Horns of course are understood.[106]

Anne Parten writes,

> In the preposterous world of the skimmington, the new symbols
> of authority are skillets and pots and ladles. The battle for the
> breeches has been won, and their unmanned former owner
> is reduced to that epitome of masculine futility, the cringing
> cuckold.[107]

The parade would end at the local pond, with the castigated individual dumped in the water.

Numerous elements of the Skimmington appear in Shakespeare's *Othello*, which begins with Iago directing the bachelor Roderigo to raise a late-night clamor outside the home of Desdemona, who has eloped with an older man. *Othello* is best known for its presentation of an interracial marriage, but the script itself gives equal or greater weight to the age difference: the older general making Desdemona unavailable to younger suitors. Iago goes on to hamper the honeymoon, blocking the couple from sexual consummation, convincing Othello he has been cuckolded, and eventually maddening the groom to the point where he murders the bride.

There's an old saying that "Shakespearean comedy ends in marriage because that is where Shakespearean tragedy begins," and *Othello* is perhaps the best illustration. From various character remarks we piece together the Romantic Comedy that just ended: Desdemona feared the battle-scarred warrior, but his friend Cassio wooed her in his name, they fell in love and eloped, outwitting her racist father. Happily ever after! ...Except that this comical trickery leaves a lingering aftertaste of distrust. Did Cassio woo for himself? And will a girl who fooled her father be honest with her husband? Iago hijacks the narrative and we see the marriage unmade, the courtship in reverse: Desdemona's father is again denied the right to choose her husband, Cassio charms Desdemona to get his job back, and in the end Desdemona's fear of Othello returns.

Desdemona's father was horrified by the idea of interracial marriage, his fear amplified by Iago's evocative imagery: "*an old black ram / Is tupping your white ewe...making the beast with two backs.*" (OTH I.i)

The coupling will be frustrated by repeated interruptions, but the marriage will then consummate itself in something much darker, a grotesque distortion of sex where Desdemona is suffocated, and the sexually frustrated Othello will penetrate himself with a knife.

In terms of stagecraft, *Othello* is highly ritualistic. Like any great tragedy, we know from the start that the turning clockwork gears will eventually grind the hero to death, and this one is particularly somber because there will be a virgin sacrifice, the honeymoon bed becoming a ghastly sacrificial altar. While modern audiences want to disappear into the depths of its characters, the original audience would have been far more aware of these characters as masque personae – Othello in face-paint,

Desdemona played by a boy (like the Skimmington drag-queen) and Iago the priest/emcee who narrates directly to the audience. Recently watching a dull video I impatiently said "just kill her already!" I knew—spoiler-alert—that Desdemona would die. Although there's a funny story about a Baltimore production in 1822 when a soldier in the audience, sensing Othello's murderous intent, fired a gun and broke the actor's arm.[108] Anyone who considers producing *Othello* in 2022 should take heed.

We can see traces of Iago in prince Hamlet, who also expresses his disapproval of a wedding in rancid terms like *"the rank sweat of an enseamed bed, stew'd in corruption, honeying and making love over the nasty sty."* (HAM III.iv) Hamlet resents Claudius, not for being old, but for being too jolly (unlike either Hamlet Sr. or Jr., Claudius thinks royalty should be fun!). The artsy prince expresses his embitterment by hijacking a theatrical production and inserting some lines to torment his mother and stepfather. Unfortunately, the trick backfires—instead of a play about murder by a usurping brother, Hamlet selects one about a nephew killing his royal uncle, and this alerts Claudius to plot his demise.

Shakespeare puts a more comical twist on the *Charivaris* in *The Merry Wives of Windsor* where, instead of bachelors punishing a husband, two local wives orchestrate an elaborate ritual to shame the attempted seducer Falstaff. Mrs. Ford and Mrs. Page are "merry" in that they are light-hearted and sociable, and the wandering knight mistakenly misreads their playfulness as sexual availability. This was apparently a common assumption in Shakespeare's time, and the play culminates in the moral that:

> *We'll leave a proof, by that which we will do,*
> *Wives may be merry and yet honest too.*
> *We do not act that often jest and laugh.* (MWW IV.ii)

In their merry conspiracy to humiliate him, they challenge the people of Windsor to reconsider this attitude toward women, and defend not only their honor/reputation, but the honor of all merry women.

Rather than have a man in drag beating a husband, they dress Falstaff as a woman who gets beaten by a jealous husband, but the cross-dressed man still remains part of the ritual. *"I went to her,"* Falstaff laments, *"like a poor old man; but I came from her...like a poor old woman."* (MWW V.i)

Later, they convince him to hide in a buckbasket ("buck" here meaning bleach: a basket for dirty underwear, but also a play on the buck as symbol of the cuckold) and have him thrown in the Thames river. Falstaff who assumed he'd make saucy gossip literally becomes dirty laundry.

> *I suffered the pangs of three several deaths: first, an intolerable fright*
> *to be detected with a jealous rotten bell-wether; next, to be compass'd*
> *like a good bilbo in the circumference of a peck* [barrel], *hilt to point,*
> *heel to head; and then, to be stopp'd in, like a strong distillation, with*
> *stinking clothes that fretted in their own grease... It was a miracle*
> *to scape suffocation. And in the height of this bath, when I was more*
> *than half-stew'd in grease, like a Dutch dish, to be thrown into the*
> *Thames, and cool'd, glowing...hissing hot.*[109] (MWW III.v)

After his dunking, they plan a third prank to get him wearing horns, convincing him to stand beneath a forest oak dressed like legendary Herne the Hunter. The village children then dress like fairies and jeer him in a circle dance. Elements of the Skimmington are jumbled, but they're all present in *Merry Wives*: cross-dressing, horns, beating and dunking, even the donkey when Falstaff at last admits defeat by saying *"I do begin to perceive that I am made an ass."* (MWW V.iv)

Easter | Ostara
Julius Caesar | Much Ado

The month we call April was long known as Eostre or Ostara, named for a Germanic fertility goddess, likely the same goddess known as Ishtar in ancient Babylon and Astarte in Israel. Northern European celebrations of her springtime ascendancy involved painted eggs, and a hare or rabbit (famous for its prolific breeding), and these non-Biblical traditions were merged into the Christian Easter. The early church, indignant at having their most significant holiday named after a goddess tried to re-name the day "Pasch," but it didn't catch on.

The ancient pre-Christian religions of Northern Europe generally shared a belief that sacred stories should not be written down, but only transmitted orally—once a story is written, it can no longer renew itself through adaptation and evolution, and precise fixed wordings make a sacred text vulnerable to legalistic exploitation by a scholarly elite. Think a moment about modern controversies over the Bible's creation stories and legalistic minutiae, and maybe you'll understand this ancient rationale.

So any theory about Northern European springtime-goddess-resurrection narratives must rely on a tenuous reach into probable parallels in literary cultures like ancient Babylon and Greece. The Ancient Middle Eastern version of Eostre was the goddess Ishtar, who banished her lover Dumuzi to the realm of the dead, but finally a deal was struck in which he'd spend only half of each year in the underworld: this explained the seasons, like the Greek story of Demeter, whose daughter Persephone was kidnapped by the subterranean death-god Hades, then annually released to restore fertility. Early Christianity put its own spin on this, having the crucified Christ descend into the underworld to redeem the souls of dead prophets who'd lived before him, then rising from the tomb in spring.

Shakespeare loved spring, and most of his plays conclude with springtime fertility triumphing over winter sterility—his comedies usually end with conception, and his tragedies with a promise of restored abundance. But in his entire career, he only once mentions Easter, and not in reference to a resurrection, but as a time to wear a new jacket.[110] Shakespeare and most of his characters were nominally Christian (even Shylock is forced to convert at the end of *Merchant of Venice*), some of his characters who lived before Jesus even paraphrase Gospel quotes, but the whole Christology of passion-crucifixion-resurrection is glaringly absent even from his priestly and puritanical characters. I find only two fleeting references, when a king briefly alludes to *"the world's ransom, blessed Mary's Son,"* (R2 II.i) and when a man pleads with his assassins:

> *I charge you, as you hope to have redemption*
> *By Christ's dear blood shed for our grievous sins,*
> *That you depart and lay no hands on me.*"[111] (R3 I.iv)

And his plea is in vain; they kill him anyway.

A shaky case could be made for Julius Caesar as Shakespeare's male Christ-figure: He is thrice tempted to accept a crown, and three times refuses. Brutus speaks of the assassination in sacrificial terms: *"Let us be sacrificers, but not butchers... Caesar must bleed* [but] *Let's carve him as a dish fit for the gods.*" (JC II.i) Like Jesus, JC is killed by Romans who then *"bathe our hands in Caesar's blood."* (JC III.i) His death is preceded by apocalyptic signs and portents: *"Graves have yawn'd, and yielded up their dead; / Fierce fiery warriors fight upon the clouds... / Which drizzled blood upon the Capitol."* (JC II.ii) And his ghost appears to his former disciple, Brutus who, like his rhyme-mate Judas, commits suicide. But that's an awfully selective reading of a play full of pagan rituals and gods, diviners, ghosts, etc.

Shakespeare did write plenty of resurrections that are accompanied by joyful forgiveness and reconciliation. But his risen saviors are all women, and their resurrections owe more to the goddess traditions from which Easter took its name. The famous one is Hero, the bride in *Much Ado About Nothing*, whose name derives from kings who will be sacrificed for the goddess Hera (like Heracles) and then replaced/resurrected. She is framed for premarital sex and collapses during the accusation at her wedding. The word then spreads that she is dead, the conspiracy to slander her is exposed, and her fiancée is instructed to *"Hang her an epitaph upon her tomb, and sing it to her bones: sing it tonight."* (MAAN V.i) The song for this nocturnal ritual contains no reference to Christian salvation or paradise, but rather beseeches a goddess to raise the dead:

> *Pardon, goddess of the night,*
> *Those that slew thy virgin knight;*
> *For the which, with songs of woe,*
> *Round about her tomb they go.*
> *Midnight, assist our moan;*
> *Help us to sigh and groan,*
> *Heavily, heavily:*
> *Graves, yawn and yield your dead,*
> *Till death be uttered,*
> *Heavily, heavily.* (MAAN V.iii)[112]

The night-time funeral is followed by a morning wedding, where the living Hero is unveiled as a bride, saying *"One Hero died defiled, but I do live."* (MAAN V.iv) Unfortunately she then marries the gullible gold-digger Claudio and the audience goes home feeling vaguely sickened. But really Hero and Claudio are just a subplot in a play about Beatrice and Benedick.

When Shakespeare's mother died, he wrote a trilogy of plays where the woman is resurrected: *Pericles, Winter's Tale* and *Cymbeline*.[113] For *Pericles* he recycled elements of *Comedy of Errors*: the mother is lost in a wreck at sea, presumed dead, but later turns up as a priestess at Diana's temple in Ephesus. For *Winter's Tale*, Shakespeare rewrote Robert Greene's popular 1588 pastoral romance *Pandosto*, about a jealous king who kills his wife and banishes his daughter, then later tries to seduce his unrecognized child and commits suicide. But Shakespeare put his own twist at the end, where the wife Hermione reappears sixteen years after the declaration of her death, as a stone statue which is then brought back to life. Her resurrection is half-heartedly explained away (she's been hidden in a basement for sixteen years!), although this contradicts a sighting of her ghost shortly after her death. The writer seems to be presenting two possibilities – a magical resurrection for the peasantry, and a rational explanation for educated patrons. Either way, the queen's return signals a religious reconciliation, and the coming of spring. Imogen in *Cymbeline* will be poisoned, buried, and awaken in a cave with a headless corpse in her husband's clothing. It's not as wild and fun as it sounds.

Ancient myths of rescues from the underworld have some curious echoes in Shakespeare's work. Isabella, the heroine of *Measure for Measure* must venture into the depths of a prison to visit her death-sentenced brother. She is even offered a chance to save his life by surrendering her virginity to the Puritan judge Angelo. In the source story, Cinthio's 1565 "Story of Epitia," the heroine sleeps with the judge and he kills her brother anyway. But Shakespeare's novice nun Isabella refuses, and when her brother pleads poetically she basically tells him: go to hell. In this way Shakespeare's heroine is more like Ishtar, abandoning Dumuzi to spend half the year underground.[114]

The tomb scene in *Romeo and Juliet* is more complex: Juliet fakes her death and descends into the underworld, to be resurrected and reunited with Romeo (alive), he descends to be reunited with her (in death) and she awakens just too late to save him (they both die). But in Shakespeare's time, the performance would end with the two dead lovers leaping onto the stage and dancing a jig, like the resurrection of Pyramus and Thisbe in *Midsummer Night's Dream*.

Ted Hughes proposes that some of Shakespeare's male characters are not resurrected but reincarnated, as in a Hindu epic, living a series of lives to get something right.[115] An easy example would be Lear, doomed by his neediness and unrealistic expectations, returning as Timon of Athens, and finally incarnated as Prospero in *The Tempest*, able at last to control the weather and his beloved daughter. The hesitant Hamlet is reincarnated as the action-hero Coriolanus–no curiosity about his father's death, no great malice toward his wife and mother, he falls in love with Laertes (Aufidius) who then kills him anyway. Leonato, the father in *Much Ado*, returns as Posthumous Leonatus in *Cymbeline*, and finally as Leontes in *The Winter's Tale*–Shakespeare didn't even bother changing the name. I'm sure a long and super-tedious book could be written on this topic of Shakespearean reincarnation, but I think the few examples here cover it.

Hocktide
ALL'S WELL THAT ENDS WELL | LOVE'S LABOUR'S LOST

Like Yule or Christmas, Easter was a multi-day event in the medieval and renaissance periods. The second Tuesday after Easter was known as Hocktide or Hoke Day. "Hock" seems to have been meant in the sense of ransom, as it survives today when someone "hocks" something at a pawn shop, possibly with the hope of buying it back later. The central event of Hocktide was a sort of bachelor auction – village women would go out with ropes and playfully abduct a man, put a sack over his head, tie him up and ransom the "Hoodman" to raise funds for the local church.

Elements of this tradition make up the plot of *All's Well That Ends Well*. The play begins with a king terminally ill, and a young maiden with the power to cure him on the condition that the king grant her any bachelor she chooses to marry (this is not so much an extortion, but a twist on the legend of the Fisher King where the innocent fool accomplishes what the experts cannot[116]). Unfortunately, the man she chooses is awful and hates her, refusing to accept her as his wife unless she can procure the ring he'll never part with, *and* asexually conceive his offspring. Fortunately, she's Helena, Shakespeare's most monomaniacal strategist. Disguised, she stalks him on a military campaign, finds a woman he's trying to seduce, convinces her to demand the ring in exchange for sex, then Helena switches places with her in the dark to get pregnant by her husband. This all sounds like such a feisty comedy but unfortunately the guy Bertram is such a prick that the whole show is more like a tricycle-accident in slow motion.

In a subplot, Bertram's fellow soldier Parolles goes on a sort of capture-the-flag mission and his own comrades in disguise abduct and interrogate him, to prove how cowardly he is (having been blindfolded, they call him the "Hoodman").[117] Like all of Shakespeare's "Festive" plays *All's Well* does not explicitly link itself to a specific holiday; elements of ritual are flexed to fit into the context of a story. But all the integral elements of Hocktide are here: the king held for ransom, the fool hooded, the ring that is pawned by Bertram and redeemed by Helena, the man blindfolded by darkness, and the woman triumphantly fulfilled—rich, married, and pregnant.[118] And because she knows he's an unscrupulous toad, she ends with a death threat:

> BERTRAM. *I'll love her dearly, ever, ever dearly.*
> HELENA. *If it appear not plain, and prove untrue,*
> *Deadly divorce step between me and you!* (AWTEW V.iii)

Though it was less commonly practiced, men could also playfully kidnap and ransom women, as Shakespeare shows with the wedding scene in *Taming of the Shrew*: Petruchio charges in like an invader and abducts Katherina, then holds her hostage deprived of food and sleep. In the end, she learns to manipulate him: in the final scene Petruchio is willing to let Kate hold his honor/reputation hostage, and his faith in her is rewarded with the winning of a bet.

Love's Labour's Lost similarly features a mock invasion by the four wooers disguised as Russians, playfully coercing four maidens to dance with them (yes it sounds creepy now, but the guys are harmless fops).[119] The four women, knowing their plot, also disguise themselves and fool each Jack into professing his love to the wrong Jill, shaming the suitors with the charge that their boyish "love" is superficial. In this play, everyone is comically confined—the king and his friends by an oath to spend a year living like monks, the ladies awaiting the receipt for a missed mortgage payment, even the clown Costard finds himself in jail.

The play also has deeper themes of ransom, connected with the two central romances. In this light comedy, Shakespeare delves into his boldest exploration of sadomasochism, the relationship between the sharp Rosaline and the boisterous Berowne (who are a bit like *Much Ado's* Beatrice and Benedick, but with darker undertones). Rosaline delights in confining and abusing her victim:

> *That same Berowne I'll torture ere I go...*
> *How I would make him fawn, and beg, and seek,*
> *And wait the season, and observe the times,*
> *And spend his prodigal wits in bootless rhymes,*
> *And shape his service wholly to my hests,*
> *And make him proud to make me proud that jests!*
> *So pertaunt-like would I o'ersway his state*
> *That he should be my fool, and I his fate.* (LLL V.ii)

She's met her match in the masochistic Berowne, who pleads:

> *Here stand I, lady - dart thy skill at me,*
> *Bruise me with scorn, confound me with a flout,*
> *Thrust thy sharp wit quite through my ignorance,*
> *Cut me to pieces with thy keen conceit.* (LLL V.ii)

The princess is also a hostage—her father has sent her in lieu of a missed mortgage payment, clearly with the understanding that her marriage to the king of Navarre would cancel his debt. She cleverly avoids making any such promise, and at the last possible moment news of her father's death puts her in a position to take control of her own destiny. As the title warns, *Love's Labour's Lost* is unique among Shakespeare's comedies in that it does not end with a wedding: Cupid has been busy but then the messenger Mercury arrives in the grim form of Marcadé, bearing news of death, and the ladies leave. In an extension of the Hocktide hostage theme, the women confine the men in promises to spend a year doing their bidding, and in exchange they promise to withhold sex. Suspending disbelief we can leave the theater thinking this will come true, but then we remember these men all broke their prior oaths within the first five minutes of the play, and are highly unlikely to make it a year. Regardless, the play ends with men held for ransom by women.

Interesting side note: lists of Shakespeare's play productions printed in 1598 and 1603 contain references to a *Loue Labours Wonne* or *Loves*

Labor Won [sic]. No play by this name has ever been published, so it's unknown whether he wrote a direct sequel where the characters reunite a year later, or if *Love's Labour's Won* was an alternate title for a comedy later published under the name of *Much Ado About Nothing* or *Taming of the Shrew,* or revised and re-released as *All's Well That Ends Well.* All three candidates have intriguing thematic ties with *Love's Labour's Lost.*

St. George's Day
MERRY WIVES OF WINDSOR

There's a common mythic archetype of a hero rescuing a nation (sometimes represented by a princess) from a serpent who threatens an apocalyptic degeneration to swampy chaos. In Mesopotamia this was Marduk slaying Tiamat in the *Enuma Elish,* in Egypt it was *Ra and the Serpent,* in the Bible God slays the sea monster Leviathan, the Greeks produced many versions including Heracles and the Hydra, Perseus and the Kraken, the list goes on. The common core of these myths is a culture of sky-worshiping male dominance violently subduing a culture of earth-worshiping matriarchy – essentially some barbarians attack a convent, and *then* claim that the nuns were a nine-headed monster or whatnot. I've compiled evidence in support of this thesis in my books *Genesis and the Rise of Civilization* and *Romancing the Minotaur: Sex and Sacrifice and some Greek Mythology.*

Whether intentional or not, Shakespeare twists the basic outline of this myth into the plot of *Taming of the Shrew.* Access to the fertile princess (Bianca) is blocked by the chimera/sphinx/man-eating-dragon (Katherina, *"Kate the curst"*), but instead of hacking her head off, the knight (Lucentio) enlists the fool (Petruchio) to transform the gorgon into a bride. We in the audience might even say she's been dismembered and reassembled into a *subservient* wife, a fate worse than death. But a closer look reveals that she's fooled the fool into thinking himself a king—she'll have what she wants, and let him take the credit. As her first trick, she'll use Petruchio's pugnacity as a tool to publicly trounce her sister, *and* win a round of applause for it, not to mention a two-hundred-crown bet. In other Shakespearean plays, the damsel-in-distress is held hostage by another kind of dragon, the widower (the man emotionally scarred by the death of the wife/mother) who must be defeated or subverted so that potential fertile energy can be released.

The English version of this hero myth is Saint George and the Dragon – a legend about a Christian knight rescuing a princess from a dragon that demanded human sacrifice. This story was told featuring various saints for centuries, but eventually became attached to a Greek knight, George, fighting a dragon in Turkey. Then during the crusades, the tale became a hit in England, and George became the patron saint of the nation. This was a natural fit on an island that was sometimes called the dragon in legends–King Arthur's surname Pendragon meant "lord of the dragon," and his myths generally concern the transition from indigenous Paganism to Christianity. Shakespeare's pre-Christian King Lear refers to himself as the dragon ("*Come not between the dragon and his wrath.*" KL I.i[120]). Symbolizing the victory of militant Christianity over Paganism, Saint George and the parade-float dragon became a regular fixture at national pride events. The story was also presented in Mummer's Plays, in which a Christian knight battled a dragon *or* pagan, his hard-won triumph resulted in near-fatal wounds, and then a healer would magically restore him to full health.

The Feast-Day of Saint George also became associated with the Garter Knights. This was a special fraternity of royal retainers and friends sworn to uphold the chastity and majesty of the queen, and defend her reputation from any slander. Their emblem and Latin motto, *Honi soit qui mal y pense*, "evil be to him who thinks evil," derive from an old story where an English queen's garter fell during a royal procession and King Edward III picked it up, shooting nasty glances around and cursing anyone who'd peeked at it. Thus, a queen's garter became iconic of her virtue, somewhat like a king's crown symbolizes his wisdom.

Unsurprisingly, England's "virgin queen" Elizabeth took a keen interest in having a special order of knights to defend her immaculate reputation, and in 1597 she apparently commissioned William Shakespeare to write a special play for the Garter Ceremony on St. George's Day. The script had to uphold the honor of slandered women, and legend has it, Elizabeth added that she wanted to see Falstaff in love. The rotund drinking buddy from the *Henry IV* plays had been so popular, and his curt dismissal and pathetic offstage death were jarring for his fans. So the merry knight was resurrected and transported through time to engage in some apocryphal hijinks. *The Merry Wives of Windsor* is nobody's favorite Shakespeare play, and some scholars who love Falstaff just hate this. The great literary critic Harold Bloom, who strains to insert his beloved Falstaff into nearly every paragraph of his heavy tome *Shakespeare: The Invention of the Human*, will only touch *Merry Wives* for three and a half pages, and only on the condition that we accept his "firm declaration that the hero-villain of *The Merry Wives of Windsor* is a nameless imposter masquerading as the great Sir John Falstaff."[121] With all that said, I still think the play is pretty good.

Though the play debuted at the queen's palace in Whitehall, the setting is Windsor, the traditional location of the Garter celebration,[122] and the story begins with nobles arriving on a sort of religious pilgrimage to attend it. But the action takes place on the margins, largely focused on the inn where travelers are staying, and a certain mischievous knight's attempt to swindle two local men by seducing their wives. Discerning this plot, these two merry wives conspire to shame Falstaff with a series of practical jokes, incorporating elements of Skimmington, and culminating in a very public ceremony in which they defend their virtuous reputations, proving that *"Wives may be merry and yet honest too."* (MWW IV.ii)[123] The climax of their pageant is a ring of local children dancing like a garter around the knight, singing:

> *And nightly, meadow-fairies, look you sing,*
> *Like to the Garter's compass, in a ring;*
> *More fertile-fresh than all the field to see;*
> *And 'Honi soit qui mal y pense' write* [Latin: "evil be to him who thinks evil"]
> *In em'rald tufts, flow'rs purple, blue and white;*
> *Like sapphire, pearl, and rich embroidery,*
> *Buckled below fair knighthood's bending knee.* (MWW V.v)

This climactic dance neatly links the themes of the play: that what makes England special is a combination of male chivalry and female chastity, all under the supervision of a fairy queen representing the magic of royalty.

Royalty

The Hollow Crown
RICHARD II | HENRY IV

Shakespeare wrote many royalty plays, most of which are excruciatingly dull if you try to slog through them today, but they were wildly popular at the time. He was establishing himself as a writer during Queen Elizabeth's twilight years, and a big question on the English mind was: when will the childless queen name a successor? She never did, and thus the Scottish King James got a promotion, but for decades Englishmen went to bed wondering if they'd awaken to hear the queen was dead and England had been plunged into a bloody civil war. So there was a great deal of public interest in plays about the history of royal succession, and Shakespeare the shrewd businessman provided many: the whole nine-play series of Richards and Henrys, plus *King John*.[124]

He also delved farther into the past. When King James ascended to the throne, Shakespeare celebrated with *Macbeth* (retrojecting the royal destiny of James's ancestor Banquo) and *King Lear* (with its message that the United Kingdom *must* remain united). And let's not forget *Cymbeline*, or better yet, yes let's forget it. Shakespeare's royal plays can be dull, but we should remember that other playwrights of his time were censured for writing royalty plays that were too exciting: "Three of Shakespeare's contemporaries did time in jail for putting into a play a couple sentences that sounded like satire on the Scotsmen coming to England in the train of king James I, and worse things, like cutting off ears and noses, could be threatened."[125] The most amazing thing about Shakespeare's royalty plays is that they're so pragmatically *un-political*.

I guess I may as well admit that when it comes to folk-superstitions in Shakespeare I've got more patience for ghosts, witches and fairies than I do for a "divine right" of kings. But let's do this.

We may not immediately think of royalty as supernatural, but when we look at it rationally, what separates a king from a peasant is really just a bunch of hocus-pocus mumbo-jumbo generating an imaginary aura of superiority. Arthurian legends abound with supernatural elements: the sword in the stone, lady of the lake, Holy Grail, etc. Stories of transformation from peasant-girl to princess are commonly called a "fairy tales," though most don't contain fairies. This classification simply denotes a supernatural element: one minute you're nobody, and the next, everyone obeys your commands. And to this day, princess-fantasy is a major industry, so well packaged by Disney that when I'm trying to pay for my groceries I find myself surrounded by magazine pictures of England's royalty, getting all dressed up in fancy clothes paid for by English taxpayers. I will never understand what could possibly possess an American to trade U.S. currency for pictures of these smug, uninteresting people. But that's the supernatural element of royalty.

After watching Disney's *Frozen* with my daughter, I asked her: Why does this guy want to be king? Being very young at the time, she admitted she hadn't thought much about it, but assumed that royalty was worth pursuing for its own sake, and you get to live in a castle. Then I asked: Who paid for this castle? Did the king build it himself? Did he chop the trees and haul the stones and weave the curtains? Ah, then we got somewhere—people had done this for him. Why did they do it? We had to work on this a little, but finally we came around to: Extortion by threat of violence. Soon, with a sheet of paper, we'd charted a feudal economy (if you're unfamiliar with "feudal," you can substitute "mafia"). I assume all Daddies do this after watching a Disney movie with their little girl.

The earliest known kings won their crowns through violence and used them to extort food and labor from surrounding people. But violence can only get you so far. If you burn a village every time a peasant won't pay up, you'll soon find you have to pick your own damned cotton. So you need something else—a supernatural aura, a "divine right" that will make peasants pay taxes for fear of supernatural punishments, like gods who threaten plague and famine if you don't obey your king. *Or*, if you obey a king who turns out to be illegitimate.

Shakespeare's Richard II is tragically poetic and whiny, and while tearfully passing the crown to Henry IV, he snivels out an inventory of royal rights and privileges:

> *I give this heavy weight from off my head,*
> *And this unwieldy sceptre from my hand,*
> *The pride of kingly sway from out my heart;*
> *With mine own tears I wash away my balm,*
> *With mine own hands I give away my crown,*
> *With mine own tongue deny my sacred state,*
> *With mine own breath release all duteous oaths;*
> *All pomp and majesty I do forswear;*
> *My manors, rents, revenues, I forgo;*
> *My acts, decrees, and statutes, I deny.*
> *God pardon all oaths that are broke to me!*
> *God keep all vows unbroke are made to thee!*
> *...God save King Henry, unking'd Richard says,*
> *And send him many years of sunshine days!* (R2 IV.i)

If we played this sad ballad backward it would be a coronation: "*sceptre...pride of kingly sway...balm* [anointing oil]*...crown...sacred state... duteous oaths* [of loyalty]*...pomp and majesty...manors, rents, revenues...acts, decrees, and statutes...God save King...years of sunshine days!*" (R2 IV.i)

The king's aura is symbolized by a golden circle, like a halo in a Christian icon: the crown.[126] Henry IV wearily says, "*Uneasy lies the head that wears the crown.*" (2H4.III.i) His son Hal, soon to be Henry V, speaks to the crown as though it were some demonic parasite that had drained his father to death:

> *Coming to look on you, thinking you dead...*
> *I spake unto this crown as having sense,*
> *And thus upbraided it: 'The care on thee depending*
> *Hath fed upon the body of my father;*
> *Therefore thou best of gold art worst of gold.*
> *Other, less fine in carat, is more precious,*
> *Preserving life in med'cine potable;*

But thou, most fine, most honour'd, most renown'd,
Hast eat thy bearer up.' (1H4 IV.iv)

The crown is indeed dangerous: very few Shakespearean kings die of old age. But still there's plenty of conniving, conspiring, plotting and scheming to get one.

Magic Words
King John | Macbeth | Midsummer

Every utterance of a king becomes "magic words." A king orders something be done, and someone does it because they believe the king's commands are backed by some higher power. There's a darkly comical moment in *King John* when the king has ordered a young boy's execution, then changes his mind but is informed that the sentence was already carried out. He then whines:

> *It is the curse of kings to be attended*
> *By slaves that take their humours for a warrant*
> *To break within the bloody house of life,*
> *And on the winking of authority*
> *To understand a law; to know the meaning*
> *Of dangerous majesty, when perchance it frowns*
> *More upon humour than advis'd respect.* (KJ IV.ii)

For most of Shakespeare's life, the English crown belonged to Queen Elizabeth. Her word was law, and she was surrounded by an aura of supernatural power. The Protestant Reformation meant a demotion of the Virgin Mary (the mother-goddess of Catholicism and inheritor of old Pagan fertility-goddess reverence), so it's no surprise to see the Virgin Queen Elizabeth benefiting as a new recipient of this veneration. When in 1588 a storm at sea prevented the Spanish Armada from penetrating England, many saw this as a manifestation of the Virgin Queen's magical chastity. A "chastity" that, apparently, was magically renewed every time she tired of a lover, like the Classical "virgin" huntress Artemis/Diana. Like other English monarchs, Queen Elizabeth was believed to have a special touch that could cure scrofula, which we now call tuberculosis but was long known as "the King's Evil."[127]

In *Macbeth*, Malcolm returns from England and reports having witnessed this cure there (the unnamed King is Edward the Confessor):

> *'Tis call'd the evil:*
> *A most miraculous work in this good King,*
> *Which often, since my here-remain in England,*
> *I have seen him do. How he solicits heaven,*
> *Himself best knows; but strangely-visited people,*
> *All swol'n and ulcerous, pitiful to the eye,*
> *The mere despair of surgery, he cures,*
> *Hanging a golden stamp about their necks*
> *Put on with holy prayers; and 'tis spoken,*
> *To the succeeding royalty he leaves*
> *The healing benediction.* (MAC IV.iii)

King James initially resisted this power, arguing "the age of miracles being past," but eventually relented under pressure and began touching for the Evil.

Kings were believed to have some control over weather. For example, Hamlet says of his dead father, "*That he might not beteem* [allow] *the winds of heaven visit her face too roughly.*" (HAM I.ii)

And Lear spends a good deal of his play outside railing against his lost ability to control weather, "*Thunder would not peace at my bidding.*" (KL IV.vi) He does command the winds to blow during the storm, but they're doing that anyway. In *Macbeth*, the weather is bad from Duncan's death until Macbeth dies. Although it *is* Scotland, which is not really famous for sunny days. Shakespeare often uses a storm or long sterile winter as a symbol of unworthy royalty, giving way to spring/summer fertility when legitimate rule is restored.

> *Now is the winter of our discontent*
> *Made glorious summer by this sun of York;*
> *And all the clouds that lour'd upon our house*
> *In the deep bosom of the ocean buried.* (R3 I.i)

In *A Midsummer Night's Dream*, royal discord (a bitter custody dispute) between the fairy king and queen causes unseasonable weather, crop failure and livestock disease:

> TITANIA. *These are the forgeries of jealousy...*
> *Therefore the winds, piping to us in vain,*
> *As in revenge, have suck'd up from the sea*
> *Contagious fogs; which, falling in the land,*
> *Hath every pelting river made so proud*
> *That they have overborne their continents.*
> *The ox hath therefore stretch'd his yoke in vain,*
> *The ploughman lost his sweat, and the green corn*
> *Hath rotted ere his youth attain'd a beard;*
> *The fold stands empty in the drowned field,*
> *And crows are fatted with the murrion flock...*
> *The seasons alter: hoary-headed frosts*
> *Fall in the fresh lap of...spring, the summer,*
> *The childing autumn, angry winter, change*
> *Their wonted liveries; and the mazed world,*
> *By their increase, now knows not which is which.*
> *And this same progeny of evils comes*
> *From our debate, from our dissension;*
> *We are their parents and original.* (MND II.i)

In the first half of the *Winter's Tale*, King Leontes becomes infected with delusional jealousy that causes sixteen years of sterile winter throughout his realm. This curse is not lifted until he reunites his family.

Cry Havoc
MACBETH | KING JOHN | HENRY V

The primary power of a king's "magic words" is a monopoly on violence. In a ritual involving some lofty-sounding abracadabra and a touch with a sword, a king can transform a peasant into a knight, earl, duke or thane. These were all fancy words for tax-collector, or mafia leg-breaker, someone who could extort goods from the peasantry by legitimized force, as long as they kicked up some percentage to the crown.

Only a king (or a king's appointed henchmen) can legally sentence someone to death. At the start of *Macbeth*, king Duncan has been pouring soldiers into a slaughter and it's no problem, then he declares a death sentence on the Thane of Cawdor and nobody bats an eye. That's the power of the king. But when Macbeth slays Duncan all hell breaks loose (literally!), and then we cringe as the usurper sends assassins after all his suspected rivals. Executing subversives is perfectly legal for a "true" king, but the play has established that Macbeth is an illegitimate imposter. Actually, the historical Macbeth slew the historical Duncan fair-and-square in battle, then reigned legitimately for seventeen years.

In *King John*, Faulconbridge the Bastard muses on the power of kings to declare war:

> *Ha, majesty! how high thy glory tow'rs*
> *When the rich blood of kings is set on fire!*
> *O, now doth Death line his dead chaps with steel;*
> *The swords of soldiers are his teeth, his fangs;*
> *And now he feasts, mousing the flesh of men,*
> *In undetermin'd differences of kings.* (KJ II.i)

The Bastard is sarcastic about how idiotic royal disagreements can cause mass slaughter. All the blood and butchery in *Henry V* begins with a French king sending a gift of two tennis balls, playfully implying that young Henry lacks testicles. But Henry is also guided by his father's dying advice that war abroad is the only way to maintain peace at home:

> *Come hither, Harry; sit... God knows, my son,*
> *By what by-paths and indirect crook'd ways*
> *I met this crown; and I myself know well*
> *How troublesome it sat upon my head...*
> *And I had many living to upbraid*
> *My gain of it by their assistances;*
> *Which daily grew to quarrel and to bloodshed,*
> *Wounding supposed peace... Therefore, my Harry,*
> *Be it thy course to busy giddy minds*

With foreign quarrels, that action, hence borne out,
May waste the memory of the former days. (2H4 IV.iii)

This speech sounds eerily prophetic today. Securing domestic peace through foreign warfare has become a great American pastime.

William Shakespeare was able to tread a fine line in his royalty plays – he humanized kings but never criticized the entitlements of monarchy. Theater goers in his time must have been curious about what goes on inside the head that wears the crown, and Shakespeare gratified audiences with long introspective speeches, sometimes strident like Henry V, sometimes self-pitying like Richard II, sometimes playful like Richard III. These characters harbor no illusions about themselves or their fathers being magical. Shakespeare himself almost certainly knew Queen Elizabeth and King James personally, and he does seem to have worshiped Elizabeth a bit. But while Shakespeare writes convincingly of fairies, witches and ghosts, he treats the divinity of kings as peasant folklore.

Fairies

n 1689, John Aubrey wrote "Before Printing, Old-wives Tales were ingeniose, and since Printing came in fashion, till a little before the Civill-warres, the ordinary sort of People were not taught to read. Now-a-dayes Bookes are common, and most of the poor people understand letters; and the many good Bookes, and variety of Turnes of Affaires, have putt all the old Fables out of doors: and the divine art of Printing and Gunpowder have frightened away Robin-goodfellow and the Fayries." [sic][128]

Roger Lancelyn Green cautions us against any fanciful attempt to use Shakespeare's work as sacred, systematic scripture on English fairy-lore.

> The one danger of such a study is to assume that Shakespeare knew his sources: I don't think that he did in any scholarly sense, and I'm certain that he didn't bother to do one scrap of homework before writing *A Midsummer Night's Dream*, 'our greatest Fairy poem.' But of course he had behind him two very important sources: on the one hand the actual superstitions still alive in Warwickshire when he was a boy, and on the other the general literary tradition which he seems to have soaked in at every pore when he was serving his apprenticeship to the theatre during his first ten or twelve years in London. He had also an advantage which no writer of fairy literature has ever had since— he hadn't read Shakespeare![129]

As a people who value (and even worship) the written word, we may feel a temptation to think of Shakespeare's work as a sort of scripture:

definitive, authoritative, canonical, inerrant, even divinely inspired. And this might mislead us into seeking a comprehensive systematic fairy-ology in his works. But as with all supernatural phenomena, Shakespeare cherry-picked from a wide range of folk and literary traditions, and then shaped the selected fragments in accordance with particular plots of particular plays. The fairies he creates follow no strict pattern.[130]

He did live during a major turning point in English-lore and its transmission, and he left a significant mark upon it. The "fairy tale" or "old wives' tale" had been an oral tradition primarily transmitted by women – medicine women, shamans, "witches," grandmothers, midwives, babysitters, etc., as acknowledged in Chaucer's *Canterbury Tales* and the pulp pamphlet *Robin Good-Fellow, His Mad Prankes and Merry Iests*. But during the reign of Queen Elizabeth, who was widely believed to have supernatural powers (for example, her magical chastity was credited with protecting the island from penetration by Spanish invaders), there developed a fairy literature including Edmund Spenser's 1590 epic *The Faerie Queene*, then Shakespeare's *A Midsummer Night's Dream*, and then a whole slew of plays and poems constituting a literary genre. The most significant change here is from female oral transmission to male literary transmission. And in a culture that values scripture over hearsay, the male literature version has generally been considered definitive ever since. But really the mass-produced literature is a knock-off, what we might call the "sell-out" version, packaged for the masses, censored down to PG-13, less authentic, less fluid and sacred than the improvisatory ramblings of old wives. Unfortunately, we don't have Shakespeare's mom or granny or nanny here to tell us the old tales - the text is all that survives, and Shakespeare is arguably our best specimen of it.

Pixies

MIDSUMMER

"The Wife of Bath's Tale," one of Geoffrey Chaucer's *Canterbury Tales* from the late 1300s, is an "old wives' tale" in multiple ways: the story she tells is a fairytale fantasy romance (with the moral of not judging a woman by her looks), and it also contains a fascinating synthesis of medieval fairy-lore:

Now in the olden days of King Arthur,
Of whom the Britons speak with great honour,
All this wide land was full of faery.
The elf-queen, with her jolly company,
Danced oftentimes on many a green mead;
This was the old opinion, as I read.
I speak of many hundred years ago;
But now no man can see the elves, you know.
For now the so-great charity and prayers
Of limiters and other holy friars
That do infest each land and every stream
As thick as motes are in a bright sunbeam,
Blessing halls, chambers, kitchens, ladies' bowers,
Cities and towns and castles and high towers,
Manors and barns and stables, aye and dairies -
This causes it that there are now no fairies.
For where was wont to walk full many an elf,
Right there walks now the limiter himself...
As he goes round his district in his gown.
Women may now go safely up and down,
In every copse or under every tree;
There is no other incubus, than he,
And would do them nothing but dishonour.[131]

The "olden days of King Arthur" is, on the one hand, British code for "once upon a time," the misty, mysterious past. But Arthurian legend is almost always connected with the Christianization of Britain, often involving some merger with indigenous paganism.[132] This seems to be the sense of it here, since the narrative concerns Roman Christianity persecuting native beliefs, and the priesthood replacing fairies as sexual predators.

It's possible that this medieval legend of Britain having once belonged to elves and fairies refers to a historical race of natives, short in stature, with large blue eyes, curly blond hair, and pale skin that they tattooed and painted blue. Robert Graves theorizes that these were relatives of a people encountered by the Athenian soldier/historian Xenophon 400 years before the common era, who describes a woodland warrior race "with their backs variegated and their breasts tattooed with patterns of all sorts of flowers. They sought after the women in the Hellenic army, and would fain have laid with them openly in broad daylight, for that was their custom. The whole community, male and female alike, were fair-complexioned and white-skinned. It was agreed that this was the most barbaric and outlandish people that they had passed through on the whole expedition, and the furthest removed from the Hellenic customs, doing in a crowd precisely what other people would prefer to do in solitude, and when alone behaving exactly as others would behave in company, talking to themselves and laughing at their own expense, standing still and then again capering about, wherever they might chance to be, without rhyme or reason, as if their sole business were to show off to the rest of the world."[133]

By the time the Romans arrived in Britain, these had been mostly displaced by the arrival of the larger Druidic Celts, but centurions in the woods would still catch the odd glimpse of small, blue-painted people whom they called the "Picts," meaning "Painted." And Roman soldiers in all their heavy battle-armor were still terrified at the prospect of being ambushed by tiny women wearing nothing but blue paint who would tear them to pieces (or sometimes force the soldiers to mate with them and *then* tear them to pieces) and vanish into the shadowy woods. Ultimately the only way to get rid of these natives was to destroy the forests of Britain. But the legends remained, of small semi-magical forest people, regionally known by various names. Being light-skinned and blond, they were most popularly called the fair-folk or "fairies," the equivalent of "blondies." The Pictish origin survives in the word "pixies." And elsewhere they were known as elves, Sidhe, Leprechauns, Brownies, etc.[134] To this we could even loosely add Smurfs, but gender reversed. Who on earth came up with the idea that a community could survive with a hundred males and only one female?

Reginald Scot, in his 1584 book *Discouerie of Witchcraft*, inadvertently preserves a fascinating catalogue of "Old Wives' Tale" mythical forest creatures:

> "In our childhood our mothers maids have so terrified us with
> [tales of] bull beggers, spirits, witches, urchens, elves, hags,
> fairies, satyrs, pans, faunes, sylens, kit with the cansticke, tritons,
> centaurs, dwarfes, giants, imps, calcars, conjurors, nymphes,
> chang-lings. Incubus, Robin good-fellowe, the spoorne, the mare,

the man in the oke, the hell waine, the fierdrake, the puckle, Tom thombe, hob gobblin, Tom tumbler, boneles, and such other bugs, that we are afraid of our owne shadowes. [sic]"[135]

William Shakespeare would then combine several of these into the *Midsummer Night's Dream's "shrewd and knavish sprite / Call'd Robin Goodfellow* [and] *Hobgoblin...and sweet Puck."* (MND II.i)

True to Robin Goodfellow's "Old Wives' Tale" origins, his story in *Mad Prankes* is told by a tavern hostess "to passe the time withall, and make our selves merry." Puck in *Midsummer* will poke fun at Robin's folktale origins by transforming into a stool and then causing such a storyteller to fall:

> *The wisest aunt, telling the saddest tale,*
> *Sometime for three-foot stool mistaketh me;*
> *Then slip I from her bum, down topples she...*
> *And then the whole quire hold their hips and laugh,*
> *And waxen in their mirth, and neeze, and swear*
> *A merrier hour was never wasted there.* (MND II.i)

The fairy as mischievous shapeshifter corresponds with "trickster" figures in tribal folklores from around the world. Puck speaks of his ability to take plant and animal forms. But one thing Shakespeare's fairies can't do is fly: Mab needs a chariot, Puck never speaks of transforming into any sort of bird, Oberon and Titania have to walk everywhere (Titania does have one retainer named "Moth," so that's debatable, but she also has one named "cobweb" and it's doubtful she's a real cobweb). A stage direction mentions that Ariel can put on harpy wings, but Ariel speaks of riding on a bat's back. In general, fairies in literature don't tend to have wings until a century after Shakespeare wrote. Shakespeare's water-fairies are hitch-hikers too, as we learn when Oberon reports on having heard a siren's song:

> *Once I sat upon a promontory,*
> *And heard a mermaid on a dolphin's back*
> *Uttering such dulcet and harmonious breath*
> *That the rude sea grew civil at her song,*
> *And certain stars shot madly from their spheres*
> *To hear the sea-maid's music.* (MND II.i)[136]

Fairies in the oral traditions had generally been mischievous tricksters led by their appetites, causing trouble, sometimes stealing babies, sometimes helping with chores. Most so-called "fairy tales" do not feature fairies, but one of the few that does, "Rumpelstiltskin," sums it up pretty well – he can magically help with an impossible task but demands a firstborn child. He's an extreme example, though: common fairies were believed to help out with basic household chores and maybe even leave a gold coin in your shoe if you left out a bowl of milk. Who drank the milk? Who left the coin? We don't know.[137] But these traditions – the bowl of milk and gift in the footwear – later became associated with Santa Claus and the Tooth Fairy, last survivors of Christianity's war on fairy-lore.

Robin Goodfellow

MIDSUMMER

> *FAIRY. Either I mistake your shape and making quite,*
> *Or else you are that shrewd and knavish sprite*
> *Call'd Robin Goodfellow. Are not you he*
> *That frights the maidens of the villagery,*
> *Skim milk, and sometimes labour in the quern,*
> *And bootless make the breathless housewife churn,*
> *And sometime make the drink to bear no barm,*
> *Mislead night-wanderers, laughing at their harm?*
> *Those that Hobgoblin call you, and sweet Puck,*
> *You do their work, and they shall have good luck.*
> *Are not you he?* (MND II.i)

Shakespeare's most memorable fairy, Puck, comes primarily from medieval English folklore about a forest bandit prankster with a lengthy rap-sheet and list of aliases: Robin Goodfellow, AKA Robin Hud ("Hud" here meaning a piece of sacred oak, and from this we get "Robin Hood"), AKA Hob Goblin, AKA Puck (from the Celtic "Púca" meaning "nature spirit," related to the Dutch word "spook"). Then as Renaissance England appropriated Greek and Roman mythology, Robin also inherited elements of the Classical tricksters with their combination of goat-man-deity, known variously as fauns, satyrs, Pan, Dionysus and Bacchus.

According to his 1628 biography, the popular pulp pamphlet *Robin Good-Fellow, His Mad Prankes and Merry Iests*, Robin was half human, but nonetheless considered "a hee fayrie" whose fairy father "did love a proper young wench, for every night would hee with other fayries come to the house, and there dance in her chamber...and at his departure would hee leave her silver and jewels, to expresse his love unto her. At last this mayde was with childe, and being asked who was the father of it, she answered a man that nightly came to visit her, but earely in the morning he would go his way, whither she knew not, he went so suddainly." [sic]

Mad Prankes itself seems to be a combination of two different regional portraits.[138] In the first half he's all appetite, a hedonist who'd fit in well among Native American Trickster figures: he's a shapeshifter who kisses the weaver's wife, transforms into a bear to steal food, misleads travelers, and occasionally helps out with housework, grinding malt and spinning hemp. His catch-phrase is "hempen hampen," which Shakespeare alludes to by having Puck call the artisans *"hempen homespuns."* The second half of *Mad Prankes*, perhaps influenced by *A Midsummer Night's Dream*, has him stealing babies, cavorting with a fairy king and queen, and punishing "sluttery," a word that originally meant domestic sloppiness but quickly gained the connotation of sexual promiscuity:

> When house or harth doth sluttish lie,
> I pinch the maids there blacke and blew;
> And, from the bed, the bed-clothes I
> pull off, and lay them naked to view:
> twixt sleepe and wake I doe them take,
> And on the key-colde floore them throw. [sic]

In the early 1600s, as fairy-lore transitioned from oral folktales to written literature, Robin underwent an identity change. The hairy forest bandit, core of the Robin Hood legends, was inducted into the court of a fairy royalty as a jester or fool (and meanwhile Robin Hood was being disassociated from his pagan fairy origins and rehabilitated as a slumming nobleman who redistributed ill-gotten wealth). The pagan witch-god was essentially being put into witness protection in the fairy kingdom, which was considered relatively harmless. The domestication of Robin seems to have been a defense against the Reformation charge that this lusty, goaty little guy was Satan. And indeed, Christian visual representations of Satan were greatly influenced by popular images of Robin Goodfellow with goat-horns and legs, a torch and broom, a permanent erection, and a circle of black-clad witches dancing a circle around him.[139]

Robin Goodfellow would become a kind of patron saint of good housekeeping, with the rise of a "middling sort" of class in England. Members of this emerging middle class could afford to own their homes, but most were not wealthy enough to hire a housekeeper, so the lady of the manor was also the maid. Wendy Wall proposes that fairy-lore was adapted to add a touch of glamor to domestic drudgery: "Pinching maids, grinding meal, and scrubbing the kitchen, he makes eroticism and work seem natural allies."[140]

In *A Midsummer Night's Dream*, Puck does retain a hint of his prankster past, but Shakespeare has taken away the incubus/trickster's appetite for food and sex. He is primarily concerned with restoring order in the fairy kingdom, and promoting monogamous human marriage. At the end, he uses his broom to *"sweep the dust behind the door"* to ensure that the midsummer night's rule-breaking, boundary crossing and partner-swapping are over. *A Midsummer Night's Dream* will have a sequel, *Merry Wives of Windsor*, in which re-named older versions of Helena and Hermia will once again venture into the forest and produce a fairy pageant to protect their reputations from charges of sluttery (in the sense of infidelity) and Puck will make a brief cameo appearance at the end of it.

Cupid and Hymen
Love's Labour's Lost | Tempest | As You Like It

Cupid and Hymen were minor Greek gods but in Shakespeare's plays they have been adopted as honorary English fairies. Berowne, who has sworn off romance in *Love's Labour's Lost*, berates Cupid for his domineering ways:

> *This wimpled, whining, purblind, wayward boy,*
> *This senior-junior, giant-dwarf, Dan Cupid;*

Regent of love-rhymes, lord of folded arms,
Th' anointed sovereign of sighs and groans,
Liege of all loiterers and malcontents,
Dread prince of plackets, king of codpieces, [141]
Sole imperator, and great general
Of trotting paritors. (LLL III.i)

Berowne describes Cupid in alliterative terms similar to the Lord of
Misrule, the mock-king of *Mardi Gras,* and indeed Cupid will cause quite a
bit of carnival-mischief in *Love's Labour's Lost.* [142] Berowne may not believe
in the *literal* existence of this god, but this is the play where Shakespeare
creates his clearest physical manifestation of Cupid, in the form of Boyet the
love-messenger. Unfortunately, this Cupid's labors will be lost when another
messenger, Mercury (Marcadé) spoils the mood with news of death. [143]

Cupid is real, though unseen, in *Midsummer Night's Dream.* The
fairy king Oberon reports having watched him miss a shot at *"a fair vestal*
[virgin], *throned by the west"* - an inside joke about the unmarried Queen
Elizabeth. When she visited Elvetham in 1591, she was seated at the west
side of a garden lake for a fairy pageant, and there was some unsuccessful
attempt to set her up with a suitor. [144]

That very time I saw, but thou couldst not,
Flying between the cold moon and the earth
Cupid, all arm'd; a certain aim he took
At a fair vestal, throned by the west,
And loos'd his love-shaft smartly from his bow,
As it should pierce a hundred thousand hearts;
But I might see young Cupid's fiery shaft
Quench'd in the chaste beams of the wat'ry moon;
And the imperial vot'ress passed on,
In maiden meditation, fancy-free.
Yet mark'd I where the bolt of Cupid fell.
It fell upon a little western flower,
Before milk-white, now purple with love's wound,
And maidens call it Love-in-idleness. [145] (MND II.i)

Cupid is distinct from other fairies in *Midsummer Night's Dream*: He
can fly, humans and Puck can't see him, but Oberon can. Puck and Oberon

will "play Cupid" by using this love-juice to drug Titania and the teenagers, but they can't create a love potion on their own. Cupid is also a celebrity; he needs no introduction.

Cupid was a Classical god, son of the erotic goddess Venus and the war-god Mars – it's from his father's side he gets the weapon, a symbol of conquest and penetration. In *Love's Labour's Lost*, when the four wooers decide to become Cupid's army, they use militaristic terms to describe romantic aggression: *"Saint Cupid, then! and, soldiers, to the field! ...Advance your standards, and upon them, lords; Pell-mell, down with them!"* (LLL IV.iii) The popular image of Cupid has since been softened into a baby (symbolizing a potential child that could be born of love) but for Shakespeare's original audience the name was more likely to conjure images of a spiteful, armed pre-teen sociopath, who sometimes shot his arrows at random – several of Shakespeare's characters complain that Cupid does his dirty-work "blind." Even Puck says: *"Cupid is a knavish lad, thus to make poor females mad."* (MND III.ii)

Prospero in *The Tempest* will employ a somewhat playful fairy, Ariel, but Cupid is banned from the island – even his name cannot be uttered. When Prospero produces a goddess pageant to celebrate his daughter's engagement, he conjures visions of Ceres (harvest), Iris (rainbow) and Juno (matrimony), but *not* Venus (physical attraction) or her son Cupid. Ceres announces that she has forsworn Venus and *"her blind boy's scandaled company"* and Iris assures her they will not show up and spoil the engagement party with any thoughts of sex:

> *Here thought they to have done*
> *Some wanton charm upon this man and maid,*
> *Whose vows are that no bed-rite shall be paid*
> *Till Hymen's torch be lighted; but in vain.*
> *Mars's hot minion is return'd again;*
> *Her waspish-headed son has broke his arrows,*
> *Swears he will shoot no more, but play with sparrows,*
> *And be a boy right out.* (TEM IV.i)

Shakespeare does not seem to have been a fan of Cupid, and this appears to be his last written reference to him: Cupid breaks his arrows and becomes an ordinary boy.

While Cupid is the god of irrational desire, Hymen is the god of the wedding contract, sealed in the blood of maidenhood – the anatomical hymen is named after this deity. The narrator of *Pericles* sums it up: *"Hymen hath brought the bride to bed, where, by the loss of maidenhead, a babe is moulded."* (PER II.v[146])

Prospero, like Shakespeare himself, is obsessed with virginity and disgusted by premarital sex.[147] Shakespeare's characters often speak of Cupid with resentment and dread, but Hymen is another matter—he physically appears in one of Shakespeare's plays, or two if we count a non-speaking cameo in *Two Noble Kinsmen*.

Hymen's big scene is the quadruple wedding at the end of *As You Like It*. There's been so much masquerade and mirth and mayhem that this deity must personally show up to straighten it all out. And his assertion that he *prevents* confusion is clearly a dig at Cupid (or Rosalind, who's been *playing* Cupid in the woods):

> *HYMEN. Peace, ho! I bar confusion;*
> *'Tis I must make conclusion*
> *Of these most strange events.*
> *Here's eight that must take hands*
> *To join in Hymen's bands,*
> *If truth holds true contents...*
> *Whiles a wedlock-hymn we sing,*
> *Feed yourselves with questioning,*
> *That reason wonder may diminish,*
> *How thus we met, and these things finish.* (AYL V.iv)

Then everyone bursts into song, and as in *The Tempest*, Juno/Hera and Hymen (representing marriage) are celebrated while Venus/Aphrodite and Cupid (representing physical attraction) are left out:

> *Wedding is great Juno's crown;*
> *O blessed bond of board and bed!*
> *'Tis Hymen peoples every town;*
> *High wedlock then be honoured.*
> *Honour, high honour, and renown,*
> *To Hymen, god of every town!* (AYL V.iv)

Rosalind

As You Like It

Shakespeare had a special fondness for putting a female character in male clothing, likely because he and his audience enjoyed the inside-joke of a boy playing a woman playing a boy. Most of his cross-dressed heroines use the disguise to hide (Julia in *Two Gentlemen*, Viola in *Twelfth Night*, Imogen in *Cymbeline*) and their masculine persona is more genderless than male. Portia and her servant, cross-dressed in *Merchant*, are assertive and have a certain homoerotic sexual chemistry with their hoodwinked husbands, but they run their errand and hang up the costumes. Rosalind in *As You Like It* is something else entirely. For her male persona she chooses a flashy and flamboyant gay man, a self-described *"saucy lackey"* pushing the clever transvestite joke into the realm of transexuality. And that's not the only boundary she messes with.

Rosalind is a genuine shapeshifter – she doesn't just put on male clothing, she *becomes* something else, a sort of wood-nymph in the forest of Arden. She's a better fit in the category of fairies like Puck and Ariel than with Shakespeare's other transvestite heroines. While other cross-dressed heroines hide, Rosalind needs to be the center of attention. The persona she chooses for herself is Ganymede, a beautiful Trojan boy whom the Greek God Zeus fell in love with and drew up to Olympus to become the semi-divine cupbearer of the gods. Shakespeare hints that Rosalind has some supernatural power when she first meets Orlando, and he's about to wrestle the local champion. *"The little strength that I have, I would it were with you,"* she says, *"Now, Hercules be thy speed, young man!"* And the young man triumphs.

Rosalind uses her powers to influence and shape the man she intends to marry.[148] As the boy Ganymede she offers to tutor him on romance, on the condition that he call her Rosalind: a boy playing a girl playing a boy playing a girl. In this double disguise she breaks him of his silly romantic notions of *"heavenly Rosalind"* with the warning that as a wife she will still be a shapeshifting trickster, more animal (and Greek huntress-goddess) than angel:

I will be more jealous of thee than a Barbary cock-pigeon over his hen, more clamorous than a parrot against rain, more new-fangled than an ape, more giddy in my desires than a monkey. I will weep for nothing, like Diana in the fountain, and I will do that when you are dispos'd to be merry; I will laugh like a hyen, and that when thou are inclin'd to sleep. (AYL IV.i)

Think a moment about Shakespearean wooers, seeking pure demure maidens – would Claudio or Orsino put up with this? Romeo would kill himself within a month of this wedding (perhaps it's for the best he didn't marry his Rosaline).

Rosalind does more than house-train her pet Orlando – she also exerts power over other characters. Rosalind's cousin Celia accompanies her disguised, but not as a man. Yet Rosalind momentarily transforms her into a (male) priest, despite Celia's protests. She also has a power over Phebe the shepherdess, who falls in love with Ganymede, spurning the shepherd Silvius. Like Cupid or Puck, Rosalind manages to transfer the shepherdess' affections and match-make this marriage. And in the final wedding scene, her metamorphosis from male to female produces a tangible manifestation of the Greek marriage-god Hymen.

Camille Paglia writes, "Rosalind's magic is real, for she produces Hymen, the marriage spirit who enters with her in the last scene...a by-product of the play's psychoalchemy... He is the ghost of her maleness, exorcised but lingering on to preside over her exit from Arden...a visible distillation of her transsexual experience. In her romantic conspiracies, Rosalind has impersonated Hymen and hence invoked his presence."[149] Seeing her in a wedding dress, the mesmerized Orlando stutters *"If there be truth in sight, you are my Rosalind."* (AYL V.iv) That's a big *"If,"* since Rosalind has been such a trickster with *"truth"* and *"sight"* for most of the play. And Rosalind's game is not over. Generally, at the end of a Shakespeare play we expect the lovers to stop changing but Rosalind has already warned Orlando (and us) that she won't.

Fairy Royalty

MIDSUMMER

The old rural fairies and sprites and pixies were anarchic in nature—the survival of popular fairylore was a form of resistance to England's urbanization and solidifying social class system. The "Fairy Tale," whether it contained fairies or not (most don't), was an underdog genre: old wives' and nannies' stories about peasant-girls becoming princesses, honest villagers finding fairy gold, and legends of babies being switched at birth all involve magical social elevation.

The idea of fairy royalty was a recent innovation in Shakespeare's time: it gained popularity with the publication of Edmund Spenser's *The Faerie Queene*, essentially a piece of Elizabethan propaganda in which a fairy king was succeeded in power by a queen (as Henry VIII was succeeded by Elizabeth). Retrojecting this story into the misty past magically enhanced the legitimacy of the monarchy, implying that Henry VIII and Elizabeth were a *restoration* of the old normalcy. And sprinkling the story with fairy-dust suggested a return of the magic of monarchy, which had been long dimmed or usurped by Roman domination.

Adding a king and queen into "Faerieland" introduces hierarchy into what had been a subversive storytelling genre, turning a mischievous trickster like Robin Goodfellow into a loyal court jester. In the popular pulp-pamphlet *Robin Good-Fellow, His Mad Prankes and Merry Iests*, Robin even becomes a son of the fairy king (but significantly *not* the fairy queen, who could still be considered virginal). "While the fairies of folk tradition complemented the workaday existence of commoners, courtly fairylore elevated the aristocracy into a realm of mythical origins superior to popular culture."[150]

King James did not take fairies seriously, but mentioned them among popular beliefs in his 1597 *Daemonologie*: "That fourth kind of Spirites, which by the Gentiles [pagans] was called *Diana* and her wandring court, and amongst us was called the *Phairie*...or our good neighboures... To speake of the many vain trattles founded upon that illusion: How there was a King and Queene of *Phairie*, of such a iolly court & train as they had a teynd, & dutie, as it were, of all goods: how they naturallie rode and went, eate and drank, and did all other actiones like naturall men and women."

[sic]¹⁵¹ These fairy-courts were under hills and mortals could enter them at certain times of the year (James conflates fairyland with ancient passage-tombs like Newgrange in Ireland).

Since fairyland was subterranean, the fairy king was identified with mythical lords of the underworld: the Germanic dwarf-king Albrecht/Alberich (spelled Oberon in French) and the Greco-Roman Hades/Pluto. And from there it was no great leap for Thomas Hobbes to write that fairies "have but one universal king, which some poets of ours call King Oberon, but the Scripture calls Beelzebub."¹⁵² If the fairy king was nocturnal, subterranean and non-Christian, he must have been the Devil. Shakespeare's Oberon is called *"king of shadows"* by Puck, who uses the word *"shadows"* to refer to fairies and spirits. Oberon and Puck are nocturnal, although Oberon claims to have some limited tolerance for daylight:

> *We are spirits of another sort* [from ghosts]:
> *I with the Morning's love have oft made sport...*
> *But, notwithstanding, haste, make no delay;*
> *We may effect this business yet ere day.* (MND III.ii)

Where he spends his days we are not told, but probably underground.

Oberon seems to own Fairyland (Titania says she wouldn't trade her adopted child for it) but he does not own the fairy queen. He spends the early scenes sullenly sulking around because she won't give him what he wants—a changeling child, but more importantly her unconditional devotion. And it's only by drugging her that he's able to exchange a changeling, the ass-headed Bottom, for the child he wants. Then he runs out the clock of a Shakespearean comedy so that there must be a reconciliation.¹⁵³

Shakespeare, like King James, loosely equates the fairy queen with the Roman virgin huntress-goddess Diana, the name Titania being a variant designation of Diana in Ovid's *Metamorphoses* ("Titania" means "of the Titans," pre-Olympian gods). The ass-headed Bottom bumbling into Titania's bower comically parallels medieval representations of the stag-headed Actaeon stumbling into the forest fountain of the goddess Diana. Shakespeare also follows Chaucer by mixing in elements of the Greek Persephone, the underworld god's wife who oversees crop growth.¹⁵⁴ In *Midsummer Night's Dream*, a marital spat between the fairy king and queen causes blight and famine.

Like Oberon and Puck, Titania is nocturnal, although her sleep schedule makes the pacing of the play a bit confusing. She sleeps and awakens twice in what seems like a single night. But this is just a grammatical issue with the play's title, which implies a singular midsummer night. We're told at the start that the action of the play will take four days, and three of these are spent in the woods. So Titania is up three nights, interspersed with two days of sleep.

Oberon and Titania's relationship is generally referred to as a marriage, but the text is sketchy on that. When Oberon insists *"Tarry, rash wanton* [slut]*! Am I not thy lord?"* Titania huffs back at him *"Then, I must be thy lady."* (MND II.ii) "Lord" is a common title for husband in Shakespeare's writing, but it also means king, and this is as close as we get to defining their relationship. If they're married, it's an open marriage: Oberon's been romantically involved with human women including Hippolyta, and Titania's had a fling with Theseus. They live and sleep separately and oversee different elements of forest life: Oberon speaks of predatory animals and takes an interest in human matchmaking, Titania speaks of plants and insects. When the play opens it seems they've been separated since last summer, a full year. They have separate attendants. In Puck's first scene he meets one of Titania's fairies who fawns like he's a celebrity but doesn't know him personally. Puck seems to be Oberon's only henchman, while Titania has a whole train of followers. And then there's a fascinating twist at the end of *Merry Wives of Windsor* (a sort of sequel to *Midsummer Night's Dream*) when the Fairy Queen and Puck appear at a forest dance and Oberon is not seen or even mentioned.

Mab

ROMEO AND JULIET

In *Romeo and Juliet*, the manic-depressive Mercutio explodes in a tirade against Romeo's belief in ominous dreams. His monologue is long, and likely familiar, but it's worth another look to see how different this fairy *"queen"* is from Titania in *A Midsummer Night's Dream*, especially since the two plays were written at about the same time.

MERCUTIO. *O, then, I see Queen Mab hath been with you.*
She is the fairies' midwife, and she comes
In shape no bigger than an agate-stone
On the fore-finger of an alderman,
Drawn with a team of little atomies
Over men's noses as they lie asleep:
Her waggon-spokes made of long spinners' legs;
The cover, of the wings of grasshoppers;
Her traces, of the smallest spider's web;
The collars, of the moonshine's watery beams;
Her whip of cricket's bone; the lash, of film;
Her waggoner, a small grey-coated gnat,
Not half so big as a round little worm
Prick'd from the lazy finger of a maid:
Her chariot is an empty hazelnut,
Made by the joiner squirrel or old grub,
Time out o' mind the fairies' coachmakers.
And in this state she gallops night by night
Through lovers' brains, and then they dream of love;
O'er courtiers' knees, that dream on curtsies straight;
O'er lawyers' fingers, who straight dream on fees;
O'er ladies' lips, who straight on kisses dream,
Which oft the angry Mab with blisters plagues,
Because their breaths with sweetmeats tainted are:
Sometime she gallops o'er a courtier's nose,
And then dreams he of smelling out a suit;
And sometime comes she with a tithe-pig's tail,
Tickling a parson's nose as a lies asleep,
Then dreams he of another benefice:
Sometime she driveth o'er a soldier's neck,
And then dreams he of cutting foreign throats,
Of breaches, ambuscados, Spanish blades,
Of healths five fathom deep; and then anon
Drums in his ear, at which he starts and wakes;
And, being thus frighted, swears a prayer or two,
And sleeps again. This is that very Mab
That plats [braids/dreadlocks] the manes of horses in the night;

And bakes the elf-locks in foul sluttish hairs,
Which, once untangled, much misfortune bodes:
This is the hag, when maids lie on their backs,
That presses them, and learns them first to bear,
Making them women of good carriage:
This is she. (R&J I.iv)

The principal difference is that Titania is a woodland fairy, while Mab belongs to the city. Marjorie Swann writes, "Shakespeare's Mab is a fairy queen for the Elizabethan urban jungle, an accomplice of greed and worldly ambition far removed from the hearths and dairies of rural domestic production. No sixpences in shoes here: Mab races through a world of avaricious professionals, not householders for whom a coin is a windfall."[155] The monologue bustles like a metropolis with courtiers, lawyers, ladies, parson, soldier, and they all dream of consumption and predation. Titania is a nurturer of nature, and we also see her strong maternal streak with the changeling child and Bottom. We see none of this with Mab, cracking her whip, inspiring people to exploit and dominate each other.

Mab herself is only briefly described. In the text she is largely defined by her possessions, especially the chariot that is explained in minute detail. She's "a cutting-edge consumer who flaunts her aristocratic status by displaying her newfangled mode of transportation"[156]

Titania is more down-to-earth, her courtiers are named after common rural household items, her bed is a flower, and she listens to music played with tongs and bones. Her quarrel with king Oberon concerns *his* materialistic desire to possess an Indian changeling child as an exotic collectible, a conversation piece, and he's willing to exchange goods for it. But Titania refuses to make a deal, *"The fairy land buys not the child [from me... Not for thy fairy kingdom."* (MND II.i) Her attachment is sentimental, because the mother who died in childbirth was a friend of hers.

Mab's tiny chariot and accessories represent a change in English conceptions of wealth. Wealth had always been the ownership of land – productive farmlands for nobles, and the most elite form of wealth was forest-as-private-hunting-preserve, which could only be owned by royalty. But wealth kept getting smaller in the form of jewels and spices (and would soon become imaginary, with the invention of "stock" by the Dutch East India Company). Shakespeare himself profited greatly from stock in a theater company, but being old-fashioned, he used the profits to buy up large tracts of farmland.

"English fairylore was traditionally bound up with normative concepts of a precapitalist social formation; thus, as England shifted from a rural, household-based mode of production to an urban, commercial, and increasingly mercantile economy, fairylore became a particularly apt vehicle for mystifying the profound socioeconomic changes of the early modern period."[157] Fairies of rural folk legend had been mischievous and subversive, but Shakespeare was part of a literary movement to rehabilitate them from trickster incubi into guardians of propriety, and eventually into capitalist consumers, collectors of novelty items. Mab is compared to a jewel, and her flashy chariot is a symbol of conspicuous consumption.

The name "Mab" comes from the Irish Medb (or Maeve, related to the word "Mead" meaning intoxication), a legendary queen famous for her exploits on the battlefield and in the bedroom. This fairy queen is wild and adventurous, more like a female Puck than another Titania. And like Shakespeare's other fairies she cannot fly on her own, hence the fancy chariot.

Scholars in this last four centuries have put forth numerous proposals to harmonize Mab and Titania, scrambling to defend the semi-divine Shakespeare from charges of inconsistency.[158] But here, as in all of his supernatural references, Shakespeare flexes the lore in service of the specific plot and character. The "Mab" speech is not a professorial lecture about systematic fairy-ology. In the context of *Romeo and Juliet* it's a satire of fairy fantasy, expressing Mercutio's toxic cynicism about dreams and desire (and if Romeo's mercurial friend did not die early in the play, he likely would have become an Iago figure, poisoning Romeo's brain with doubt and distrust. ...Or, who knows? A healthy dose of skepticism might have saved the impulsive Romeo's life).

These plays were written at about the same time, and one required a forest-fairy-queen while the other required a city-fairy-queen. Shakespeare does appear to be treading relatively new ground with relocating a fairy from the countryside to the urban landscape. And this speech, fixating on Mab's tiny size, was highly influential in the further development of fairy literature. Unlike Titania who must be played by a human being, Mab does not physically appear, so Shakespeare could let his imagination run wild without theatrical constraints.

Ariel

TEMPEST

Shakespeare's final fairy is Ariel in *The Tempest*. Like Puck, he/she is a prankster, shapeshifter, and master of illusion. Unlike Puck, Ariel is genderless–the only gendered pronouns about Ariel are in stage directions, which may have been added by someone other than Shakespeare. Puck's playful nature and comical miscommunications with Oberon add a great deal of fun to *Midsummer Night's Dream*, but Prospero keeps Ariel on a very short leash. Ariel's pranks are precise expressions of Prospero's punitive spite, and there's definitely no allowance for any romantic-comedy confusion concerning Prospero's daughter. Ariel does not seem to take any particular joy in his/her work, desiring only to be free of the gloomy Prospero: the only times we see Ariel happy are when he/she extracts another promise of liberation.

Whether or not *The Tempest* was Shakespeare's grand finale script, there's definitely some exhaustion here. Shakespeare himself couldn't work up the interest to write the first half of the story, where Prospero loses everything but gains the audience's sympathy. Instead, the play begins with the banished, abandoned, bitter man briefly narrating the slights against him and then joylessly trudging through his revenge.[159] It would be nice to care about Prospero and *want* him to get his old job back, but he doesn't even bother to report that he was any good at it. Shakespeare/Prospero's exhaustion is contagious. We get the sense that Ariel *could be* sprightly and charismatic, but under the strict guidance of these tired men he/she is also exhausted. The play does end with a note of hope when the fairy becomes free, but it's hard to imagine Ariel having much fun on this unpeopled island.

Fairy Dancing

MIDSUMMER NIGHT'S DREAM | MERRY WIVES

Chaucer's "Wife of Bath" reported that in the old days, "All this wide land was full of faery. / The elf-queen, with her jolly company, / Danced oftentimes on many a green mead." The belief was influenced by the mysterious appearance of "Fairy rings" on the ground, actually circles of darkened grass caused by nocturnal fungus growth, referred to in *Midsummer Night's Dream* as *"orbs upon the green."* (MND II.i) But like crop circles, they inspired a good deal of supernatural speculation.

The Fairy Queen Titania calls for circular dances, *"Come now, a roundel and a fairy song,"* (MND II.ii) and invites Oberon into one: *"If you will patiently dance in our round / And see our moonlight revels, go with us; / If not, shun me, and I will spare your haunts."* (MND II.i) And his stubborn refusals seem to be why time is out of joint:

> *The spring, the summer,*
> *The childing autumn, angry winter, change*
> *Their wonted liveries; and the mazed world,*
> *By their increase, now knows not which is which.*
> *And this same progeny of evils comes*
> *From our debate, from our dissension;*
> *We are their parents and original.* (MND II.i)

She goes on to describe bad weather, crop failure and livestock death very much like the problems facing English agriculture in 1594-1596. This play, which may have premiered in 1595, accredited current weather events to fairy discord. Within the logic of the script, circular fairy dancing stabilizes the cycle of seasons, and Titania is warning Oberon that the whole clockwork is broken because he refuses to stay in the circle. But Oberon's interest is more in the processional march: he wants Titania to get in line and follow his lead (and watching Helena beg to follow Demetrius like a spaniel gets Oberon interested in influencing the procession of human genetic succession).

At the end of the play, Oberon finally accepts the invitation into the dance:

> *Come my queen, take hands with me,*
> *And rock the ground whereon these sleepers be.*
> *Now thou and I are new in amity,*
> *And will to-morrow midnight solemnly*
> *Dance in Duke Theseus' house triumphantly,*
> *And bless it to all fair prosperity.* (MND IV.i)

Oberon is finally willing to accept equality with Titania, and within the circle. This will restore prosperity to the natural world, and also bless human childbirth. It may be this compromise that gives them the power to bring their woodland fairy dance into the city, infiltrating the indoor realm of Theseus' castle. And Titania gets to call the tune:

> First rehearse your song by rote,
> To each word a warbling note.
> Hand in hand, with fairy grace,
> Will we sing, and bless this place. (MND V.i)

Merry Wives of Windsor deals with a later stage in life: the two women are in relatively happy marriages (only one has a child) and a trickster comes to shake things up. Falstaff rides into town and convinces himself he can seduce both women, and thereby swindle their husbands. He's not a shapeshifter, but through a series of pranks they transform him into a woman, a load of dirty laundry, and finally a horned forest king. For his final humiliation they lure him into a wood and make him the center of a circular fairy dance.

These "fairies" are village children in disguise, but somehow in the midst of this, the Fairy Queen and Puck show up to lead a song, and the defeated Falstaff says, *"I am made an ass."* (MWW V.v). And in this woodland confusion, a young lady manages to escape her parents' calculated matchmaking schemes and elope with her true love. Numerous elements of *Midsummer Night's Dream* are reprised here, so although the characters have different names, it makes sense enough to think of this as a continuation.

This dance contains a brief synthesis of the fairy-lore of *Midsummer Night's Dream*: the circular motion *"about, about,"* the entry into houses to assist with housework, the punishment of lazy housekeepers, and the use of flowers and glow-worms. We also see a couple other superstitions about fairies: Falstaff's fear that no mortal can look upon a fairy and live, and also that they might transform him into a piece of cheese:

> FAIRY QUEEN. Fairies, black, grey, green, and white,
> You moonshine revellers, and shades of night,
> You orphan heirs of fixed destiny,

Attend your office and your quality.
Crier Hobgoblin, make the fairy oyes.
PUCK. Elves, list your names; silence, you airy toys.
Cricket, to Windsor chimneys shalt thou leap;
Where fires thou find'st unrak'd, and hearths unswept,
There pinch the maids as blue as bilberry;
Our radiant Queen hates sluts and sluttery.
FALSTAFF. They are fairies; he that speaks to them shall die.
I'll wink and couch; no man their works must eye...
FAIRY QUEEN. About, about;
Search Windsor castle, elves, within and out;
Strew good luck, ouphes [oafs], on every sacred room,
That it may stand till the perpetual doom
In state as wholesome as in state 'tis fit,
Worthy the owner and the owner it...
And nightly, meadow-fairies, look you sing,
Like to the Garter's compass, in a ring;
Th' expressure that it bears, green let it be,
More fertile-fresh than all the field to see...
Fairies use flow'rs for their charactery.
Away, disperse; but till 'tis one o'clock,
Our dance of custom round about the oak
Of Herne the Hunter let us not forget.
EVANS. Pray you, lock hand in hand; yourselves in order set;
And twenty glow-worms shall our lanterns be,
To guide our measure round about the tree.
But, stay. I smell a man of middle earth.
FALSTAFF. Heavens defend me from that Welsh fairy, lest he
transform me to a piece of cheese!
PUCK. Vile worm, thou wast o'erlook'd even in thy birth. (MWW V.v)

The reference to Falstaff as a *"man of middle earth"* likely refers to a belief that the skies were for angels and the underground for fairies, with humanity in the middle. It's chronologically doubtful that Shakespeare was referring to *The Lord of the Rings*.

Changeling

Winter's Tale | Midsummer

In *The Winter's Tale*, an elderly shepherd finds an abandoned baby near the sea:

> *Mercy on's, a barne! ...A very pretty one – sure, some scape. Though I am not bookish, yet I can read waiting-gentlewoman in the scape. This has been some stair-work, some trunk-work, some behind-door-work; they were warmer that got this than the poor thing is here. I'll take it up for pity; yet I'll tarry till my son come.* (WT III.iii)

He immediately identifies this abandonment as an infanticide, and he's right—this newborn has been left to die because the father delusionally believes her to be illegitimate. However, when his dim-witted son approaches, the shepherd gives a different explanation for the baby and the small box by its side:

> *Look thee here; take up, take up, boy; open't. So, let's see – it was told me I should be rich by the fairies. This is some changeling. Open't... This is fairy gold, boy... We are lucky, boy; and to be so still requires nothing but secrecy.* (WT III.iii)

The child turns out to have been abandoned with gold, which is good news as long as the shepherd's son can keep his mouth shut about it. But more significant, the shepherd has altered the baby's back-story from a seamy sexual tryst to *"this is some changeling,"* meaning a child left by fairies.

In the literature of Shakespeare's time, no doubt owing to oral traditions going back much further, we encounter this concept of the "changeling" to explain a variety of phenomena. It seems to have been rural code for "I don't want to talk about it" in cases of birth defects, effects of parental neglect, and infant mortality, to say that night-time fairies had stolen a healthy baby and left a deformed or dead one in its place.[160] [161] It could also cover deliberate infanticide in cases of premarital, extramarital or non-consensual pregnancies.

To what extent anyone took the "changeling" belief literally is debatable. At best, it could encourage extra night-time vigilance in new mothers. And it could be used to defend the reputation of an ill-begotten baby, as we see in the 1628 pamphlet, *Robin Good-Fellow, His Mad Prankes and Merry Iests*: "Many old women, that then had more wit than those that are now living and have lesse, sayd that a fayry had gotten her with childe; and they bid her be of good comfort, for the childe must needes be fortunate that had so noble a father as a fayry was, and should worke many strange wonders. [sic]" Robin Goodfellow himself was said to have been conceived in a mortal maiden's rendezvous with the fairy king.

A Midsummer Night's Dream contains two "changelings." The fairy queen has adopted the child of a follower who died in childbirth: *"a lovely boy, stolen from an Indian king. / She never had so sweet a changeling,"* (MND II.i) with an implication she's had other changelings in the past. And in order to acquire this child for himself, the fairy king Oberon substitutes the ass-headed Bottom to distract Titania's foster-maternal affections. The Indian child is not shown or physically described in the play, nor do we get any hint about what manner of substitute may have been left for the Indian king.

When the conflict between Titania and Oberon has been resolved and he joins her dance, they enter into the Duke's house and he adds an interesting twist: fairylore often involves mischievous interference with human reproduction, but Oberon leads the fairies in a song promising unblemished offspring:

> *Now, until the break of day,*
> *Through this house each fairy stray.*
> *To the best bride-bed will we,*
> *Which by us shall blessed be;*
> *And the issue there create*
> *Ever shall be fortunate...*
> *And the blots of Nature's hand*
> *Shall not in their issue stand;*
> *Never mole, hare-lip, nor scar,*
> *Nor mark prodigious, such as are*
> *Despised in nativity,*
> *Shall upon their children be.* (MND V.i)

The intrusion of a "changeling" into his own relationship (and his own substitution of another changeling into Titania's maternal affections) seems to have convinced Oberon that healthy babies will cause greater marital stability.

In *Midsummer* the "changeling" is literal, and we accept it within the magical conventions of the play. *The Winter's Tale* is much later in Shakespeare's career, and "changeling" is clearly a metaphor—even the shepherd who speaks of the tradition clearly does not believe he's found an actual fairy baby. But he uses the fairy-lore in much the same way that a modern parent would talk about Santa Claus or the Tooth Fairy, to explain something mysterious to a child.

Bottom's Dream

MIDSUMMER | COMEDY OF ERRORS

In Shakespeare's time, mysterious or distasteful episodes could be explained or dismissed with the popular expressions "taken by the fairies" or "pixy-led" when someone returned from the woods. This covered a wide variety of phenomena including intoxication, illicit sex, or just missing a shift of work because of an afternoon nap. In an American folktale, Rip Van Winkle disappears for twenty years, offering no explanation but that he was enchanted by mysterious little men. Marshy areas contained methane gasses that could resemble lanterns (called Will-o-the-Wisp or Jack-o-Lanterns) that could mislead a traveler. Puck in *Midsummer* and Ariel in *The Tempest* both lead unsuspecting travelers on roundabout misadventures.

> PUCK. *I'll follow you; I'll lead you about a round,*
> *Through bog, through bush, through brake, through brier;*
> *Sometime a horse I'll be, sometime a hound,*
> *A hog, a headless bear, sometime a fire;*
> *And neigh, and bark, and grunt, and roar, and burn,*
> *Like horse, hound, hog, bear, fire, at every turn.* (MND III.i)

"Taken by the fairies" could also mean "I don't want to talk about it" to cover illicit sexual encounters, whether consensual or non-consensual.

Demetrius in *Midsummer* warns Helena that by wandering alone at night she makes herself vulnerable to *"mischief in the wood."* A rape victim who could not identify her attacker, or feared reprisal, could use this as a code for silence.[162] Or someone who'd had sex with someone of a different social rank, or an affair that could produce an illegitimate child could evade questioning with this excuse. Bottom the weaver, having disappeared into the woods, would have sounded more credible saying he'd spent the night with a fairy than reporting an affair with an upper-class married woman.

In one of Shakespeare's first plays, *Comedy of Errors*. Antipholus and his servant Dromio venture from Syracuse to Ephesus, unaware that they both have identical twins living there. Antipholus fears he's being pixy-led during an encounter with his twin brother's wife Luciana, who mistakes him for her husband:

> *ANTIPHOLUS OF SYRACUSE. To me she speaks; she moves me*
> *for her theme.*
> *What, was I married to her in my dream?*
> *Or sleep I now, and think I hear all this?*
> *What error drives our eyes and ears amiss?*
> *Until I know this sure uncertainty,*
> *I'll entertain the offer'd fallacy.*
> *DROMIO OF SYRACUSE. ...This is the fairy land. O spite of spites!*
> *We talk with goblins, owls, and sprites.*
> *If we obey them not, this will ensue:*
> *They'll suck our breath, or pinch us black and blue.*
> *...I am transformed, master, am not I?...*
> *LUCIANA. If thou art chang'd to aught, 'tis to an ass.* (COE II.ii)

Here it's just a quick joke, but later this becomes a rough outline of Shakespeare's most elaborate fairytale—Bottom the weaver in *Midsummer* being "taken" by the fairy jester Puck and queen Titania, and *literally* transformed to an ass. To flesh out the encounter, Shakespeare draws from the bawdy second century Roman novel *The Metamorphoses of Apuleius*, which the famous theologian Augustine of Hippo mockingly called "The Golden Ass." The story follows a man obsessed with magic, who tries to transform himself into a bird but accidentally becomes a donkey instead, then undergoes various misadventures before the goddess Isis restores his manhood. In one of the tales, Lucius the ass becomes a famous sideshow attraction, and a wealthy woman rents him for a sexual encounter. But then, realizing she's a killer, he runs away at the last minute. Some of her seduction speech makes its way almost word-for-word into *A Midsummer Night's Dream:* "Thou art he whom I love, thou art he whom I onely desire, without thee I cannot live."[163]

While the scenes of Titania and Bottom are certainly titillating (in a bestiality sort of way), it's doubtful they do the deed. Titania is married, and despite his male characters' obsession with being cuckolded, Shakespeare is very anxious about extramarital affairs. The key to this relationship is Titania's maternal affection for the changeling child, which started her marital conflict in the first place. Her all-consuming love for the Indian changeling is punished by the substitution of an ass-man changeling.

Titania's love for Bottom is maternal and infantilizing. She brings him to her bower, which is called a *"cradle,"* and orders her fairies to gather *"aprococks and dewberries, With purple grapes, green figs, and mulberries,"* items commonly used by mothers to treat childhood constipation (which seems to be the meaning when she says *"I will purge thy mortal grossness."*).[164]

Some commentators have noted that Titania's nurture of Bottom is like the Elizabethan servant-women who told fairy-tales in the nurseries of wealthy young noblemen: "What, after all, is the fairy Titania but a shadow of the servant surrogate mothers whom humanists love to censure, a creature marked in this play by her shameful desire to eroticize, infantilize, and dominate a male child?"[165] Certainly she is in charge of this semi-domestic sphere, and her servant fairies are named after common household items.

And like a young nobleman coming of age, Bottom must then leave the nursery for Theseus' court, transition from the old wives' tales to the mens' realm of classical literature. *"The most Lamentable Comedy and most Cruel Death of Pyramus and Thisby"* is a story from Ovid's *Metamorphoses,* a Roman medley of popular Greek myths. The production we see is ridiculous, but if it weren't for bungling production, it would essentially be *Romeo and Juliet.* As Bottom prepares for the transition, he marvels:

> *I have had a dream, past the wit of man to say what dream it was. Man is but an ass if he go about to expound this dream... The eye of man hath not heard, the ear of man hath not seen, man's hand is not able to taste, his tongue to conceive, nor his heart to report, what my*

dream was. I will get Peter Quince to write a ballad of this dream. It shall be call'd 'Bottom's Dream,' because it hath no bottom; and I will sing it in the latter end of a play, before the Duke. Peradventure, to make it the more gracious, I shall sing it at her death. (MND IV.i)

Bottom envisions a mash-up of nursery folklore and court literature, but Theseus prevents him from performing the epilogue. The joke is, of course, on Theseus, who *"never may believe / These antique fables, nor these fairy toys,"* and yet he, himself, is a Greek myth, whom Shakespeare has mixed into this cocktail of pop and high art.

Fairy Erotica
MERRY WIVES

Although Titania's feelings toward Bottom are mostly maternal (he is given to her as a "changeling" replacement for her adopted Indian child), there's definitely an undercurrent of eroticism to it. Stage and film adaptations will generally put in some unspoken joke that Bottom is anatomically "like a horse" in areas besides his head. And *Midsummer Night's Dream* has already established that Titania and Oberon have been involved with humans in the past. We can add to this that the belief in fairies switching babies with human beings is a transgression against rules of patriarchal legitimacy, "fairy tales" often involve peasants mixing genes with royalty, and "taken by the fairies" was sometimes used to cover illicit or unintended sexual encounters.

Robin Goodfellow in *Mad Prankes* has a touch of erotic sadism in him, to punish young women who are "sluttish" (domestically and/or sexually untidy):

> When house or harth doth sluttish lie,
> I pinch the maids there blacke and blew;
> And, from the bed, the bed-clothes I
> pull off, and lay them naked to view.

Shakespeare repeats this in *Merry Wives of Windsor*, when Puck shows up at a fairy pageant:

Where fires thou find'st unrak'd, and hearths unswept,
There pinch the maids as blue as bilberry;
Our radiant Queen hates sluts and sluttery. (MWW V.v)

Likewise, the man Falstaff is pinched as punishment for his adulterous fantasies while (children dressed as) fairies sing:

Fie on sinful fantasy!
Fie on lust and luxury!
Lust is but a bloody fire,
Kindled with unchaste desire,
Fed in heart, whose flames aspire,
As thoughts do blow them, higher and higher.
Pinch him, fairies, mutually;
Pinch him for his villainy;
Pinch him and burn him and turn him about,
Till candles and star-light and moonshine be out. (MWW V.v)

Just as the slut is punished, the chaste and diligent maiden is rewarded with dreams of happy eroticism:

Go you, and where you find a maid
That, ere she sleep, has thrice her prayers said,
Raise up the organs of her fantasy.
Sleep she as sound as careless infancy. (MWW V.v)

Mercutio in *Romeo and Juliet* takes this even farther when he speaks of Queen Mab:

And in this state she gallops night by night
Through lovers' brains, and then they dream of love...
O'er ladies' lips, who straight on kisses dream,
Which oft the angry Mab with blisters plagues,
Because their breaths with sweetmeats tainted are...
This is the hag, when maids lie on their backs,
That presses them, and learns them first to bear,
Making them women of good carriage. (R&J I.iv)

Women who have been seduced with sweetmeats wake up with cold sores and maidens who dream of marriage will awaken with their hips widened for pregnancy.

Shakespeare was part of a literary movement to domesticate and rehabilitate the fairy-lore, to clean up their lusty and promiscuous reputation. He, personally, had a great anxiety about loose sexuality and illegitimate children, so all of his fairies take a profound interest in *"Jack shall have Jill; / Nought shall go ill; / The man shall have his mare again, and all shall be well."* (MND III.ii) And his prudish fairies have had a profound influence on the continuing development of fairy-lore, to the point where entertainment corporations can mass-produce "fairy tales" that even the most puritanical parents deem appropriate for small children. The fairy is no longer explicit, no longer subversive, and no longer socially relevant. The printing press (and other forms of mass media) have circumscribed the freedom of the old wives' tale, and there went the improvisatory magic. Shakespeare may be the best fairy-writer ever, and what he wrote is great, but it's also a bit like encasing a butterfly in glass: fascinating to study, but unlikely to surprise.

Early in the 1600s, Richard Corbett wrote:

> FAREWELL, rewards and fairies,
> Good housewives now may say,
> For now foul sluts in dairies
> Do fare as well as they.
> And though they sweep their hearths no less
> Than maids were wont to do,
> Yet who of late for cleanness
> Finds sixpence in her shoe?
>
> ...
>
> Witness those rings and roundelay
> Of theirs, which yet remain,
> Were footed in Queen Mary's days
> On many a grassy plain;
> But since of late, Elizabeth,
> And later, James came in,
> They never danced on any heath
> As when the time hath been.[166]

Summer Festivals

Mayday | Beltane

Get up! Get up for shame! the blooming morn
Upon her wings presents the god unshorn.
See how Aurora throws her fair
Fresh-quilted colors through the air:
Get up, sweet slug-a-bed, and see
The dew bespangling herb and tree...
Rise, and put on your foliage, and be seen
To come forth, like the springtime, fresh and green,
And sweet as Flora. Take no care
For jewels for your gown or hair;
Fear not; the leaves will strew
Gems in abundance upon you...
Come, let us go while we are in our prime
And take the harmless folly of the time...
Our life is short, and our days run
As fast away as does the sun...
Then while time serves, and we are but decaying,
Come, my Corinna, come, let's go a-Maying.[167]

Beltane, more commonly known as Mayday, is a Northern European festival for which the United States has no clear parallel – while other Pagan seasonal traditions could be disguised as Christian holidays (like Samhain/Halloween, Yule/Christmas and Ostara/Easter), Mayday does not, and was thus effectively stamped out by new-world Puritans.

This was a festival of greenery, an acknowledgment of connection with the wild forest, symbolized by people decking themselves in flora, and bringing a tree to the most prominent place in the community (often the churchyard, since churches had been strategically built over central, elevated, sacred sites). It also involved games and activities of a more animal nature, ritual combat to establish a community's alpha-male, and various games and dances to encourage romantic friskiness. One survivor of this is the merritotter, a log balanced on top of a stump which a young man and maiden could straddle at either end and bounce up and down as a form of foreplay, which today can still be found on certain playgrounds, called a see-saw.

The festivities were largely geared toward equality, symbolized by circular dances and forest finery (wearing leaves and flowers instead of expensive clothes and jewels). But there was also some playful hierarchy. The loveliest maiden in the village would be crowned the May-queen or May-bride, and the community's best wrestlers and archers could compete for a favor, a ring or a kiss, with the further possibility of a trip into the woods to elope.

The dancing, teeter-tottering and playful mating were accompanied by ale and folk songs, like this one from 1600:

> Trip and go, heave and hoe,
> Up and downe, to and fro.
> From the towne, to the grove.
> Two and two, let us rove,
> A Maying, the playing;
> Love hath no gainsaying:
> So merrily trip and go. [sic][168]

The festivities would begin on May-eve, the last night of April (in the ancient world, days began and ended at sundown). In condemning the Rites of May, the stodgy Puritan Philip Stubbes accidentally provided our most detailed surviving eyewitness account. He had no intention of being an impartial anthropologist, but it's easy (and fun!) to disregard his personal opinions and catch a glimpse of this lively folk tradition. On the eve:

> ...all the young men and maids, old men and wives, ran gadding over night to the woods, groves, hills and mountains, where they spend all night in pleasant pastimes; and in the morning they return bringing with them birch and branches of trees, to deck their assemblies withall... The chiefest jewel they bring from thence is their May-pole, which they bring home with great veneration, as thus. They have twenty or forty yoke of oxen, every ox having a sweet nose-gay of flowers placed on the tip of his horns, and these oxen draw home this May-pole (this stinking idol, rather), which is covered all over with flowers and herbs, bound round about with strings, from the top to the bottom, and sometimes painted with variable colours, with two or three hundred men, women and children following it with great devotion. And thus being reared up, with handkerchiefs and flags hovering on the top, they strew the ground round about, bind green boughs about it...and then they fall they to dance about it like as the heathen people did at the dedication of the Idols.[169]

The procession of the Maypole is a fascinating mix of human, animal and plant energy: it seems the pole is meant to absorb this cocktail of fertility power.[170] Thus imbued with vitality, the tree is sunk part-way into a hole in the ground: a phallic symbol connecting earth and sky. One Maypole was so tall that it dwarfed the steeple of a nearby church, which became playfully known as St. Andrew Undershaft.

The Maypole is a symbol of fertility for women, crops and livestock. And the circular dance around it symbolizes the cyclic nature of life: birth, reproduction and death of the individual, and a ritualistic connection across temporal boundaries, linking the present generation of dancers with dancers from the past and future in a continuous circle. The Maypole dance involved many colored ribbons tied to the top, each dancer taking hold of one, and two rings of dancers circling in opposite directions, swerving around each other, and thus weaving a colorful braid around the pole. This not only decorated the tree but also consecrated it: wrapping the trunk in colorful ribbons symbolized imbuing the dead tree with supernatural life. But in case this all sounds solemn, we should not forget the noise and merriment: "their pypers pypyng, their drummers thundering, their stumps dauncing, their bells jyngling, their handkerchiefs fluttering about their heads like madmen." [sic][171]

The pole could be left standing up to a year and was considered to have a special aura. Being a phallic symbol, its magic was tied up in fertility, and a court testimony survives from the early 1600s alleging that a man and woman were caught committing improprieties against it: "on the said feast daie at night he had the carnall knowledge of her bodie agains the Sommer pole which made a bell hanging on top of the pole to ring out whereby he was alsoe discovered & by some seene." [sic][172] In *A Midsummer Night's Dream* Hermia insults her rival Helena as *"Thou painted maypole."* (MND III.ii) Isaac Asimov observes, "Not only does Hermia in this way refer to disparagingly to Helena as tall and skinny (and perhaps with as little figure as a maypole), but she also implies that the men, Lysander and Demetrius, are dancing about her with immoral intent."[173]

Mayday seems to have been Shakespeare's favorite holiday–the festival of fertility and coupling, loosening the bonds of parental control over marriage arrangements, and giving young people, particularly young women, some choice in who to love. This will be central in Shakespeare's most festive plays, like *Midsummer Night's Dream* and *As You Like It* (a title that refers both to the popularity of Mayday pastoral romance, *and* to Rosalind's choice of a husband). He'll also use symbolic elements of Mayday fertility-power as a cure for winter sterility in plays like *Macbeth* and *King Lear*.

Trial by Combat
As You Like It | King Lear | Macbeth | King John

One of the central events of Mayday was wrestling to determine who was the toughest lad in the village, who could win the title "Little John," and attract the attention of the local maidens. Shakespeare's *As You Like It* begins with a match in which the young underdog Orlando wrestles the local champion. The heroines Rosalind and Celia watch from the side uttering blessings of strength on the challenger and curses to sabotage the contender, and when Orlando succeeds in the overthrow, Rosalind gives him a symbolic love-token, a necklace. (AYL I.ii) Later, they woo and wed in the woods.

In *The Two Noble Kinsmen*, Arcite wins in a Mayday wrestling match, and as reward he becomes the personal bodyguard of Emilia, whom he has a crush on. But his cousin Palamon loves her too, and in the end her suitor must be determined by another round of ritual combat—not just two guys bashing at each other to prove who's strongest, but a form of divination to ascertain *"He whom the gods do of the two know best."* (TNK V.iii) When Arcite wins, Theseus tells Emilia, *"The gods by their divine arbitrament have given you this Knight; he is a good one."[174]* (TNK V.iii)

Similarly, the climactic duel in *King Lear*, between the half-brothers Edgar and Edmund, is not just a brawl but a trial-by-combat. The quickening pace of the play is stopped so a trumpet can be blown, a herald can read a proclamation, and the trumpet is blown three more times. The herald's speech publicly declares that Edmund is innocent of treason, and therefore a rightful heir to Gloucester, unless someone challenges by mortal combat. The true heir Edgar enters with a trumpeter, and both brothers give lengthy speeches before fighting (and all this while we in the audience worry about Lear and Cordelia in peril–she dies during this duel, but the ritual must commence uninterrupted to be effective). The fighters understand that the gods already know who is true and who is a traitor and will reveal this judgment by fixing the fight: it's not so much a brawl as a litigation. Verdant Edgar's defeat of sterile Edmund finally ends the stormy winter of the play, and fertility can recommence! Except that poor Cordelia is dead.

The final showdown between Macbeth and Macduff is likewise predetermined: the audience has heard the witches' prophecies and the sword fight only confirms what we already know. Meanwhile the approach of Birnam wood (soldiers dressed in foliage approaching the city) reminds us of the Mayday custom of villagers returning from the forest wearing weeds and flowers. Macbeth's reign which seems to have begun on Halloween and lasted through a dark Scottish winter, gives way to the coming of fair weather and greenery.

These can easily be distinguished from impulsive grudge-matches, like Romeo vs. Tybalt, and fencing-as-entertainment, like Hamlet vs. Laertes. Duels of honor, like Andrew vs. Viola-as-Cesario in *Twelfth Night*, have legalistic elements but don't seem like ritual. Although one witness murmurs this particularly silly match is *"matter for a May morning."* (TN III.iv)

In some of Shakespeare's royal plays, ritual combat is conducted with large-scale battles to determine whom the gods have chosen as rightful king or blessed with the divine right to tax some territory. Rather than meet in single combat, these parasitic monarchs will throw thousands of knights and conscripted farmers at each other (imagine—we in the audience weep for two dead teens at the end of *Romeo and Juliet*, but Henry V marches twelve thousand peasants against sixty thousand French peasants and we yawn through a pep-rally speech).

The second act of *King John* is a legalistic trial between the kings of England and France, to determine who has the right to tax the city of Angiers. Each king states his claim outside the city walls: *"I bring you witnesses, twice fifteen thousand hearts of English breed...to verify our title with their lives."* The citizens within declare that they won't pay taxes *"till you compound whose right is worthiest."* (KJ II.i) So the rival kings each send thirty thousand men to hack each other to pieces on a field.

Each king then dispatches a trumpeter and herald to announce his victory, but the citizens who've watched from the walls *"as in a theatre"* do not see a clear winner. King John takes the French king aside and yawns, *"France, hast thou yet more blood to cast away?"* The French king is just as bored of *"this hot trial."* The scene is lightened by sarcastic commentary from Faulconbridge the Bastard, who proposes the two kings join together, destroy the town, and *then* fight over who owns the rubble:

> *Be friends awhile, and both conjointly bend*
> *Your sharpest deeds of malice on this town...*
> *Even till unfenced desolation*
> *Leave them as naked as the vulgar air.*
> *That done, dissever your united strengths*
> *And part your mingled colours once again,*
> *Turn face to face and bloody point to point;*
> *Then in a moment Fortune shall cull forth*
> *Out of one side her happy minion,*
> *To whom in favour she shall give the day,*
> *And kiss him with a glorious victory.* (KJ II.i)

The Bastard alone understands that the resources at stake (taxes from the city, plunder of maidens, lives of soldiers) don't matter–this is just a gamble to see who Fortune likes better. By imagining lady fortune on standby to kiss the victor, he likens it to a Mayday wrestling match.

The rural May Games also featured large-scale ritual combat in team-sports like tug-of-war and Barley-Break, an ancestor of "Red Rover" where two opposing lines call so-and-so to run over and tackle through their locked arms. This game is dangerous for children, but now imagine burly milkmaids and ploughmen at full sprint getting clothes-lined by muscular shepherds and laundry wenches. This was a bone-breaking good time. Rival towns would also play an older version of soccer/football, where the field was the full length between one village and the next.

The Green Gown
MIDSUMMER NIGHT'S DREAM | AS YOU LIKE IT

Come, woo me, woo me; for now I am in a holiday humour,
and like enough to consent. (AYL IV.i)

The morning after the forest misadventures of *Midsummer Night's Dream*, Theseus discovers four grubby and perhaps partially dressed teenagers sleeping at the edge of a forest, and remarks *"No doubt they rose up early to observe the rite of May."* (MND IV.i) Early indeed if it was late June and they were preparing for Mayday! The duke knows that Hermia's father has ordered her to marry Demetrius or die, and now sees that she has escaped into the forest to elope with her true love Lysander, or at least sleep with him, frustrating her father's plan to market her as a virgin (Theseus doesn't know he's in a Shakespeare play where virginity is not lost till after curtain). Theseus has correctly guessed the intention: in the opening scene, Lysander had proposed that they run away:

If thou lovest me then,
Steal forth thy father's house to-morrow night;
And in the wood, a league without the town,

Where I did meet thee once with Helena
To do observance to a morn of May,
There will I stay for thee. (MND I.i)

This was a common May-eve tradition at a time when proper marriage was essentially a form of human trafficking: daughters were traded, bartered or outright sold like farmland or livestock, seldom to the young man they might have selected for themselves. So it should be no surprise if a lass ran off into the woods against her father's wishes, to mate with whom she pleased.

The folksong "Fetching Home of May" depicts a merry competition between village maidens to earn the "green gown"—a white dress grass-stained from sex in the field or forest:

> Pan leave Piping, the Gods have done feasting,
> There's never a Goddess a Hunting to Day:
> Mortals marvel at Coridon's Jesting,[175]
> That gives the assistance to entertain May.
> The Lads and the Lasses, with Scarfs on their Faces,
> So lively as passes, trip over the Downs:
> Much Mirth and Sport they make, running at Barley-break;
> Lord what haste they make for a Green-gown!
> ...
>
> Now the Youngsters had reach'd the green Meadow,
> Where they intended to gather their May,
> Some in the Sun-shine, some in the Shadow,
> Singled in couples did fall to their Play;
> But constant Penelope, Faith, Hope and Charity,
> Look'd very modestly, yet they lay down;
> And Prudence prevented what Rachel repented,
> And Kate was contented to take a Green-gown.
> ...
> There was no speaking, they answer'd with squeaking,
> The pretty Lass breaking the head of the Clown;
> But some were wooing, while others were doing,
> Yet all their going was for a Green-gown...

Thus they did gather May, all the long Summer-day,
And at night went away with a Green-gown.[176]

This song is likely related to the folk song "Greensleeves"—another possible reference to grass stains from rolling in the woods. In *Merry Wives* when Falstaff eagerly expects illicit sex in the forest at night, he says *"Let the sky rain potatoes! Let it thunder to the tune of 'Greensleeves'!"* (MWW V.v)

The crusty Puritan Philip Stubbes again, disgusted with May-eve revels: "I have heard it credibly reported by men of great gravity and reputation, that of forty, threescore, or a hundred maids going to the woods overnight, there have scarcely the third part of them returned undefiled. These be the fruits which these cursed pastimes bring forth."[177] I once lived in a small Christian farm town in Western New York where, the night before the homecoming football game, youngsters danced around a bonfire, and our county topped national lists for teen pregnancy. So it's not hard to imagine the kind of revelries that would cause a satirist in the 1600s to dryly remark, "the maids after their downe-falls, being astonied, shall rise sooner than they would"[178] ("rise" in the sense of "a bun in the oven").

Robert Graves writes that illicit couplings in the forest, playfully called Mad-Merry Marriages or Greenwood Marriages, "blessed by a renegade friar styled Friar Tuck, were afterwards formally confirmed in the church-porch," *not* inside the church. "But very often 'merrybegots' were repudiated by their fathers. It is probably because each year, by old custom, the tallest and toughest village lad was chosen to be Little John (or 'Jenkin') Robin's deputy in the Merry men masque, that Johnson, Jackson and Jenkinson are now among the commonest English names—Little John's merrybegots. But Robin did as merrily with Robson, Hobson, Dobson (all short for Robin), Robinson, Hodson, Hudson, and Hood; [surnames] Greenwood and Merriman were of doubtful paternity."[179]

Shakespeare's wild Mayday forest romp *As You Like It* contains three variations on the Greenwood Marriage theme.[180] The clown Touchstone encounters a comely lass in the forest and, to succeed in a quick seduction, proposes a hasty wedding with *"no temple but the wood, no assembly but horn-beasts."* He enlists an assistant vicar called Martext (faulty-words) to bungle the ceremony, and when a melancholy by-passer objects that the wedding should take place inside a church with a priest, Touchstone explains, *"I were better to be married of him than of another; for he is not like to marry me well; and not being well married, it will be a good excuse for me hereafter to leave my wife."* (AYL III.iii) Later in the play, Shakespeare arranges a gender-bending wedding where Rosalind-pretending-to-be-a-man-pretending-to-be-Rosalind exchanges vows with Orlando, with her cousin Celia playing a male priest (and the further complexity that Rosalind and Celia were both originally played by boys). (AYL IV.i) Both of these marriages (and two others) are further formalized in the climactic finale, when the wedding-god Hymen materializes to bless four weddings in the name of the marriage-goddess Juno.[181] (AYL V.iv)

Robin Hud

Two Gentlemen | As You Like It

> Let us talk of Robin Hoode
> And Little John in merry Shirwood,
> Of poet Skelton with his pen,
> And many other merry men,
> Of May-game Lords, and summer Queenes
> With Milke-maides, dancing o'er the Greenes...
> Of May-poles and merriments
> That have no spot of ill pretence.
> But I wonder now and then,
> To see the wise and learned men,
> With countenance grim, and many a frowne
> Cries, Maisters, plucke the May-pole downe
> To heare this news, the Milke-maid cries
> To see the sight, the plough-man dies. [sic][182]

Medieval English royalty preserved certain stretches of forest between cities and villages for royal sport-hunts, and even during seasons of extreme privation it was illegal for peasants to hunt there. Then during the Protestant Reformation, hybrid Pagan-Catholic rituals were increasingly hounded by Puritans, and the forests at night were natural hiding places to conduct them.

These become familiar elements in legends of Robin Hood and his merry men, poaching the king's deer and hiding out in Sherwood. To these were added elements of the May Games, like an archery contest with Will Scarlet, ritual wrestling with Little John, and a kiss from the May-bride Marian.[183]

Robin Hood, AKA Robin *Hud* (*Hud* being a sacred oak), AKA Hobgoblin, AKA Robin Goodfellow, originated as a satyr with horns and goat-legs - Disney's fox Robin Hood preserves this animal-man tradition. Christianity would eventually separate these personae, adopting Robin Goodfellow as the iconic image of the Devil, and turning Robin Hood into an exiled nobleman, further bolstering his Christian credentials by making him a veteran of the Crusades. William Shakespeare inherited these two separate cultural icons and used both in different ways.

The shapeshifting trickster in *Midsummer Night's Dream* is *"call'd Robin Goodfellow. [Some] Hobgoblin call you, and sweet Puck."* (MND II.i) Puck assumes numerous animal forms including a horse, hound, hog and headless bear, and he transforms the weaver into a hybrid ass-man. Puck can also become a wooden stool, a roasted crab-apple and a fire (a will-o-the-wisp, a combustible burst of swamp-gas).

Shakespeare handles Robin Hood the banished nobleman separately. In *As You Like It*, a French Duke is exiled into the forest and establishes a woodland communalism:

> *he is already in the Forest of Arden, and a many merry men with him; and there they live like the old Robin Hood of England. They say many young gentlemen flock to him every day, and fleet the time carelessly, as they did in the golden world."* (AYL I.i)

In *Two Gentlemen of Verona*, the exiled Valentine falls in among bandits. They try to rob him, but when he tells them he's killed a man, they adopt him: *"By the bare scalp of Robin Hood's fat friar, this fellow were a king for our wild faction!"* He agrees to lead these merry outlaws *"Provided that you do no outrages on silly women or poor passengers."* (TGV IV.i) Robin Hood the banished nobleman represents chivalry in contrast to the predatory nobles at the urban court.

While planning a mischievous swindle in *Merry Wives of Windsor*, the wandering knight Falstaff refers to his two accomplices as *"Scarlet and John,"* (MWW I.i) and has another servant called *"little Robin,"* but "after 181 lines of the first scene...Shakespeare wearies of trying to make it a play about Falstaff and his latter-day merry men, and drops the whole thing."[184] However, Shakespeare later picks up the other side of the Robin Hood legend: at the play's end, Falstaff is a horned man by a forest oak with the village youth dancing circles around him, like an image of Robin Goodfellow.

Robin's "Merry Men" were familiar characters of the May games: Will Scarlet the bowman, the local wrestling champion "Little John," a mock friar called Tuck, and Maid Marian—not a damsel-in-distress, but an English version of the Greek huntress goddess Artemis/Diana. In a folk-song, she is "Marian...sovereign of the woods, chief lady of the game her clothes tucked to the knee, and dainty braided hair, with bow and quiver armed, she wandered here and there amongst the forest wild; Diana never knew such pleasure, nor such [deer] as Mariana slew."[185]

The mock Friar, apparently named after the "tuck" of a Franciscan robe, is a symbol of authority, but also an outlaw; many monasteries were closed down during the Reformation. Among Christian saints, Francis is particularly associated with flora and fauna, even in modern times he is generally depicted with small animals, and statues of him are believed to bring blessings on gardens (never mind that *two* of the Biblical Ten Commandments explicitly forbid using a graven image to encourage crop fertility. And this applies equally to garden idols of fertility goddesses thinly disguised as the Virgin Mary).

Gradually in the 1500s these characters were combined. The Beltane huntress and May-bride Morris-dancer Marian became a single figure, bringing with her the Morris hobby horse and fool. Local village May-game champions Will Scarlet and Little John became friends of the mischievous forest-spirit Robin Goodfellow. And the Friar was added to jokingly legitimize unmarried couples having sex in the forest. Turning these to a merry bandit-gang playfully acknowledged the forbidden nature of it, and explicitly Pagan fertility elements were smoothed out to present it as harmless entertainment, to the point where the witch-hating King James himself defended the peoples' right to continue the Morris Dance.

The Morris Dance
Two Noble Kinsmen

A pamphleteer in 1614 wrote:

> It was my hap of late, by chance,
> To meet a Country Morris-dance,
> When, cheefest of them all, the Foole
> Plaied with a ladle and a toole;
> When every younger shak't his bells
> Till sweating feet gave fohing smells;
> And fine Maide Marian, with her smoile,
> Shewed how a rascall plaied the voile;
> But, when the Hobby-horse did wihy,
> Then all the wenches gave a tihy;
> But when they gan to shake their boxe,
> And not a goose could catch a foxe,
> The piper then put up his pipes,
> And all the woodcocks look't like snipes. [sic]186

The Morris was a springtime fertility dance associated with Mayday and Whitsun. Shakespeare refers to both, a *"Whitsun morris-dance"* (H5 II.iii) and *"a morris for Mayday."* (AWTEW II.ii) In Elizabethan England the Morris Dance needed no introduction or instruction – it was the popular dance that concluded many theatrical productions. As hard as it might be to imagine, original productions of tragedies like *King Lear* could very well have concluded with the dead king and fool and the rest of the cast hopping onto the stage and circle-dancing to a jaunty tune. King James himself was known to sit through a tragic performance and then shout, "Why don't they dance? What did you make me come here for? Devil take you all, dance!"187 We have a good illustration of this in *Midsummer Night's Dream*, the workmen's production of the tragic Pyramus and Thisbe concludes with the dead lovers rising for a lively rustic dance, likely accompanied by the lion and other cast members.188 Structurally, *Midsummer Night's Dream* contains many elements of the Morris, re-imagined to fit the particular story – a sort of Morris remix.

The most comprehensive and systematic staging of the Morris Dance is in *The Two Noble Kinsmen*, co-written by Shakespeare and John Fletcher. The scenes of rehearsal and performance are generally agreed to be Fletcher's writing, and this play is not included in anthologies of "Complete" Shakespeare, so lengthy excerpts of the two scenes follow, abbreviated to focus on the logistics of the dance:

> THIRD COUNTRYMAN. Do we all hold against the Maying?
> ...Arcas will be there.
> SECOND COUNTRYMAN. And Sennois and Rycas; and three better lads ne'er danced under green tree. And you know what wenches, ha! But will the dainty domine, the Schoolmaster, keep touch, do you think? For he does all, you know...
> FOURTH COUNTRYMAN. Shall we be lusty?
> SECOND COUNTRYMAN. ...I'll be and there I'll be, for our town, and here again, and there again. Ha, boys, hey for the weavers!
> FIRST COUNTRYMAN. This must be done i' th' woods...
> THIRD COUNTRYMAN. We'll see the sports, then every man to 's tackle [props/costume]. And, sweet companions, let's rehearse, by any means, before the ladies see us, and do sweetly, and God knows what may come on 't.
> ARCITE. ...Are there such games today? ...What pastimes are they?
> SECOND COUNTRYMAN. Wrestling and running.
> (TNK II.iii Fletcher)

Like the mechanics in *A Midsummer Night's Dream*, these workers intend to perform for Duke Theseus and hope to be *"made"*—become professional performers. To do this dance right, they'll need the local schoolmaster as emcee, a *"bavian"* (man dressed as a baboon), and a number of *"wenches"* corresponding the number of men. Indeed, the whole structure of the dance will be threatened if they can't convince enough women to join them. *"For our town"* and *"for the weavers"* are both references to the competitive nature of this dance, like a talent show or cheerleading tournament, towns or guilds could compete against each other with some nobleman as the judge. After this first meeting to discuss logistics, the dancers leave to watch Mayday footraces and wrestling matches. When they reconvene in the forest, the schoolmaster directs a quick rehearsal before the Duke Theseus arrives.

(Enter a Schoolmaster and six Countrymen, one dressed as a Bavian [baboon])

SCHOOLMASTER. ...Here stand I; here the Duke comes; there are you, close in the thicket; the Duke appears; I meet him and unto him I utter learnèd things and many figures; he hears, and nods, and hums, and then cries 'Rare!' and I go forward. At length I fling my cap up - mark there! Then [you] break comely out before him; like true lovers, cast yourselves in a body decently, and sweetly, by a figure, trace and turn, boys...

SECOND COUNTRYMAN. Draw up the company. Where's the taborer?

TABORER. ...Here, my mad boys. Have at you!

SCHOOLMASTER. But I say, where's their women?

(Enter five Wenches.)

SCHOOLMASTER. ...Where be your ribbons, maids? Swim with your bodies, and carry it sweetly and deliverly, and now and then a favor and a frisk.

NELL. Let us alone, sir.

SCHOOLMASTER. Where's the rest o' th' music?

THIRD COUNTRYMAN. Dispersed, as you commanded.

SCHOOLMASTER. Couple, then, and see what's wanting. Where's the Bavian? My friend, carry your tail without offense or scandal to the ladies; and be sure you tumble with audacity and manhood, and when you bark, do it with judgment. ...Here is a woman wanting [missing]... Our business is become a nullity, yea, and a woeful and a piteous nullity.

(Enter Jailer's Daughter.)

THIRD COUNTRYMAN. ...There's a dainty madwoman, master, comes i' th' nick, as mad as a March hare. If we can get her dance, we are made again. I warrant her, she'll do the rarest gambols.

(TNK III.v Fletcher)

In Shakespeare's time, many of the female roles in these dances were performed by men in drag, as we see in Christopher Fetherston's 1582 *Dialogue agaynst light, lewde, and lasciuious dauncing*:

men in womans apparell, whom you doe most commonely call maymarrions... I my selfe haue seene in a may gaime a troupe, the greater part wherof hath been men, and yet haue they been attyred so like vnto women, that theyr faces being hidde (as they were in deede) a man coulde not discerne them from women. [sic][189]

However, in this scene from *Two Noble Kinsmen*, female dancers are crucial, and having too few of them dooms the whole enterprise. Fortunately, a Jailer's insane daughter happens to be wandering in the forest, and they draft her into their pageant. The female role is a ribbon dance, which in this case does not seem to involve weaving ribbons around a Maypole (the troupe will request a Maypole as payment), so perhaps here we should imagine women dancing in a circle with ribbons flowing behind them, symbolizing the flow of air and water.

There's a sharp exchange where the schoolmaster instructs the women about *"a favor and a frisk,"* which could mean dance moves or a kiss and a grope. Nell's response, *"Let us alone, sir,"* might be reminding him she knows the dance, or responding to an unwanted pinch. This exchange contains a further complexity in that women were banned from professional theatre (the role of "Nell" was played by a boy) but could still be essential in local musical pageants, what we today call "community theater."

In a pamphlet from 1600, *Kemps Nine Daies Vvonder*, William Kemp reported about a Morris Dance in which one of the men involved couldn't keep up, and "a lusty Country lasse" insisted on taking his place, saying:

> 'If I had begun to daunce, I would have held out one myle though it had cost my life...if the Dauncer will lend me a leash of his belles.' ...I lookt upon her, saw mirth in her eies, heard boldnes in her words, and beheld her ready to tucke up her russet petticoate, I fitted her with bels: which she merrily taking, garisht her thicke short legs, and with a smooth brow bad the Tabrer begin. The Drum strucke, forward marcht I with my merry Mayde-marian: who shooke her fat sides: and footed it merrily to Melfoord, being a long myle. There parting with her, I gave her (besides her skin full of drinke) an English crowne to buy more drinke, for good wench she was in a pittious heate: my kindnes she requited with dropping some dozen of short courtsies... She had a good care, daunst truely, and wee parted friendly. [sic][190]

Instruments involved included the "tabor," a hand-drum, leashes of sleigh-bells strapped around dancers' ankles, the "minikin," or lute, what we today would call an acoustic guitar, and a flute called the "fife." The phallic flute represented maleness and the guitar represented femaleness (the phrase "tickle the minikin" could mean either to strum the guitar or frisk a lass), blending together. And the lyric would be a bawdy innuendo: one surviving specimen is "Skip it, & trip it, nimbly, nimbly, tickle it, tickle it, lustily, / Strike vp the Taber, for the wenches fauor, tickle it, tickle it, lustily." [sic][191] Apparently this was intended to tread a fine line on the bounds of taste without crossing into lewdness, but if I heard my kids singing this at home I'd tell them not to sing it at school.

The schoolmaster's instruction that the *"Bavian"* (baboon) take care not to scandalize the ladies sounds a good deal like Peter Quince in *Midsummer Night's Dream* directing Snug not to frighten the women with his lion performance. But while the schoolmaster tells the baboon to carry his tail inoffensively, he later describes the baboon as having *"long tail and eke long tool,"* which could refer to nothing but its dangling wang. In both plays, the players worry about shocking the Amazon warrior-queen Hippolyta, who *"hast slain the scythe-tusked boar"* and can *"make the male to thy sex captive."* (TNK I.i) Needless to say, she doesn't seem bothered at all.

> (Enter Theseus, Pirithous, Hippolyta, Emilia, and train.)
> SCHOOLMASTER. …If you but favor, our country pastime
> made is. We are a few of those collected here
> that ruder tongues distinguish 'villager.' And to say verity, and
> not to fable, we are a merry rout, or else a rabble, or company, or
> by a figure, chorus, that 'fore thy dignity will dance a morris. And
> I that am the rectifier of all, … do here present this machine, or
> this frame… upon this mighty 'Morr,' of mickle [heavy] weight
> 'is' now comes in, which being glued together makes 'Morris,'
> and the cause that we came hither. The body of our sport, of no
> small study, I first appear, though rude, and raw, and muddy, to
> speak before thy noble grace this tenner, at whose great feet I
> offer up my penner. The next, the Lord of May and Lady bright,
> the Chambermaid and Servingman by night that seek out silent
> hanging; then mine Host and his fat Spouse, that welcomes to
> their cost the gallèd traveler, and with a beck'ning informs the

tapster to inflame the reck'ning; then the beest-eating Clown;
and next the Fool, the Bavian with long tail and eke long tool,
cum multis aliis [Latin: with a number of others] that make a
dance; say 'ay,' and all shall presently advance...
(Music. Enter the Countrymen, Countrywomen, and Jailer's
Daughter; they perform a morris dance.)
SCHOOLMASTER. Ladies, if we have been merry and
have pleased ye with a derry, and a derry and a down, say the
Schoolmaster's no clown. Duke, if we have pleased thee too and
have done as good boys should do, give us but a tree or twain for
a Maypole, and again, ere another year run out, we'll make thee
laugh, and all this rout.
THESEUS. Take twenty... Now to our sports [hunting] again.
SCHOOLMASTER. May the stag thou hunt'st stand long, and
thy dogs be swift and strong; may they kill him without lets, and
the ladies eat his dowsets.... Come, we are all made. *Dii deaeque
omnes* [Latin: all we hoped], You have danced rarely, wenches.
(TNK III.v Fletcher)

The schoolmaster playfully explains that the dance derives its name
from a *"Morr"* or Moor, a piece of uncultivated wilderness, like the Heath
from which we get the word "Heathen." Given the pastoral and pagan
elements of the dance (sharing characteristics with a Wiccan Sabbat), I
find this the most convincing derivation, but in Shakespeare's time the
word "Moor" also referred to Muslims, and some scholars propose that this
was a "Moorish" Dance inspired by the Spanish *Morisca*.[192]

The characters of the dance are introduced in a procession here, in
order of rank: Lord and Lady, their personal servants, the innkeeper and his
wife, the traveler and bartender, the clown and the baboon. This sequence
also leads from interior/civilization (the manor) to exterior/wilderness (the
wild animal), from culture to nature, a devolution to primeval chaos.[193]
The linear and hierarchical parade then becomes a circular and egalitarian
dance, the distinctions between nobleman and beast get blurry.

This scene contains no instructions for the dance itself – it was
understood that performers would already know what to do. "Plays and
pamphlets describe early modern morris dancing using the same set of
descriptive words: 'lustily', 'lively', 'merrily', 'jerk', 'trip', and 'tickle'. These
words connote immense pleasure, vitality, impatient desire and light steps

combined with sharp, abrupt leaping."[194] The circular dance and ejaculatory jumping could be related to the song "Round and round the mulberry bush the monkey chased the weasel. The monkey thought it was all in fun. Pop goes the weasel!" The mulberry bush represents the Maypole. The dance could also be related to other circle games/dances like duck-duck-goose or musical chairs.

Missing from the *Two Noble Kinsmen* Morris Dance is the hobby horse ("hobby" in the sense of Hob or *Hud*, a piece of sacred oak wood), a puppet horse worn around a man's midsection, held up by suspenders. The Jailer's Daughter does make a single fleeting reference to "He'll dance the morris twenty mile an hour, and that will founder the best hobbyhorse [that] gallops to the tune of 'Light o' love.'" (TNK V.ii Fletcher) The hobby horse was going out of style in Shakespeare's time - two of his plays contain references to a popular folksong, *"the hobby-horse is forgot."* (LLL III.i, HAM III.ii) The movement of the hobby horse in the Morris Dance might explain the jerky movement of the horse-shaped knight on a chess board. The old board game Nine Men's Morris also preserves a remnant of the dance, and was apparently once played by humans on a giant game-board carved into a field (*Midsummer Night's Dream* contains a reference to this: *"The nine men's morris is fill'd up with mud."* MND II.i).

The magic of the Morris Dance, the central theme tying all of this together, is the blurring of boundaries. The dance begins with men lined up to enter from one side and women from the other, partnering and mixing in a circle. Replacing some or all of the women with men in drag further confuses gender in the dance. Class distinctions between the elite lords, the middling innkeepers and merchants, country clowns ("clown" deriving from the Latin *colonus*, bumpkin) and animals dissolve in a colorful swirl. So does the divide between the urban, rural and forest realms: we see the dance taking place in in-between spaces, a forest or highway, or even a churchyard/graveyard, the boundary between the living and the dead. And the competitive village or guild dance-off, agonistic groups doing the same dance, blurs the boundaries between rival communities.

The theory that this dance derives from a meeting between Spanish Christians and Muslims also introduces a blurring of boundaries between religions and ethnicities. In some reports, half the dancers paint their faces, a clumsy symbol of bridging racial divides. Dancers dressed as baboons and centaur-like hobby horses, and the fool with a coxcomb (rooster hat) straddle the line between the human and the rest of the animal community.

Some recollections of the dance furthermore have participants wearing weeds and flowers: hybrid human-plants.

The content of the dance seems intended to skate a thin line between religious reverence and obscenity, faith and eroticism, sacred and profane. I doubt that many of us today would think of the Morris Dance as a "religious" ritual because we're so accustomed to "religion" being indoors, rectangular, monotonous and solemn. But the dreary solemnity of modern Christian ritual is largely a product of Puritan influence during the Protestant Reformation, a *reaction against* the sort of colorful pagan pageantry that had been blended into European Catholicism (there were numerous English Puritan attempts to ban the Morris Dance in the early 1600s, and the Pilgrims succeeded in stifling its transmission to North America).

Certainly, there's plenty for Puritans to disparage in the drunken merriment and boundary-blurring of the dance—and a licentiousness that could extend beyond the dance itself into unsanctioned sexuality. Indeed, it may have been hard to see a clear boundary between dancing and foreplay. Puritans protested that "Euery leap or skip in dance, is a leap toward hel," [sic][195] and "when as dauncinge was vsed, then men & women came abrode, and now they creep into corners, either to filtch or els to play the naughtipackes." [sic][196] What "filtch" and "naughtipackes" may have meant is anybody's guess. But the popular surnames Morris and Morrison may have originally meant "son of some random dude I met at the Morris Dance."[197] Jim Morrison might have gotten a kick out of that.

Come Now a Roundel

MIDSUMMER NIGHT'S DREAM

Although the Morris Dance is not explicitly mentioned in *A Midsummer Night's Dream*, numerous elements of it are present. *"Enter the King of Fairies, at one doore, with his traine; and the Queene, at another with hers."* (MND II.i, stage direction) We can see Oberon and Titania as King and Queen of the forest, Puck as the fool, Bottom as the hobbyhorse, and two pairs of teenaged lovers (three pairs if we count Theseus and Hippolyta).

If we were watching the play in pantomime or in another language (and for many of us today, "Shakespearean English" *is* a foreign language), it could easily be understood as a ritualistic fertility dance. Enid Welsford describes the elaborate choreography: "The plot is a pattern, a figure, rather than a series of human events occasioned by character and passion, and this pattern, especially in the moonlight parts of the play, is the pattern of a dance. The appearance and disappearance and reappearance of the various lovers, the will-o'-the-wisp movement of the elusive Puck, form a kind of figured ballet. The lovers quarrel in a dance pattern: first, there are two men to one woman and the other woman alone, then a brief space of circular movement, each one pursuing and pursued, then a return to the first figure with the position of the woman reversed, then a cross movement, man quarreling with man and woman with woman, and then, as finale, a general setting to partners, including not only the lovers but fairies and royal personages as well."[198] The story ends with couples running off to make babies, blessed by the reconciled king and queen of fairies.

Like a Morris Dance, the play is about crossing boundaries. From the restrictive city to the liberated forest (we're told the teenagers will walk *"seven leagues,"* but they get lost and accidentally cross from urban Athens to a wood in England!). Helena and Hermia, having grown up *"like to a double cherry"* in an enclosed relationship, must deal with the entry of inconstant men who want to enter both their emotional and physical boundaries.

Bottom the weaver becomes an ass, bobbing through the boundaries of Titania and Oberon's relationship, and his entry into Titania's bower represents multiple levels of interspecies intimacy: fairy/human/animal, as well as social boundaries of queen/peasant/livestock (Oberon meant to match her with a wild predator, a lynx or *"cat, or bear,* [leo]*pard, or boar,"* but the playful Puck chose a more tame creature, the ass-man[199]). Puck, AKA Robin Goodfellow, is a shape-shifter who can transform to plants, fruits, or animals, and Titania's fairies are Peaseblossom (flower), Cobweb (excrement), Moth (insect) and Mustardseed.

In the artisans' production of "Pyramus and Thisbe," two men play women, one plays a lion, one plays the moon, and the central actor, Bottom, wishes to play a man, a woman *and* a lion simultaneously. In performance he crosses the boundary between life and death, perishing as Pyramus, then leaping up to offer a dance. At the end of their performance, they break the "fourth wall" boundary between performers and audience: the lowly artisans on the stage argue with the noblemen Theseus, and he still rewards them, transforming them into professional actors.

Midsummer Night's Dream also plays loose with temporal boundaries, as J.M. Nosworthy observes. "Critics have complained that the four-day action promised at the start is, in fact, accomplished in two, while others have carped about the rites of May being observed on June 24, and Shakespeare has, as usual, been convicted of carelessness... Two days or four, it matters little since this is, by any reckoning, all too short a date for the preparation of a play by a bunch of rude mechanicals [and] that play, said to be 'some ten words long,' actually lasts about twenty minutes yet fills up the three hours from suppertime to midnight."[200]

The whole fabric of space, time, species and love—everything gets jumbled in this story, and yet we in the audience know that everything will be sorted out in the end. Everything gets rearranged in the primal chaos of the forest, then returns to the ordered city. The chaotic partner-swapping swirl finally becomes a neat wedding march. But Shakespeare then surprises us with one more crossing, when the forest fairies enter Theseus' Athenian manor to bless the beds and sweep the dust.

Whitsun
WINTER'S TALE | ROMEO AND JULIET

Whitsuntide is an old English name for the Christian Holiday Pentecost, celebrated fifty days after Easter, sometime in late May or early June. The good weather made this a popular day for baptism in rivers and lakes, and white baptismal garments led to calling the day "White Sunday," or in peasant slang, "Whitsun." The good weather also lent itself to outdoor games, "like the Olympic games of the ancients... manly sports, such as wrestling, leaping, pitching the bar, handling the pike, dancing, and hunting."[201]

There were various dances and community theater pieces associated with Whitsun. During the sheep-shearing festival in *Winter's Tale*, twelve herders have prepared a touring dance of satyrs:

Master, there is three carters, three shepherds, three neat–herds, three
swineherds, that have made themselves all men of hair; they call
themselves Saltiers, and they have dance which the wenches say is a
gallimaufry of gambols, because they are not in't; but they themselves
are o' th' mind, if it be not too rough for some that know little but
bowling, it will please plentifully. (WT IV.iv)

The satyr is a mythological hybrid goat-man, and this dance symbolizes an integration of the human and animal realms.

The day could also feature Morris Dances[202] and folk pageants: pastoral folk-plays celebrating fertility, and masques/masquerades celebrating ancient heroes and heroines. These were not necessarily Christian in nature, but often involved a mix of Biblical and Classical Greek/Roman personages. The "Masque of Nine Worthies" in *Love's Labour's Lost* included Judas Maccabaeus, Pompey the Great, Hercules, Alexander the Great and Hector of Troy. The pageant is interrupted and we never find out whom the other worthies were, although hecklers refer to Saint George and Julius Caesar, who would make sense in this context.[203] We may further note here an appropriation of Biblical and classical history: the "Masque of Nine Worthies" essentially adopts Israelite and Greco-Roman heroes as honorary Englishmen or proto-Englishmen.

Whitsun pageants could also include tragic historical heroines, sometimes played by women or boys. In *Two Gentlemen of Verona*, a woman named Julia is disguised as a boy named Sebastian who... This is difficult to explain. "Sebastian" claims to have once worn Julia's clothing:

at Pentecost,
When all our pageants of delight were play'd,
Our youth got me to play the woman's part...
And at that time I made her weep a good,
For I did play a lamentable part.
Madam, 'twas Ariadne passioning
For Theseus' perjury and unjust flight. (TGV IV.iv.157-172)

Ariadne was the Cretan princess who helped Theseus escape the Minotaur's maze, and in thanks he gave her passage from the island, but then raped and abandoned her and she committed suicide.[204]

A pastoral pageant in *Winter's Tale* features a shepherdess playing the fertility goddess Flora, merged with the Greek goddess Persephone.[205] Prince Florizel comments on Perdita's costume:

> FLORIZEL. *These your unusual weeds to each part of you*
> *Do give a life - no shepherdess, but Flora*
> *Peering in April's front...*
> PERDITA. *...Poor lowly maid,*
> *Most goddess-like prank'd up. But that our feasts*
> *In every mess have folly, and the feeders*
> *Digest it with a custom.* (WT IV.iv.1-14)

Perdita feeling silly in her party dress (*"Prank'd up"* may refer to the tradition of a goddess played by a jovial drag-queen) is one of many references to costumes and cheeky role-play in the *Winter's Tale*. In the pastoral Bohemian scenes, prince Florizel dresses as a country boy, the king and his advisor dress down to spy on the prince, and find him courting a lowly shepherdess dressed as a goddess (they disapprove of this match, but it's later revealed she's a true princess after all).[206] The merry conman Autolycus, named after a shapeshifting trickster from Greek mythology, appears in rags as a robbery victim, then trades clothes with a nobleman, appears later as a mountebank peddling trinkets, broadside ballads (the tabloids of the time), and dildos.[207] Then he appears as himself again, and gets recommended for a job at the royal court. Believe it or not, if you can choke down the dull, cold opening half of *The Winter's Tale* it becomes a lush and cheery pastoral in the second half.

Whitsun was a popular time to throw a masquerade ball, giving young people a chance to mingle anonymously. Leading Romeo to a masque, his friend refers to this as *"Cupid hoodwink'd with a scarf."* (R&J I.iv) The party reminds Juliet's father of a Whitsun wedding when he was younger: *"Tis since the nuptial of Lucentio, / Come Pentecost as quickly as it will, / Some five and twenty years; and then we mask'd."* (R&J I.v) But the action of that play takes place in July, with Lammas approaching. A masquerade could also be a chance to pursue a crush without fear of crushing rejection—in *Much Ado About Nothing*, Claudio sends a masked friend to find out of Hero likes him, and in *Henry VIII* the masked king makes adulterous advances on Anne Bullen.

Sometime around Whitsun the shepherds would shear their sheep and sell the wool, and this big annual payday would be celebrated with further outdoor festivities. Whoever owned the sheep who had given birth earliest in the year would be shepherd king for the day, and his wife or daughter would be mistress of the sheep-shearing feast. Not only was this considered a great honor, but generosity toward neighbors and visiting strangers was believed to influence future flock prosperity.

In *Winter's Tale*, a widower shepherd tells his adopted daughter about his late wife's energetic generosity:

> *Fie daughter, when my old wife liv'd, upon*
> *This day she was both pantler, butler, cook;*
> *Both dame and servant; welcom'd all; serv'd all;*
> *Would sing her song and dance her turn; now here*
> *At upper end o' th' table, now i' th' middle;*
> *On his shoulder, and his; her face o' fire*
> *With labour, and the thing she took to quench it*
> *She would to each one sip. You are retired,*
> *As if you were a feasted one, and not*
> *The hostess of the meeting. Pray you bid*
> *These unknown friends to's welcome, for it is*
> *A way to make us better friends, more known.*
> *Come, quench your blushes, and present yourself*
> *That which you are, Mistress o' th' Feast. Come on,*
> *And bid us welcome to your sheep-shearing,*
> *As your good flock shall prosper.* (WT IV.iv)

Midsummer | Litha

KING LEAR

The Summer Solstice, which we consider the beginning of summer, was formerly known as Midsummer – in an agricultural year with three seasons, "summer" included what we now call spring. On the eve of the solstice, it was customary to build a fire mostly composed of animal bones (the bonefire from which we get the word bonfire) and dance around it, to magically coerce the sun to rise and shine through the longest day of the year. The fires would also be built upwind of grain-fields, so that the smoke could purify the crops and protect them from pests and blight. Cattle born that winter would likewise be purified with this smoke, to protect them from sickness (untreated cattle were prone to convulsions that looked like dancing, perhaps an ancestor of Mad Cow Disease.)

This might sound ridiculous now, but it does make a certain scientific sense. An old folksong from 1616 went:

> A thousand sparks dispersed throughout the sky
> Which line to wandering stars did fly,
> Whose wholesome heat, purging the air, consumes
> The earth's unwholesome vapours, fogs and fumes.
> (Anonymous, 1616)

Summer is the time of year when crops are most vulnerable to drought, insects and blight. It's also the time when growing insect populations present the greatest danger of spreading plague, typhus and malaria. Not to mention dragons, which were believed to mate in the sky on this night, dripping poisonous dragon love-juices into wells and lakes. The fire smoke was meant to chase these pests away. It was also believed to cure *"Midsummer Madness"* (mentioned in *Twelfth Night*[208]), which seems to be a festive medieval phrase for heat-stroke, and to purify community relations. As neighbors all contributed to the communal fire, the cooperation would symbolically burn away feuds and grudges from the previous year. The housewives would bring an ember home to re-light their home-fires, making all the village hearth-fires related.

Another Midsummer fire custom was to wrap a wagon-wheel in straw, set it ablaze on a hilltop and roll it toward a lake in order to ensure agricultural bounty. The idea seems to have been that crops were dependent on stable weather, caused by consistency of celestial movements, and so a straight roll of this flaming wheel was a reminder to the stars and planets, to stay their courses. *King Lear* contains numerous references to this wheel-of-fortune, *"Fortune, good night: smile once more, turn thy wheel!"* (KL II.ii) The Fool encourages Lear to accept his fate, saying *"Let go thy hold when a great wheel runs down a hill, lest it break thy neck with following it; but the great one that goes upward, let him draw thee after."* (KL II.iv) And Lear himself later despairs *"I am bound / Upon a wheel of fire, that mine own tears do scald like molten lead."* (KL IV.vii)

François Laroque further proposes that the maddened Lear's crown of weeds and flowers might signify his transformation from a political king to the mock carnival-king of a solstice pageant.[209] Lear imagined his retirement as an orderly royal procession of himself, followed by his hundred mounted knights, followed by their squires and attendants. But instead he is reduced to the leader of a ragtag roving shambles. In Lear's aimless march through the storm we see a mock king (Lear), a pedant (Gloucester), a brave knight (Kent), a fool, and "Poor Tom" the madman who has forsworn his own humanity (a sort of Baboon). If you added in some women or boys in women's clothing (Goneril and Regan) you'd have a Morris Dance. Throw in a dragon (which Lear calls himself[210]) and it would be a Midsummer parade. Midsummer parades featured loud music, dancing, elaborate floats of Saint George and the Dragon, and men in drag. Some of these traditions survive in modern Gay Pride parades.

Lammas | Lughnasadh

TEMPEST

Lammas or Lughnasadh was an August harvest festival, originally commemorating the warrior-king Lugh (from whom we get the word "Loaf"). Lugh was something like an Irish English King Arthur, whose bravery in battle was rewarded with a promise that the land would become so fertile that there would be four harvests a year. Lugh refused, saying one harvest was enough, but demanded instead the knowledge of how to plough the ground and plant grain. With only one harvest season to worry about, Lugh dedicated himself to inventing games, and his holiday, celebrating the completion of harvest labors, was time for an Irish Olympics.

Medieval Christianity begrudgingly adopted this holiday, inviting farmers to bring half of a loaf baked from the first harvested grains, to be blessed in church. Asimov proposes that "Half-Mass," "*hlaf-maesse*" in old Anglo-Saxon, was abbreviated to Lammas.[211] The harvest was a merry time – for subsistence farmers it was the big annual payday, and it involved the whole community: artisans would hire themselves out for reaping, village maidens would thresh the grains, and when the job was done everyone would be invited for a drinking party. There was a friendly competition about the harvest – the last sheaf cut on the last farm to be reaped would be bound up and called The Old Maid, a bad-luck charm (this is the likely origin of the Old Maid card-game). Beatrice in *Much Ado About Nothing* speaks of herself as the last unharvested sheaf when she says *"Thus goes everyone to the world but I, and I am sunburnt. I may sit in a corner and cry heigh-ho for a husband!"* (MAAN II.i)

This harvest festival marked the end of summer, as Labor Day does in the USA. An observer wrote in 1598, "In the holy dayes all sommer, the yoouths are exercised in leaping, dancing, shooting, wrastling, casting the stone, and practising their shieldes; the maidens trippe it with their Timbrelles, and daunce as long as they can well see." [sic][212] But Lammas festivities were declining in Shakespeare's time, when land-barons were consolidating family plots into massive cash-crop plantations. For many dispossessed peasants in the city slums, harvest-time was only a reminder of what they'd lost. Shakespeare names Lammas only once, in *Romeo and Juliet*, when Lady Capulet and the nurse discuss Juliet's upcoming birthday on *"Lammas Eve."* (R&J I.iii) But the plot has no strong ties to a Lammas festival.[213]

Shakespeare re-creates a harvest fertility-pageant in *The Tempest*, when Prospero conjures the goddesses Juno, Ceres and Iris. These were the Roman versions of the Greek Hera (goddess of wives) and Demeter (goddess of grain). The sex goddess Venus/Aphrodite would have made sense to round out this trinity, but the squeamish Prospero replaces her with Iris, the goddess of rainbows. Prospero's harvest pageant links together numerous themes of the play: like Demeter's daughter he has been banished to a sort of underworld and now looks forward to a return, and his daughter who's been fending off sexual advances from death-scented Caliban will now marry a bright, shining prince.

Prospero is also anxious that this romance will quickly burn itself out and become cold after marriage. Shakespeare expresses this anxiety in *As You Like It: "Men are April when they woo, December when they wed. Maids are May when they are maids, but the sky changes when they are wives."* (AYL IV.i) So the pageant suggests that, in this marriage, harvest season will always go straight into spring, skipping winter.

> IRIS. *Ceres, most bounteous lady, thy rich leas*
> *Of wheat, rye, barley, vetches, oats, and pease;*
> *Thy turfy mountains, where live nibbling sheep,*
> *And flat meads thatch'd with stover, them to keep;*

Thy banks with pioned and twilled brims,
Which spongy April at thy hest betrims,
To make cold nymphs chaste crowns; and thy broom groves,
Whose shadow the dismissed bachelor loves...
CERES. Earth's increase, foison plenty,
Barns and gamers never empty;
Vines with clust'ring bunches growing,
Plants with goodly burden bowing;
Spring come to you at the farthest,
In the very end of harvest!
Scarcity and want shall shun you,
Ceres' blessing so is on you...
IRIS. You nymphs, call'd Naiads, of the wind'ring brooks,
With your sedg'd crowns and ever harmless looks,
Leave your crisp channels, and on this green land
Answer your summons; Juno does command.
Come, temperate nymphs, and help to celebrate
A contract of true love; be not too late.
(Enter certain NYMPHS)
You sun-burnt sicklemen, of August weary,
Come hither from the furrow, and be merry;
Make holiday; your rye-straw hats put on,
And these fresh nymphs encounter every one
In country footing.
(Enter certain REAPERS, properly habited; they join with the
NYMPHS in a graceful dance). (TEM IV.i)

The sheer vivacity Shakespeare brings to his treatments of summer festivity make it clear that this was his favorite time of year. In stark contrast with a winter huddled indoors, drinking hot ale by the fireplace, Mayday marked a time of wild abandon on the border between civilization and the wilderness. This was a season when anything seemed possible, young love could blossom with unbridled freedom, so it's only natural that Shakespeare should choose this season for his liveliest and most optimistic stories. Then the August harvest festival of Lammas represents the in-gathering of wheat, in preparation for bracing through another hard winter.

The Enchanted Forest

Arden | Eden
AS YOU LIKE IT | LOVE'S LABOUR'S LOST | TEMPEST | MIDSUMMER

This royal throne of kings, this scept'red isle...
This other Eden, demi-paradise,
This fortress built by Nature for herself
Against infection and the hand of war...
This blessed plot, this earth, this realm, this England,
This nurse, this teeming womb of royal kings. (R2 II.i)

How use doth breed a habit in a man!
This shadowy desert, unfrequented woods,
I better brook than flourishing peopled towns. (TGV V.iv)

    William Shakespeare lived in a time of change: Land-barons were gobbling up family farmsteads in the countryside, evicting subsistence farmers who had no choice but to seek degrading work in filthy cities. Shakespeare himself relocated from a farm-town to London and used his success as a playwright to buy up lands in his hometown, becoming a notorious miser. He was frequently dragged to court for crop-swindles, then paid the fines and kept going. In his lifetime he was a sort of

Heathcliff (from *Wuthering Heights*) or Citizen Kane, more famous as a robber baron than as a playwright, which is why his epitaph was a curse on any who came to desecrate his grave. No doubt he knew they'd be lining up. He seems to have been slowly eaten alive by venereal disease, and eventually crawled off to his ill-gotten country estate to drink himself to death. But in his big-city celebrity years he always retained a fondness for the countryside, and his plays have a running theme of the forest as a cure for the sickness of the city.

Shakespeare's forest is always an English forest. *A Midsummer Night's Dream* begins with four Athenian teenagers trapped by ancient laws, but they run off toward the woods and suddenly they're in England. In *Love's Labour's Lost* the king of Navarre walls himself off with a monastic code and forces a visiting French princess to camp out in the woods, but going to see her he's magically transported from northern Spain to England. In *Winter's Tale* a Sicilian princess is banished to Bohemia, but the forest there is England again (Shakespeare even gives landlocked "Bohemia" an English sea coast). In *As You Like It*, exiled French nobles disappear into the forest...you guessed it–England. An Italian nobleman in *Two Gentlemen of Verona*, more Athenians in *Two Noble Kinsmen*, shipwrecked Italian nobles in *The Tempest*, Shakespeare keeps drawing his characters into the enchanted English forest where they can recover from urban competition and cruelty. Even the mad King Lear eventually finds peace in the woods, and let's not forget it's a walking forest that finally heals Scotland from Macbeth's reign of terror. There's magic in the Shakespearean forest.

In *As You Like It*, a French Duke usurped and exiled by his younger brother has established a woodland commune:

> *He is already in the Forest of Arden, and a many merry men with him; and there they live like the old Robin Hood of England. They say many young gentlemen flock to him every day, and fleet the time carelessly, as they did in the golden world.* (AYL I.i)

The *"golden world"* here is the age of innocence before agriculture and cities–the Biblical Eden or Greek "Golden Age." The refugees are compared to Robin Hood's merry men, Robin Hood being a sort of patron-saint of English forests. Because the play is set in France, the speaker specifies *"Robin Hood of England,"* and yet the woodland itself is English–Arden was a forest just north of Shakespeare's birthplace (Arden was also his mother's maiden name, a symbol of virginal innocence). When we meet the Duke a few scenes later, he is giving a sermon about how the forest is teaching him how to be a human being:

> *Now, my co-mates and brothers in exile,*
> *Hath not old custom made this life more sweet*
> *Than that of painted pomp? Are not these woods*
> *More free from peril than the envious court?*
> *Here feel we not the penalty of Adam,*
> *The seasons' difference; as the icy fang*
> *And churlish chiding of the winter's wind,*
> *Which when it bites and blows upon my body,*
> *Even till I shrink with cold, I smile and say*
> *'This is no flattery; these are counsellors*
> *That feelingly persuade me what I am.'*
> *Sweet are the uses of adversity...*
> *And this our life, exempt from public haunt,*
> *Finds tongues in trees, books in the running brooks,*
> *Sermons in stones, and good in everything.*
> *I would not change it.* (AYL II.i)

The theme of escaping the *"penalty of Adam"* (toiling for food as punishment for the crime in Eden) is hammered home with the appearance of an elderly farm-laborer *named* Adam who quits his job to follow the Prodigal Son Orlando in search of a better life. In the forest of Arden/Eden they quickly discover that the wages of Adam's lengthy toil have no value – they can't find anyone who'll trade food for money. Stumbling into the exiled Duke's commune, Orlando demands food with threats of violence, but he's invited to share in the meagre feast of the forest dwellers. And after this initial welcome of the Prodigal Son, Orlando becomes the Duke's son-in-law in the play's resolution. You don't exactly need a degree in poetry or Bible-study to get the symbolism here. But just in case anyone in the original audience might have missed it, Shakespeare personally played the role of Adam.[214]

Although Shakespeare played Adam, the character with which he most identified was Jaques, whom he inserted into the story he took from

Lodge's *Rosalynde,* and playfully named after himself – Jakes/Shakes.[215] This sarcastic and disease-ridden philosopher provides a jaded commentary on the comical commonwealth, inserting a verse into a hippie sing-along:

> SONG *(All together here)*
> *Who doth ambition shun,*
> *And loves to live i' th' sun,*
> *Seeking the food he eats,*
> *And pleas'd with what he gets,*
> *Come hither, come hither, come hither.*
> *But winter and rough weather.*
> JAQUES. *I'll give you a verse to this note that I made yesterday in despite of my invention.*
> AMIENS. *And I'll sing it.*
> JAQUES. *Thus it goes: [sings]*
> *If it do come to pass*
> *That any man turn ass,*[216]
> *Leaving his wealth and ease*
> *A stubborn will to please,*
> *Ducdame, ducdame, ducdame;*
> *Here shall he see*
> *Gross fools as he,*
> *An if he will come to me.*
> AMIENS. *What's that 'ducdame'?*
> JAQUES. *'Tis a Greek invocation, to call fools into a circle.* (AYL II.v)

Jaques' infections from the city are *almost* healed in the forest, and he suspects that he could be purified by becoming a clown, one who can bring the outsider (natural) perspective into the city. But then, in a fascinating final twist when the exiled refugees are restored to court, Jaques chooses instead a new level of exile, hobbling off to become a monk.

The play ends with the forest-magic version of a fireworks finale. Orlando's oppressive older brother Oliver ventures into the forest and instantly falls in love with the refugee Celia, abruptly deciding to share the inheritance with his younger brother. The Duke's usurping brother pursues him into the wood, but the forest magic heals him of all his ambition and cruelty. He gives the dukedom back and banishes himself to a life of religious contemplation. And somehow Rosalind's repressed sexuality manifests itself in the *Deus-ex-machina* form of the marriage-god Hymen, who blesses a mass wedding.

While the forest in *As You Like It* gives refuge from the *"penalty of Adam,"* *The Winter's Tale* explores the penalty of Eve. The drama begins with a man and woman alone in an enclosed garden. The Bohemian king is recalling his boyhood bond with the king of Sicily, the innocence that gave him a feeling of eternal life:

> We were, fair Queen,
> Two lads that thought there was no more behind
> But such a day to-morrow as to-day,
> And to be boy eternal...
> We were as twinn'd lambs that did frisk i' th' sun
> And bleat the one at th' other. What we chang'd
> Was innocence for innocence; we knew not
> The doctrine of ill-doing, nor dream'd
> That any did...O my most sacred lady,
> Temptations have since then been born to us. (WT I.ii)

The Sicilian queen cheerfully responds that growing up and getting married does not necessarily mean a fall to temptation:

> Grace to boot!
> Of this make no conclusion, lest you say
> Your queen and I are devils. Yet, go on;
> Th' offences we have made you do we'll answer,
> If you first sinn'd with us, and that with us
> You did continue fault, and that you slipp'd not
> With any but with us. (WT I.ii)

Unfortunately, there's a snake in this garden – the anxious eye and jealous heart of king Leontes, watching his wife and best friend talking, and becoming convinced that they have fallen in lust with each-other. He tries to kill his friend, imprisons his wife (which causes the death of their only son), banishes their newborn daughter, and then gets the news that his wife has died. This all happens very suddenly as if death itself had newly emerged, hungry, into the world. And the kingdom of Sicily is cursed with winter until innocence is restored.

Sixteen years go by. The banished daughter is a shepherdess in rural Bohemia, handing out flowers at a fertility pageant. The prince has fallen in love with her, but his father disapproves, assuming this is only lust that will cause the boy's downfall. They flee to Sicilia and must prove that their love is innocent and pure in order to restore balance, which incidentally lifts the winter-curse and restores spring in Sicilia. The shepherdess doesn't know she's meeting her own father, and the king sees only a stranger, but acknowledges the lovers' healing purity:

> *Welcome hither,*
> *As is the spring to th' earth... The blessed gods*
> *Purge all infection from our air whilst you*
> *Do climate here!* (WT V.i)

And like the Biblical Job who lost everything, his family is restored to him.[217]

Love's Labour's Lost contains Eden/Arden symbolism of the forest as a paradise where the curses on Adam and Eve can be escaped. It begins with four men deciding to live like monks, studying ancient texts and forswearing the company of women for three years. Their written contract is a harsh covenant or testament, and once signed it becomes a rigid scripture. But barely five minutes pass before they remember a visit from the Princess of France and her three friends. They cannot allow these women into the castle, so offer to lodge them in the *"curious-knotted garden"* of the adjacent state park. Surveying this, the princess sneers *"The roof of this court is too high to be yours."* This untamed land does not *really* belong to the king, and she'll use this to her advantage. Driven by lust, the men fall from grace, abandoning their studies to seek the forbidden knowledge of love in these ladies' tempting glances under the trees. The poet Berowne then uses his acrobatic logic to contort his Old Testament fall-from-grace into a form of New Testament salvation:

> *From women's eyes this doctrine I derive...*
> *They are the books, the arts, the academes,*
> *That show, contain, and nourish, all the world,*

Else none at all in aught proves excellent.
Then fools you were these women to forswear;
Or, keeping what is sworn, you will prove fools...
Let us once lose our oaths to find ourselves,
Or else we lose ourselves to keep our oaths.
It is religion to be thus forsworn;
For charity itself fulfils the law,
And who can sever love from charity? (LLL IV.iii)

English forests in Shakespeare's time belonged exclusively to the royalty as private gaming reserves, which added to the public view of forests containing a special aura. This puts a sinister spin on *Love's Labour's Lost*: a French king sends his daughter as partial payment of a debt, and the king of Navarre confines her in his gaming reserve, then keeps stalking her with predatory advances. But the whole action of the play is the princess and her ladies evading the king and his hunting buddies (and a fascinating scene is devoted to the women learning to bow-hunt deer). It's the only Shakespearean comedy where the heroines do not marry the heroes, hence the title. The hunters are captured by the prey. At the conclusion, each of the four heroines imposes a year of confinement on her would-be wooer, ranging from remedial study to Peace Corps-style volunteer labor.

Shakespeare's woodland is primarily a feminine space, in contrast to the male-dominated city. In the forest of Arden (and really *all* of Shakespeare's forests are Arden), Rosalind can choose and mold her own mate in *As You Like It*. Hermia in *Midsummer Night's Dream* flees the city in which her father can rule her through ancient law, to elope with her chosen man in the woods—the same forest where the fairy queen Titania challenges the rule of king Oberon. In the source for *King Lear*, the banished princess runs off into the forest, disguises as a shepherdess and marries a disguised French King, but Shakespeare changed that ending. Then he retooled *King Lear* into *A Winter's Tale* where the prince proposes to the lowly shepherdess in the forest against his father's wishes, and then it's revealed she's a banished princess. The forest is also a place where women can transcend other boundaries: Rosalind becomes a young man, and her cousin Celia momentarily becomes a priest.

The forest in *The Tempest* is post-apocalyptic—the feminine forest-guardian Sycorax has died and Prospero has moved in.[218] As a hermit he is somewhat genderless and manipulates the enchanted forest to win an exiled prince for his daughter (he even briefly disguises the prince as a lumberjack). The Eden theme is present: a man and woman banished because of an exploration of forbidden knowledge, and the "natural" man Caliban is exiled for lust.[219] Prospero uses his powers to create a Purgatory to punish and purify the royal party shipwrecked there. But while wrongdoers see the island as a barren and cursed place, the kindly Gonzalo sees it as a perfect site to establish a utopia.

> *Had I plantation of this isle...what would I do?*
> *...I' th' commonwealth I would by contraries*
> *Execute all things; for no kind of traffic*
> *Would I admit; no name of magistrate;*
> *Letters should not be known; riches, poverty,*
> *And use of service, none; contract, succession,*
> *Bourn, bound of land, tilth, vineyard, none;*
> *No use of metal, corn, or wine, or oil;*
> *No occupation; all men idle, all;*
> *And women too, but innocent and pure;*
> *No sovereignty...*
> *All things in common nature should produce*
> *Without sweat or endeavour. Treason, felony,*
> *Sword, pike, knife, gun, or need of any engine,*
> *Would I not have; but nature should bring forth,*
> *Of its own kind, all foison, all abundance,*
> *To feed my innocent people...*
> *I would with such perfection govern, sir,*
> *T' excel the golden age.* (TEM II.i)

Gonzalo is drawing from Greek myths: Hesiod's *Theogony* reports a long-gone Golden Age when people lived "with carefree heart, remote from toil and misery... All good things were theirs, and the grain-giving soil bore its fruits of its own accord in unstinted plenty, while they at their leisure harvested their fields in contentment amid abundance."[220] The Roman mythographer Ovid further elaborates in his *Metamorphoses*: "Then living creatures trusted one another; people did well without the thought of ill: nothing forbidden in a book of laws, no fears, no prohibitions...no cities climbed behind high walls and bridges; no brass-lipped trumpets called, nor clanging swords, nor helmets marched the streets, country and town had never heard of war: and seasons traveled through the years of peace. The innocent earth learned neither spade nor plough; she gave her riches as fruit hangs from the tree."[221]

When Prospero produces a fertility pageant to celebrate his daughter's engagement, he takes paradise/perfection one step further: the Roman grain-goddess Ceres promises that the autumnal harvest will be followed by spring:

> *Earth's increase, foison plenty,*
> *Barns and garners never empty...*
> *Spring come to you at the farthest,*
> *In the very end of harvest!* (TEM IV.i)

In Shakespeare's time, winter was considered a punishment for the crime in Eden (much like the ancient Greek belief that winter was a result of the underworld god Hades kidnapping the grain-goddess's daughter, and parallel beliefs are common to other ancient cultures). During the blessing of Miranda, the Greek/Roman goddess promises to undo this curse, and her song is then followed by a dance of springtime forest nymphs and august reapers.

Arden/Eden is not always strictly a forest. Friar Lawrence's cell is a greenhouse in the city of Verona, where Romeo and Juliet can escape their parents' control. Wild young Hal is able to evade his royal father's somber guilt-tripping in the cavernous taverns of *Henry IV*. Mariana in *Measure for Measure* fools her scornful ex-fiancée into having blind sex in a walled garden locked with two keys, thus entrapping him into marriage.[222] Portia's Belmont in *Merchant of Venice* is a haven for the runaway Jessica to elope with the man of her choice (although for most of the play, Belmont is ruled by Portia's dead father and his irrational law).

A slim case could be made for Macbeth's *"blasted heath,"* the wilderness where witches' songs dictate the futures of Scottish kings. In *Antony and Cleopatra*, Egypt functions as a sort of Eden, where the love of a man and woman is creating a *"new heaven, new earth."* (A&C I.i) But this love is threatened by the long reach of Caesar Augustus, the *"universal landlord,"* Eden is besieged by Rome, and the story ends with death: Eve bitten by a snake.

The anti-Arden would be *Hamlet*'s Elsinore – a cold stony death-trap haunted by a ghost's vendetta (frigid father, rigid law), where prince charming chooses suicide and a maiden's love corrodes to madness and death. Maybe instead of tossing skulls around a graveyard Hamlet should have taken a walk in the woods.

Although Shakespeare's forest is a place of rejuvenation and reconciliation, it is not a place of permanent settlement. If the forest were to become a town it would lose its mystery and magic, and quickly become infected by the hierarchy and legalism of the city. So all of Shakespeare's forest jaunts must end with pilgrims healed, restored, and/or matched, bringing their renewed energies back to town.

The enchanted forest is not a backdrop, but an active agent: a teacher, healer and savior. If we were to assign woodland a volition and personality, it would be Oberon, Titania and Puck in *Midsummer Night's Dream*, except that they spend most of that play bickering (and their discord causes bad weather and romantic confusion). The male principle Oberon is always on the march, leading linear processions, always passing through while the female principle Titania is nesting and cradling, leading circular dances: *"a roundel."*

"There is no clock in the forest" says Orlando in *As You Like It* but really there are two: the linear time of birth-to-death, and the cyclical time of life-change-death-decay-regeneration. As king, Oberon sides with predators—leopards, bears and boars–while Titania is more attentive to the smaller (but no less significant) elements of biodiversity: bees and butterflies, fireflies, medicinal herbs and flowers, fruits and berries. Oberon takes an active interest in matchmaking[223] and Titania's interest is in nurturing babies (the changeling child, for whom Oberon and Puck substitute the ass-man Bottom).

Audience perceptions of the power dynamic between the fairy king and queen are skewed by the prank Oberon orchestrates, but it's important to note that Titania and Oberon are equally matched in a tug-of-war until he cheats (and if the Titania-Bottom relationship is viewed as sexual, then the plan backfires and he is cheated upon[224]). A very close look at their power struggle reveals that she has the upper hand: Titania wants to stabilize the climate and nurture a child, and informs Oberon that even giving all he owns will not make her budge: *"The fairy land buys not the child of me."* All that Oberon wants is Titania's obedience, and when he finds that he cannot force or purchase it he becomes sullen and immature – he needs her devotion, but she is content to set his love aside and focus her love on her adopted child. Oberon's prank of substituting a monster for the baby is meant to make her ridiculous, and yet even drugged in the scenes with Bottom she remains completely composed and in control.

Shakespeare only makes Oberon and Titania visible when they're in conflict, but we wouldn't be so far out on a limb in imagining a unified Oberon-Titania always lurking unseen in the background of Arden, gently adjusting lovers' paths to bring unity and fertility. The Shakespearean forest likewise seems to always contain an invisible Puck, playfully switching characters' loyalties and identities. They make a sort of three-in-one holy trinity. The climactic scene of *Merry Wives of Windsor* (a circle dance in a forest) contains cameo appearances by *"PUCK"* and the *"FAIRY QUEEN,"* who are not even listed among the characters on the script's title page–they just magically appear.[225] It's possible that they're always there, invisible, in Shakespeare's enchanted forest.

Conclusion

hen we consider how authoritative Shakespeare's writings on the supernatural have become, it's important to remember that he never envisioned a "Collected Works" tome of his writing. He saw his writings alive on a stage, not compiled in an old, dead text. He clearly did not believe he was writing a definitive "Bible" of fairy-lore or witches – if he had, he would have been consistent. Rather than use rigid systems of ghost-lore or fairy-ology, the author freely adapted and improvised supernatural beings to fit perfectly into individual stories. Likely it was this freedom of expression that makes these supernatural characters feel so spontaneous, autonomous, and lively.

In the last four hundred years, no other writer has had the same flexibility when writing about fairies, ghosts, and witches. As Roger Green observed, Shakespeare could play so freely because he *hadn't read Shakespeare!* He had no definitive text on these topics, just fragments of oral tradition and bits of poetry. Playfully gathering from among these fragments, Shakespeare chose pieces to assemble into mosaics, like his most famous fairy Puck (a composite bricolage from bits of English folklore and Roman literature), and Puck is astonishingly different from Ariel: each fairy was custom built to serve a specific story.

The aim of this book has been to gather some of these raw materials, fragments which Shakespeare re-shaped and assembled into his composites, to lay out the rough component parts. Then the hope is that readers examine these fragments and draw their own conclusions – even if it means using this book as a concordance and disregarding all author commentary.

In the process of disassembling Shakespeare's supernatural figures into their component parts, the purpose is not to demote Shakespeare-as-godlike-creator, but to put the spotlight on Shakespeare-the-master-craftsman who assembled these unforgettable portraits, giving them life and desire and personality. In reverse-engineering Shakespeare's creations, we can gain a greater appreciation of how imaginative, flexible, and intellectually nimble he was. That famous gleaming forehead was hard at work, we could even say fertile and frequently pregnant.

I don't personally know or care who it was that wrote these plays. But whoever it was, I assume that, if the author heard that they'd been put on a pedestal and invested with godlike perfect creative powers, he or she would protest that these plays were hard work. And, going out on a limb, I assume that the author would rather be respected as an outstanding human than idolized, Bard-olized or whatever.

Ladies and Gentlemen and Groundlings

When we imagine "The Immortal Bard" William Shakespeare as a divinely inspired or even godlike creator, then we could easily slip into envisioning this creator working alone in a darkened vacuum of empty space, generating these plots and characters from nothing. But nothing could be further from the truth. The historical author was not alone in the dark but immersed in the blurry, colorful, ever-shifting matrix of England in transition from rural medievalism to urban modernity. It was a very specific and hectic historical moment.

Shakespeare didn't just write to please himself, he wrote to impress his contemporaries, from royalty to peasantry. He wanted every seat in the theatre filled, from the most expensive box down to the penny standing-spaces. And he succeeded in impressing his contemporaries. We know this because his works survive and continue to impress us centuries later. That was an unplanned side effect; he didn't care about impressing future generations. If he had, he would have published official authorized manuscripts, but he didn't. We get to eavesdrop on his conversations with people of his own time, and that keeps getting harder as the English language continues to evolve away from primitive Elizabethan English, and as we drift further and further out of sync with Medieval English countryside superstitions and folk beliefs.

The central purpose of *Supernatural Shakespeare* has been to bridge some of the gaps between a modern reader/theatergoer and Shakespeare's target audiences, the ladies, gentlemen, and groundlings of his own time. The hope is that this will add another dimension to some familiar stories and spark some interest in further exploration of Shakespeare's works.

Notes

Introduction

1   Hughes (1992) p. 85

2   Woodbridge (1994) p. 8

3   Jonson, Ben (1640) in Eastman (1964) p. 8

4   Elements of the Hecate scenes also appear in a play called *The Witch* (1610) by Thomas Middleton. It's possible that sections of Middleton's play were inserted into a revival production of *Macbeth*, or that Middleton expanded *Macbeth* into a musical. Asimov (1970:2) p. 185

5   Frye (1965) p. 22

6   Paglia (1991) p. 195-196

7   And to maintain his rhythm, Shakespeare would sometimes arrange the parts of a sentence in funny sequences, like when Hamlet goes into Yoda-mode saying *"Sense sure you have, else you could not have motion."* (HAM III.iv)

8   When Hamlet himself speaks of attending a performance, he says *"We'll hear a play tomorrow."* (HAM II.ii) For educated audience members, a play is primarily *heard*. The groundlings were *spect*ators (those who show up to *see*) and the elite were an *aud*ience (who show up to *hear*).

9   Woodbridge (1994) p. 1

10   Hughes (1992) p. 152

11   Someone on the internet says his collected writings contain 31,534 different words, 14,376 of which he used only once.

12   Just as learning Latin used to be an initiation into the elite, now studying some Shakespeare has become a rite of passage into the adult middle class. Sinfeld in Woodbridge and Berry (1992) p. 25

13   Arnold, Matthew (1853) in Eastman (1964) p. 10

14   Frazer (1996) p. 553

15   Barber (1972) p. 169

16   Barber (1972) p. 6

17   Philip Stubbes *Anatomie of Abuses* (1583)

18   If Shakespeare's comedies had proper-noun titles they would have to

be womens' names – *Much Ado* would be "Beatrice," *All's Well* would be "Helena," *Measure for Measure* would be "Isabella." Shakespeare took the plot and characters of *As You Like It* from a play called *Rosalynde*, but changed the title. Maybe he wouldn't give the headline to a female character, unless she shared it: *Romeo and Juliet*, *Antony and Cleopatra*, *Troilus and Cressida*. The closest he gets is *"The Shrew"* and *"Merry Wives."*...Unless we say *Macbeth* was named for Lady Macbeth.

19   Laroque (1993) p. 4

20   Spens (1916) p. 50 *The moste famous Chronicle historye of Leire king of England and his Three Daughters* was published anonymously in 1594, about ten years before Shakespeare wrote *King Lear* (There's some possibility Shakespeare wrote this 1594 play and then significantly rewrote it).

21   Pope, Alexander (1725) in Eastman (1964) p. 9

22   And when Reformation Puritanism sought to banish festive decoration and pageantry from Christian ritual, it's not hard to imagine that some of these unmarriageable sons, who might have grown up to be Catholic priests, put their energies into professional theater instead.

23   The touring players in *Hamlet* first enact a scene from the Trojan War, but then Hamlet requests a more contemporary Italian piece, "The Murder of Gonzago" (by "contemporary" I mean it seems to have been based on a story from the 1500s, a thousand years after *Hamlet* takes place.

24   Order by Justices of the Peace (1612) in Laroque (1993) p. 35

25   Barber (1972) p. 110

26   In Protestant theology this took the form of Calvin's doctrine of Predestination. In theater it took the form of characters doomed to tragic ends or predestined to comic happiness.

27   Arguably there are instances where Shakespeare created a personality so deep that the character actually escaped from their conventional destiny. Shakespeare copied the plot of *King Lear* from a comedy, but in his hands it twisted into tragedy. The legendary Hamlet won the throne and the girl, but Shakespeare killed him. The source for *Winter's Tale* is a crushing tragedy for the king but Shakespeare rehabilitates him.

28   Spens (1916) p. 92 Spens adds: "Nor does Shakespeare, with one exception, ever give a full-length portrait of a woman. The exception is perhaps significant, for it is Cleopatra."

29   Shakespeare's female characters who pretend to be men are Julia in *Two Gentlemen of Verona*, Portia and her servant Nerissa in *Merchant of Venice*, Rosalind in *As You Like It*, Viola in *Twelfth Night* and Imogen in *Cymbeline*. Falstaff in *Merry Wives* is briefly dressed as a woman, and *Midsummer Night's Dream* includes a male character playing Thisbe onstage.

30   Paglia (1991) p. 195, 197

31   Rosalind's dark male shadow is Duke Vincentio in *Measure for Measure* who temporarily exiles himself from court and dons the disguise of a friar (although he does not switch genders, he becomes sexless, a sort of temporary eunuch). Playing this role in costume, he schemes behind the scenes, directing

and stage-managing a very theatrical pageant-trial to be played through the entire fifth act of the play, full of plot-twists and matchmaking. This all sounds like fun, but has sinister undertones that culminate in the silencing and entrapment of the heroine Isabella.

32 Shakespeare does show a couple of his kings being stage-managed/ directed by pompous Roman Catholic Cardinals – Pandolf in *King John* and Wolsey in *Henry VIII.*

33 Paglia (1990) p. 219

34 She also directs and stage-manges him, and there are even a few hints that she costumed Antony, at times, in her own clothing: *"O times / I laughed him out of patience; and that night / I laugh'd him into patience; and next morn, / Ere the ninth hour, I drunk him to his bed, / Then put my tires and mantles on him, whilst / I wore his sword."* (A&C II.v)

35 Asimov (1970:1) p. 22

Witches

36 After her death, Lady Macbeth is referred to as a *"fiendish queen,"* meaning possessed by spirits. Edgar, calling himself "Poor Tom" and feigning madness in *King Lear*, also speaks of being possessed by spirits: *"Poor Tom hath been scared out of his good wits. Bless thee, good man's son, from the foul fiend! Five fiends have been in poor Tom at once; of lust, as Obidicut; Hobbididence, prince of darkness; Mahu, of stealing; Modo, of murder; Flibbertigibbet, of mopping and mowing, who since possesses chambermaids and waiting women. So, bless thee, master!"* (KL IV.i) Shakespeare found these demon names in Samuel Harsnett's *A Declaration of Egregious Popish Impostures* (1603). Further exploration of musical verse/rhyme patterns in Doran, Madeleine "The *Macbeth* Music" (1983) and Kranz, David "The Sounds of Supernatural Soliciting in *'Macbeth"* (2003)

37 Hecate also appears in the Homeric *"Hymn to Demeter"* as an elderly woman who witnesses Persephone's abduction into the underworld and becomes the guide of her biannual crossings. The implication here is that she is also the elder in a trinity with Persephone (virgin) and Demeter (mother).

38 The Hecate scenes are dubious, since elements of them also appear in a play called *The Witch* (1610) by Thomas Middleton. It's possible that sections of Middleton's play were inserted into a revival production of *Macbeth*, or that Middleton expanded *Macbeth* into a musical. But regardless of authorship, these Hecate speeches do contain some insights into folk beliefs about witchcraft in Shakespeare's time. Asimov (1970:2) p. 185

39 Hughes (1992) p. 300. Shakespeare's *Pericles* contains the evil form of the three-in-one witch, a princess sexually involved with her own father, who is at once virgin, bride/mother (in the sense that she has become her own mother) and symbol of death. She is a sphynx-like riddle which Pericles solves and manages to escape, and we later hear she has been burned alive by fire from the sky.

40   Hughes (1992) p. 434

41   "Blue eye'd" in Shakespeare's time did not necessarily refer to eye-color, but to blue rings around the eyes from late-night debauchery.

42   Asimov (1970:2) p. 152

43   Calhoun (1942) p. 184-186

44   For example, Hamlet says of his dead father *"That he might not beteem [allow] the winds of heaven / Visit her face too roughly."* (HAM I.ii) And Lear spends a good deal of his play outside railing against his lost ability to control weather, *"Thunder would not peace at my bidding."* (KL IV.vi) He does command the winds to blow, but they're doing that anyway. In *Macbeth*, the weather is bad from Duncan's death until Macbeth dies. Although it *is* Scotland, which is not really famous for sunny days.

45   She turns to Queen Elizabeth (not "the Elizabethan" Elizabeth, but the wife of the doomed Edward IV), sneering *"The day will come that thou shalt wish for me / To help thee curse this poisonous bunch-back'd toad."* (R3 I.iii) And indeed three acts later this will come to pass, Elizabeth beseeching *"O thou well skill'd in curses, stay awhile / And teach me how to curse mine enemies!"* (R3 IV.iv) Lady Anne will also be the victim of a terrible curse, which she casts herself. Weeping over the corpse of Henry VI she curses the murderer (Richard) and also any woman who marries him. (R3 I.ii) Then she becomes his wife and realizes only later that her curse has come true: *"This was my wish: 'Be thou' quoth I 'accurs'd / For making me, so young, so old a widow; / And when thou wed'st, let sorrow haunt thy bed; / And be thy wife, if any be so mad, / More miserable by the life of thee / Than thou hast made me by my dear lord's death.' / Lo, ere I can repeat this curse again, / Within so small a time, my woman's heart / Grossly grew captive to his honey words / And prov'd the subject of mine own soul's curse."* (R3 IV.i) *The Winter's Tale* (WT III.ii) will contain a curse by the so-called *"mankind witch"* Paulina, punishing King Leontes for his refusal to believe in the Oracle. Her prophecy comes true, but this curse will eventually be lifted when the king repents.

46   *"KING JOHN. Though you and all the kings of Christendom / Are led so grossly by this meddling priest, / Dreading the curse that money may buy out, / And by the merit of vile gold, dross, dust, / Purchase corrupted pardon of a man, / Who in that sale sells pardon from himself – / Though you and all the rest, so grossly led, / This juggling witchcraft with revenue cherish; / Yet I alone, alone do me oppose / Against the Pope, and count his friends my foes."* (KJ III.i.162-171)

47   Woodbridge (1994) p. 7. Cerimon is an Ephesian in Shakespeare's *Pericles, Prince of Tyre*, with a sort of Shamanic knowledge: *"'Tis known, I ever / Have studied physic, through which secret art... / Together with my practice, made familiar / To me and to my aid the blest infusions / That dwell in vegetives, in metals, stones; / And I can speak of the disturbances / That nature works, and of her cures."* (PER III.ii)

48   The tragically effeminate King Richard II also dabbles in witchcraft, going so far as to call himself a mother of the land, which he then curses with sterility and pestilence toward his enemies: *"Dear earth, I do salute thee with my hand... / As a long-parted mother with her child... / And do thee favours with my royal hands. / Feed not thy sovereign's foe, my gentle earth, / Nor with thy sweets comfort his ravenous sense; / But let thy spiders, that suck up thy venom, / And heavy-gaited toads, lie in their way, / Doing annoyance to the treacherous feet / Which with usurping steps do trample thee; / Yield stinging nettles to mine enemies; / And when they from thy bosom pluck a flower, / Guard it, I pray thee, with a lurking adder, / Whose double tongue may with a mortal touch / Throw death upon thy sovereign's enemies. / Mock not my senseless conjuration, lords."* (R2 III.ii)

49   Shakespeare's *Cymbeline* also features a soothsayer, who prophesies Roman victory over an English insurrection. *"Last night the very gods show'd me a vision / I fast and pray'd for their intelligence- thus: / I saw Jove's bird, the Roman eagle, wing'd / From the spongy south to this part of the west, / There vanish'd in the sunbeams; which portends, / Unless my sins abuse my divination, / Success to th' Roman host."* (CYM IV.ii)

50   A reference to a *"huntress"* in a forest is clearly one of Shakespeare's invocations of Artemis/Diana, generally associated with virginity. But in the myth of Actaeon (which Shakespeare refers to often) she is also a symbol of death.

51   Othello goes on to explain that the handkerchief was woven by a 200-year-old Sibylene oracle and dyed with the blood of virgins: *"'Tis true; there's magic in the web of it. / A sibyl, that had number'd in the world / The sun to course two hundred compasses, / In her prophetic fury sew'd the work; / The worms were hallow'd that did breed the silk, / And it was dyed in mummy which the skillful / Conserved of maiden's hearts."* (OTH III.iv) Shakespeare would feature another such love charm in *Troilus and Cressida*.

52   Shakespeare would reuse this stage direction for an entrance of the maddened king Lear: *"Enter Lear, fantastically dressed up with wild flowers."* (KL IV.vi)

53   Laroche in Bruckner and Brayton (2016) p. 216, 220

54   John Gerard *Herball* (1597) in Laroche in Bruckner and Brayton (2016) p. 216-217

55   It seems unlikely to me that Ophelia is pregnant, since Hamlet has been studying abroad in Germany for months or years. On the other hand, Shakespeare entered into *Hamlet* having just lost both his father and son (named Hamnet), so there's a certain poetic symmetry in having Hamlet lose an unborn child.

56   Florizel comments *"These your unusual weeds to each part of you / Do give a life - no shepherdess, but Flora / Peering in April's front."* (WT IV.iv)

57   Kelley (2006) p. 141

58   Cotton (1987) p. 324

59   Knowlton-Davis (2012) p. 30

60   In terms of a trinity of "witches," it's worth noting that Perdita's birth is accompanied by a single reference to Margery the midwife, who then disappears

from the play. So we could say Margerie represents the former crone of the trinity. The virgin-mother-crone trinity appears in many more of Shakespeare's plays: three women curse Richard III and he dies, three women try to warn Hector of his death in *Troilus and Cressida* and he dies. Three women (mother, bride and virgin) conspire to save Bertram from his suicidal wanderlust in *All's Well that Ends Well*. And in a more complex scenario, the tragic hero in *Coriolanus* is confronted by his mother and bride to prevent him from penetrating the virginal city of Rome. They succeed and he is killed. The three queens who appear at the start of *The Two Noble Kinsmen* are all widows, but each in her opening line makes an appeal in the name of a life-stage: pity, motherhood, and virginity.

61   In Shakespearean English: *"Good frend, for Iesvs' sake forbeare / To digg the dvst enclosed heare / Bleste be ye man yt spares thes stones / And cvrst be he yt moves my bones."* It's worth noting here that Shakespeare did not fear his grave would be desecrated by theatrical detractors or literary critics (or frustrated high-school students), but rather by peasant farmers he'd impoverished with his robber-baron land-grabbing, crop-hoardling, stock-swindling and usury.

62 Shakespeare makes only a couple of fleeting references to Hallowmas. For example, when Richard II goes into exile and must send his wife back to France, he contrasts the cold parting with the summer of their wedding: *"She came adorned hither like sweet May, / Sent back like Hallowmas or short'st of day."* (R2 V.i)

ꟻall and ꟼinter ꟻestivals

63   Asimov (1970:2) p. 162

64 *The Tempest* contains a phantasmagorical harvest pageant in which autumn reapers dance with spring nymphs – sowing and reaping occur simultaneously – symbolizing an abolishment of winter, a restoration of an Edenic paradise.

65   For example: In *Much Ado*, Benedick says Beatrice exceeds Hero *"as much in beauty as the first of May doth the last of December."* *"Men are April when they woo, December when they wed: maids are May when they are maids, but the sky changes when they are wives."* (AYL IV.i)

66   Robert Herrick (1660) in Barber (1972) 26. Shakespeare does use the word "Wassail" in non-Christmas contexts, in *Antony and Cleopatra* where Caesar says *"leave thy lascivious wassails"* (A&C I.iv) and *Macbeth*, when Lady Macbeth uses wassail to lull Duncan's guards to sleep. (MAC I.vii)

67   Woodbridge (1994) p. 270

68   In the first four acts of the play, Hamlet is a student too young for the throne and has never been married (and his sweetheart Ophelia can't be more than 13 years old). But when he returns from England in act five he's different, not playful anymore, and when he asks the grave-digger, *"HAMLET. How long hast thou been a grave-maker? ...FIRST CLOWN. It was the very day that young Hamlet was born...I have been sexton here, man and boy, thirty years."* (HAM V.i) And Yorick the court jester, whom he knew well in childhood, *"hath lain in the earth three-and-twenty years."*

69   Laroque (1993) p. 228

70   In his mistaken belief that the lady Olivia loves him, the butler Malvolio cites precedent, saying *"There is an example for't: the Lady of Strachy married the yeoman of the wardrobe."* (TN II.v) This "Yeoman of the Wardrobe" was some henchman of the Twelfth Night Lord of Misrule according to Janet Spens, and I wish she'd elaborated further on that. If this person was locked in a closet against his will, it would further tie Malvolio's darkened confinement in with Twelfth Night tradition. Or perhaps this Yeoman of the Wardrobe was involved in some ancient form of the teenager party-game of locking a couple in a closet. Unfortunately all we know for certain is that the "Yeoman of the Wardrobe" tradition was familiar enough in Shakespeare's time that it required no explanation. Spens (1916) p. 42

71   Woodbridge (1994) p. 166

Afterlife and Ghosts

72   Northrop Frye observes that Shakespeare's *Hamlet* focuses on "an afterlife that has no infinite presence in it, only the clicking and whirring of a sacramental machine... Apparently everything depends on whether the priest gets there in time or not. So it's not very reassuring to find that the only accredited priest in the play is that horrible creature who presides over Ophelia's funeral, and who gets a concentration of malice and spite into an eight-line speech that would do credit to the Devil himself, who doubtless inspired it." Frye (1986) p. 87

73   Hamlet sort-of confesses to Horatio and Horatio sort-of absolves him (*"And flights of angels sing thee to thy rest."* HAM V.ii) but Horatio is established within the text as a philosophy student, basically agnostic, certainly not a priest.

74   *"LEAR. You heavens, give me that patience, patience I need! / You see me here, you gods, a poor old man, / As full of grief as age; wretched in both! / ...You think I'll weep; No, I'll not weep:— (*[Stage direction] *Storm and tempest.) / I have full cause of weeping; but this heart / Shall break into a hundred thousand flaws / Or ere I'll weep... / CORNWALL. Let us withdraw; 'twill be a storm."* (KL II.iv)

75   The *Tempest's* storm at sea has parallels with Clarence's dream in *Richard III* (R3 I.iv), which contains many additional nightmarish details.

76   The island is in the Mediterranean between Naples and Tunis, and yet the play contains numerous quotations from pamphlets Shakespeare read about exploratory voyages to Bermuda, including the loose anagram of Caliban / Cannibal / Caribbean. The play's geography is further complicated by Shakespeare wrongly assigning a seacoast to the inland Dukedom of Milan, so really in this play anything can be anywhere.

77   Everyone in *The Tempest* is in their own private Hell. Like the cave/grave of the archetypal mythic Hero Quest, each character is confronted by what they bring in with them. The Boatswain is called blasphemous in the first scene (perhaps he once had some blasphemous lines that were censored from the Folio script) and then spends the play with the other sailors in some nightmarish hellhole: *"We were dead of sleep...with strange and several noises / Of roaring, shrieking, howling, jingling chains, / And moe diversity of sounds, all horrible."* (TEM V.i) The clowns Stephano

and Trinculo bring a bottle of liquor, and they encounter the fish-man Caliban, then they fall in the horse-pond and get chased by hell hounds. Caliban, on his own quest, drinks like a fish and worships a Dionysian delusion–a false god of drunken cross-dressed hedonism to supplant Prospero's bookish humanism. Prince Ferdinand is briefly banished from his life of ease and forced to do the servant's job of hauling wood. The innocent Miranda is finally to be released from a penal colony where her only knowledge of sexuality has been an attempted rape by a stinking fish-man.

78   Frye (1986) p. 186

79   There have been some strained attempts to force an Eden allegory onto Prospero and Miranda's banishment as punishment for his seeking forbidden knowledge. But Milan, a den of usurping serpents, is no Eden. Nor could a case be made for the island as any sort of innocent Eden or paradise, and even the innocent joining of Miranda and Prince Ferdinand is blessed with pagan goddess-magic (a trinity of goddesses, no less).

80   Puck here refers to suicides (buried at crossroads) and people who've drowned (and therefore not received proper burial) who were believed to walk the earth at night.

81   In Purgatory they could be purged/cleansed over time and admitted into Heaven (and the Church used this for the sale of "indulgences," coupons for God's forgiveness, whereby you could pay to have a relative's Purgatory sentence shortened).

82   S. Clark Hulse quoted in Estock (2010)

83   For the sake of familiarity here, I'll call him "King Hamlet." Actually this character is based on a semi-historical Danish King Horwendil, assassinated in around 1050CE. It's also unlikely he named his son "Hamlet" (*Ameleth,* "fool," a nick-name the prince seems to have picked up for feigning madness while plotting revenge and jockeying for the throne, which he accomplished and survived). The story comes from Saxo Grammaticus' *Gesto Danorum* "Deeds of the Danes," c1200CE.

84   Bloom (1996) p. 383, 388. It's possible that the recent deaths of his father and his son (named Hamnet) brought both this old legend and its father-son connection powerfully back to him.

85   Voltaire (1748) in Lounsbury (1902) p. 143

86   Moorman (1906) p. 201. I was initially shocked by Moorman's insistence that Gertrude was unfaithful during King Hamlet's lifetime. But I looked again and when the ghost refers to Claudius as an *"adulterate beast [who] won to his lust the will of my most seeming-virtuous queen,"* (HAM I.v) it makes sense that after King Hamlet's death, she was not "his" queen anymore, and sex between Gertrude and Claudius would not be adultery (actually the Bible commands a widow's marriage to her husband's brother as a *Yibbum* or *Levirate* marriage).

87   The mysterious "armed head" that appears during the Wierd Sisters' cauldron ritual in *Macbeth* IV.i derives from King James' report that his mother's death was "spoken of in secrete by those whose power of sight presentede to them a bloodie head dancing in the aire [sic]" (Reported to Sir John Harrington in 1604, quoted in Calhoun 1942, p. 188) (Yes, apparently *the* same John Harrington who invented the English flushing toilet, which people still call "John").

88   Gruoch may be a feminine form of *Crom Cruach / Cromm Cruaich*, a pre-Christian Irish deity who demanded the sacrifice of a firstborn child in exchange for bountiful harvests (the eleventh century song about him can be found in Graves 1991 p. 130). It's doubtful Shakespeare looked into this, but an association with child sacrifice would neatly fill in the blank about the baby Lady Macbeth nursed who's no longer alive, and her numerous references to baby-killing.
89   Asimov (1970:2) p. 168

Spring Festivals

90   Plutarch *Life of Caesar* (c0096)
91   Shakespeare is here mimicking the fanfare of the Shrove Tuesday Fool, a mock king who reigns over carnival misrule and had titles like "monarch of the Mouth, high Steward to the Stomack...first Favourite to the Frying pans, greatest Bashaw to the Batter-bowles, Protector of the pan-cakes, First Founder of the Fritters, Baron of Bacon flitch, Earle of Egg-baskets, and in the least and last place, lower Warden of the Stinke-ports" -Anonymous (1622) in Laroque (1993) p. 102
92   Prospero watches his daughter instantly fall in love with a prince, then schemes: *"They are both in either's pow'rs; but this swift business / I must uneasy make, lest too light winning / Make the prize light."* (TEM I.ii)
93   It's also possible that "marriage" is a lazy twist on the Latin "matrimony," which means to make someone a mother.
94   *"BEATRICE. Therefore I will even take sixpence in earnest of the bear-ward, and lead his apes into hell. / LEONATO. Well then, go you into hell? / BEATRICE. No; but to the gate; and there will the Devil meet me, like an old cuckold, with horns on his head, and say, 'Get you to heaven, Beatrice, get you to heaven; here's no place for you maids.' So deliver I up my apes, and away to Saint Peter for the heavens: he shows me where the bachelors sit, and there live we as merry as the day is long."* (MAAN II.i) See Dyer (2017) p. 133
95   Thomas Nabbes *The Spring's Glory* (1638) in Laroque (1993) p. 102
96   John Taylor (1621)
97   Anonymous (1622) in Laroque (1993) p. 102
98   Laroque (1993) p. 49
99   Edmund Gayton (1654) in Laroque (1993) p. 99
100   Even more bizarre than this was a game in which a Hoodman tied a hen to his back, strapped sleighbells to his body, and ran through a crowd of blindfolded men who tried to beat the hen to death with sticks. The Hoodman meanwhile made it his goal to bait them into hitting each other. This tradition apparently continued into the 1800s. Hutton (1996) p. 158
101   Hutton (1996) p. 155, 160
102   Richard Carew (1602) in Hutton (1996) p. 155
103   Philip Stubbes *Anatomie of Abuses* (1583) The enduring popularity of the English football is evident in the number of times it was ineffectively banned, by

kings Edward III, Richard II, Henry IV and Henry VIII. Seeing the futility of forbidding the game, King James simply ordered that this roughhousing be taken outside the city. Ultimately, the decline of Shrovetide customs was brought on by a decline in the observance of Lent. As Catholicism lost ground and fasting became less severe (and as food importation solved the problem of late-winter scarcity), there was less general desperation, and thus less malice.

104   Prevented by law from owning land, Shylock in *Merchant of Venice* has trouble distinguishing between his daughter who's eloped, and the coins she ran off with: *"My daughter! O my ducats! O my daughter! /...My ducats and my daughter!"* (MOV II.viii) In Shylock's defense, his daughter Jessica is a wastrel, and the coins probably loved him more than she did. ...And in *my* defense, yes I did look up "wastrel" in a thesaurus but none of the alternatives were satisfactory.

105   *"DON PEDRO. Will you have me, lady? / BEATRICE. No, my lord, unless I might have another for working days: your Grace is too costly to wear every day."* (MAAN II.i) The play contains a running debate about whether Benedick will wear horns after marriage, and it's finally concluded that he will, but they'll be more like bull horns than antlers.

106   Butler, Samuel *Hudibras, the Second Part* (1664) quoted in Parten (1985) p. 187

107   Parten (1985) p. 187

108   Stendahl (1925) quoted in Bristol in Woodbridge (1994) p. 94.

109   There's a good deal of symbolism packed into this basket: Falstaff's reference to a triple death recalls old Celtic traditions of sacrificing a king by strangling, clubbing, and throat-cutting (for example, look up the "Lindow Man" who was killed three times and thrown into a bog). And the basket becomes both a stinking womb and a tomb – a place of death and rebirth (which is accompanied by a sort of baptism in the Thames). Also because Falstaff's attempted crime has been against domesticity, and in this speech the basket transforms into numerous domestic items to torment him: a pickle barrel (peck), distillery, dairy cask, bathtub and stewpot. See Wendy Wall (2001) p. 98-102

110   In *Romeo and Juliet*, Benvolio and Mercutio argue over who is more quarrelsome, and Benvolio demands, *"Didst thou not fall out* [fight] *with a tailor for wearing his new doublet before Easter?"* (R&J III.i)

111   Finding New Testament mercy ineffective, he quickly switches tactics to Old Testament judgment: *"CLARENCE. Erroneous vassals! the great King of kings / Hath in the tables of his law commanded / That thou shalt do no murder. Will you then / Spurn at his edict and fulfil a man's? / Take heed; for he holds vengeance in his hand / To hurl upon their heads that break his law."* (R3 I.iv) This is likewise ineffective.

112   The circular procession (*"round about her tomb"*) is also more associated with feminine goddess-worship than masculine god-worship, which generally features processions in straight lines (as we see in *Midsummer Night's Dream*, the contrast between Titania's *"roundels"* and Oberon's marches).

113   The resurrection trilogy of *Pericles, Winter's Tale* and *Cymbeline* is interrupted by *Coriolanus*, which deviates from the others in that the mother is

terminally overbearing and the son is symbolically resurrected. *Coriolanus* begins with Marcius (named after the Roman war-god Mars), a literal one-man-army, charging alone through the gates of Corioli and being declared slain. But he miraculously emerges – a rebirth – baptized in blood, and is re-named Coriolanus, literally "Asshole of Corioli" (penetrating the anus of Corioli is a fitting start for Shakespeare's most homoerotic play, centering on Coriolanus' tragic bro-mance with enemy general Tullus Aufidius). Later, when he threatens to bring this same doom upon Rome, some bad advice from his mother gets him killed.

114   The substitution of another maiden to sleep with the judge in *Measure for Measure* is similar to *All's Well*, where Helena must go to a dark place to conceive new life with Bertram, curing his suicidal wanderlust.

115   Hughes (1992) p. 44

116   If *All's Well That Ends Well* derives in part from the "Fisher King," Helen would be not so much the fool as the grail that heals the dying king: a literal king from literal sickness at the beginning, and then her *"lord"* Bertram, infected by lust (he longs to deflower a maiden named after the virgin goddess Diana) and a deadly petulance. Only after realizing that he has drunk from the chalice of Helen's divine love does he seem to heal.

117   Spens (1916) p. 39-41

118   There are some similarities here with *The Merchant of Venice*, where Antonio is held for ransom, and two prized rings are extorted by the disguised brides Portia and Nerissa, who then force their husbands to earn them back. It turns out Shakespeare could make not one but *two* of his most dismal comedies out of these same elements.

119   Shakespeare uses a similar plot device in *Romeo and Juliet* (Romeo and friends wearing masks to sneak into a Capulet dance) and *Henry VIII* (the king and his friends arriving masked at a party) and in both cases the masked invader will ironically become a captive in love. But these scenes seem more connected to Whitsun traditions.

120   It's worth noting that all three of Shakespeare's pre-Christian British kings – Lear, Macbeth and Cymbeline – are all in the grip of powerful witchy women. Not necessarily an intentional pattern, but a worthy representation of women having greater influence in the pre-Roman-Christian era (except that the powerful women in these plays are malevolent, owing to Shakespeare's own fear of femaleness).

121   Bloom (1998) p. 315

122   Relocating the ritual from St. George's Chapel in Windsor to Whitehall was a complex political move, touching on issues of the English Reformation (the Garter ceremony controversially retained elements of a Catholic Mass even while England turned Protestant). Leslie Katz explores this in her essay *"The Merry Wives of Windsor:* Sharing the Queen's Holiday" (1995).

123   Along with Falstaff's punishment for lust, the jealous husband Mr. Ford is also punished for his suspicions. But then Shakespeare further compicates things by having Mr. and Mrs. Page's daughter Anne elope against their wishes

(frustrating their conflicting schemes to marry her to men of their choosing). So Mr. and Mrs. Page are punished for not being suspicious *enough*.

Royalty

124   He seems to have written all these plays in the first half of his career, 1589-1599 (he may also have written an *Edward III*) except for *Henry VIII* which he wrote (or co-wrote) at the very end, around 1612.

125   Frye (1986) p. 38

126   Being a ring, the crown is also susceptible to wrongful penetration, as a French king accuses King John: *"That thou hast under-wrought his lawful king... / Outfaced infant state, and done a rape / Upon the maiden virtue of the crown."* (KJ II.i) Skulking up stairs to murder king Duncan, Macbeth compares himself to a legendary rapist stalking *"with Tarquin's ravishing strides, towards his design."* (MAC II.i)

127   Frazer (1996) p. 104

Fairies

128   John Aubrey (1689) quoted in Laroque (1993) p. 24

129   Green (1962) p. 89

130   The inconsistency of Shakespeare's fairy-lore is particularly interesting because his "fairy plays," *A Midsummer Night's Dream* and *The Tempest* were two of the very few he plotted himself. Most of his plots were adapted from the works of other writers, but with these two he had far greater freedom of expression (The "Queen Mab" speech in *Romeo and Juliet* was also likely his own invention). So if he'd *wanted* to produce patterns of fairy-lore, he could have. But he didn't.

131   Geoffrey Chaucer (c1400) translated into modern English.

132   Arthurian legends always feature Merlin, who might have been a Pictish shaman or Druid priest.

133   These are called the "Mosynoechians" ('wooden-castle dwellers') in Xenophon of Athens, *Anabasis* [March Up Country] Book V:IV (c400 BCE)

134   "Brownies" were supernatural housework helpers from Scottish folklore, from whence comes the designation for the smallest rank of girl scouts.

135   Scot in Wall (2001) p. 70 "Oke" here is "Oak," "Waine" is "Wagon," "Drake" is "Dragon."

136   Shakespeare also refers to *"sea-nymphs"* (TEM I.ii) and *"nymphs call'd naiads of the wandering brooks"* (TEM IV.i) in *The Tempest*, and these seem to be the aquatic subdivision of fairies (as Ariel is of the air and Puck is of the forest). Shakespeare's characters compare people to mermaids: an enchanting maiden in *Comedy of Errors*, Cleopatra's attendants in *Antony and Cleopatra* and the drowned Ophelia in *Hamlet*.

137   There are some fascinating theories. For example that in a time when people with dwarfism or with physical abnormalities were marginalized, a bowl of milk could be left out in exchange for domestic work under cover of night. Or

that the coin in the shoe may have been left by a poor woman's wealthy lover, to make amateur prostitution less explicit. Interesting theories for which only circumstantial evidence exists.

138   Lamb (2000) p. 297

139   Samuel Rowlands playfully distinguishes devilry from Satanism in his *More knaves yet?* (1613): "Amongst the rest was a good fellow deuill / So cal'd in kindnes, cause he did no euill."

140   Wall (2001) p. 76

141   A placket was an opening in a woman's skirt, a codpiece was like a male athlete's cup – both were designed to make it easier to go potty, but also eased access for sexual quickies.

142   The Shrove Tuesday Lord of Misrule was known by various poetic titles, including "Sole-monarch of the Mouth, high Steward to the Stomack...Protector of the pan-cakes, First Founder of the Fritters, Baron of Bacon flitch, Earle of Egg-baskets," etc. The comparison is further apt because both encourage letting the appetites of the lower half of the body rule over the reason of the mind: the Shrove Tuesday Fool puts the stomach in charge, and Cupid puts the genitals in charge. Anonymous (1622) in Laroque (1993) p. 102

143   A character named "Cupid" does appear in *Timon of Athens* (TIM I.ii) – he seems to be some sort of pimp who brings erotic dancers dressed as Amazons to entertain the guests at one of Timon's dinner-parties.

144   Barber (1972) p. 121.

145   There's a fascinating parallel here with Shakespeare's narrative poem *Venus and Adonis*, where Venus (mother of Cupid) pursues a mortal man and he rejects her. She finds him later, killed by a boar, and his blood has caused a white flower to turn purple.

146   Scholars generally agree this part was written by some co-author of the play.

147   Prospero warns Ferdinand that premarital intercourse will curse their sex-lives forever: *"Take my daughter. But / If thou dost break her virgin-knot before / All sanctimonious ceremonies may / With full and holy rite be minist'red... / Sour-ey'd disdain, and discord, shall bestrew / The union of your bed with weeds so loathly / That you shall hate it both. Therefore take heed, / As Hymen's lamps shall light you."* (TEM IV.i)

148   Orlando is the English version of Roland, essentially the same name as Rosalind (in the source play, Thomas Lodge's *Rosalinde*, Orlando is named Rosader). Both are driven into the forest by a usurping brother (in Rosalind's case her father's brother), and there she becomes masculine and he becomes effeminate. It's unclear if the similarity between the names Rosalind and Orlando/Rosader is coincidental or contains some additional hidden message about identity in the story.

149   Paglia (1990) p. 211

150   Swann (2000) p. 453

151   King James *Daemonologie* (1597)

152   Thomas Hobbes *Leviathan* (1651)

153   Perhaps we're to infer that Oberon and Titania will compromise, each

having half-year custody of the changeling child (like the compromise about Persephone spending half the year with Demeter and half with Hades)

154   Chaucer writes in the *Merchant's Tale* (from *The Canterbury Tales*, c1400) about "Pluto, that is king of Fairyland, and many a lady in his company, following his wife, the queen Proserpine [Persephone], whom he kidnapped out of Etna while she gathered flowers in the mead."

155   Swann (2000) p. 457

156   Swann (2000) p. 458

157   Swann (2000) p. 450

158   For example, that Mab is a "queen" in the sense of "quean" (an old English slang for whore) or that she is a midwife in the service of the fairy queen. I find these unconvincing, but as a Biblical scholar I'm accustomed to commentators straining unrelated ancient texts to force a unified system.

159   In terms of dramatic structure, *The Tempest* correponds with the second halves of *King Lear, Timon of Athens, Cymbeline* and *The Winter's Tale*, and Prospero seems to be a sort of reincarnation of Lear and Timon. But imagine seeing only the second half of *Lear*, meeting the character when he's already full of embitterment and self-pity: it would be harder to connect with the character.

160   "The symptoms of the inherited disease phenylketonuria, known as PKU, most common in children of English or Irish descent, begin to appear in normal-looking babies at about six months, leading to slow growth and severe retardation. Joyce Underwood Munro describes the wizened appearance of failure-to-thrive babies, who become 'psychosocial dwarves' as a result of 'parental hostility' or neglect. Susan Schoon Eberly surmises that children who survived these disfiguring disorders into adulthood may have avoided ridicule and physical persecution by keeping to themselves and, like Robin Goodfellow, performing household chores at night in exchange for a 'ritual evening dish of fresh cream.'" Lamb (2000) p. 292

161   The hunchback king Richard III is once called an *"elvish-mark'd, abortive, rooting hog"* (R3 I.iii) by an angry woman, but his mother repeatedly denies that he was a "changeling" (although Shakespeare seems to have intentionally substituted a deformed hunchback for the historical Richard III, who may have suffered scoliosis but had not been considered deformed, and the 2012 exhuming of his bones showed that he was mildly asymmetrical but basically fine). In *1 Henry IV*, the king wishes that fairies had switched his alcoholic son Hal for the princely Hotspur: *"O, that it could be proved / That some night-tripping fairy had exchanged / In cradle-clothes our children where they lay."* (1H4 I.i)

162   In Shakespeare's *Cymbeline*, the maiden Imogen prays before bedtime: *"To your protection I commend me, gods. / From fairies and the tempters of the night / Guard me, beseech ye."* (CYM II.ii) The audience knows that there's a mischievous man hiding in her trunk who will attempt to sexually blackmail her. Shakespeare seems to imply that if this all-too-human incubus were successful, she'd have no recourse but to blame fairies.

163   Note also the eunuchs, whom Shakespeare transforms into fairies: "Foure Eunuches...not minding to delay any longer the pleasure of their Mistresse closed the doores of the Chamber and departed away: within the Chamber were lamps that gave a cleare light all the place over: Then she put off all her Garments to her naked skinne, and taking the Lampe that stood next to her, began to annoint all her body with balme, and mine likewise, but especially my nose, which done, she kissed me...purely, sincerely, and with great affection, casting out these and like loving words: 'Thou art he whom I love, thou art he whom I onely desire, without thee I cannot live.' ...Then she tooke me by the halter and caste me downe upon the bed, which was nothing strange unto me, considering that she was so beautifull a Matron and I so wel boldened out with wine, and perfumed with balme, whereby I was readily prepared for the purpose: But nothing grieved me so much as to think...how I should touch her fine, dainty, and silken skinne, with my hard hoofes, or how it was possible to kisse her soft, pretty and ruddy lips, with my monstrous mouth and stony teeth, or how she, who was young and tender, could be able to receive me. [sic]" -Apuleius, Lucius *The Metamorphoses of Apuleius, Book Ten* (c150s CE) quoted in Nosworthy (1982) p. 99

164   Wall (2001) p. 86

165   Wall (2001) p. 83

166   Bishop Richard Corbet (1582–1635)

Summer Festivals

167   Robert Herrick (1591-1674) *Corinna's Going A-Maying*

168   Thomas Nashe *Summer's Last Will and Testament* (1600)

169   Philip Stubbes *Anatomie of Abuses* (1583)

170   We have no written record of what (if any) ceremony might surround the selection and cutting of the tree, but there are some interesting parallels with North America's Lakota Sun Dance, in which the central tree is blessed with energies of human fertility and ferocity before people dance around it: pregnant women dancing around the tree, then warriors charging at it, then mothers bring newborn babies to be blessed around it.

171   Philip Stubbes *Anatomie of Abuses* (1583)

172   Statement taken before William Hunt in Wells. *Bishop's Court Deposition Book* (28 May 1633) That this particular event was witnessed on All Soul's Day in November is a sign that the Maypole could be left standing all year, until being replaced the following May.

173   Asimov (1970:1) p. 45

174   Unfortunately for Arcite, "the gods" are not of one mind – the war-god Mars chooses him to win the fight, but the love-goddess Venus chooses Palamon to get the girl. So Arcite is thrown from a wild Amazonian mare and dies before he can marry Emilia.

175   "Pan" is the Roman name for a faun or satyr, a mischievous goat-man, the equivalent of the English Robin Goodfellow. The huntress is Artemis/Diana, the virgin goddess who was caught bathing by Actaeon, so transformed him into a stag to be torn apart by his hunting dogs. Coridon is a character from an English ballad who fell in love with a nymph named Parthenia (Greek: virgin), said he would die unless she slept with him, and she then proposed they die of pleasure together.

176   Anonymous *The Fetching Home of May* (c1635). Another verse of the song contains a constellation of names from the Robin Hood legend: "*John* with Gillian, Harry with Frances, / Meg and *Mary*, with *Robin* and *Will*, / *George* and Margery lead all the Dances, / For they were reported to have the best Skill." (emphases added)

177   Philip Stubbes *Anatomie of Abuses* (1583) In *Henry VIII* the birth of Queen Elizabeth inspires a peasant stampede of well-wishers, which is likened to the Rites of May: "*PORTER. Do you look / for ale and cakes here, you rude rascals? / MAN. Pray, sir, be patient; 'tis as much impossible, / Unless we sweep 'em from the door with cannons, / To scatter 'em as 'tis to make 'em sleep / On May-day morning; which will never be. / PORTER. ...Bless me, what a fry of fornication / is at door!*" (H8 V.iv)

178   Vox Graculi, or Iacke Davve [Jack Daw] (1623) in Laroque (1993) p. 113

179   Graves (1991) p. 398

180   The play contains no explicit reference to taking place in May, but there is plenty of circumstantial evidence: the banished Duke (likened to Robin Hood) speaks of having just spent a winter in the forest, Orlando engages in a wrestling exhibition, Rosalind ventures into the woods to pursue her beloved, and the play contains a bunch of forest weddings. Symbolically, the usurping Duke is a winter-king and the restoration of the banished Duke is a return of summer.

181   And because this mass-wedding is performed in a forest without a priest, the Duke's last line implies that these weddings might be performed yet again before any baby-making begins.

182   Humphrey King, from *An Halfe-Penny Worth of Wit in a Penny-Worth of Paper* (1613)

183   This Marian does not seem to be related to Miriam the mother of Jesus. It's possible this "Marian" is a distortion of "May-Rhiannon," named for a Welsh goddess.

184   Asimov (1970:2) p. 425 In *1 Henry IV*, Falstaff insulted a tavern hostess by comparing her to a man in drag playing Maid Marian. (1H4 III.iii)

185   Michael Drayton (1563–1631) from *Poly-Olbion*

186   *Cobbe's Prophecies, his Signes, and Tokens, his Madrigalls, Questions, and Answers* (1614)

187   King James (c1618) in Hiscock (2018) p. 47

188   In the play this is referred to as a "*Bergomask*," a term which applied broadly to country dances (with connotations of playful clumsiness, in contrast to rigid court dances).

189   Fetherston (1582) quoted in Kolkovich (2017) p. 169

190   William Kemp (1600) in Kolkovich (2017) p. 170

191   John Marston *Jack's Drum Entertainment* (1600) in Kolkovich (2017) p. 170

192   The Spanish *Morisca* was a dance comemmorating an encounter between Moors (Muslims) and Christians. For further exploration of this etymology, see Iyengar, "Moorish Dancing in *The Two Noble Kinsmen*" (2007) Shakespeare does mix familiar elements of the Morris Dance into *Othello* – Iago as the pedant controlling the narrative, the face-painted Moor Othello repeatedly calling himself a "fool," a cross-dressed boy as Desdemona, and a loose woman is referred to as a hobby-horse. Laroque (1993) p. 290

193   An attendee of Beaumont and Fletcher's *Masque of the Inner Temple and Gray's Inn* (1613) recalled a similar sequence of dancers: "Pedant, May Lord, May Lady; Seruingman, Chambermaide; A Countery Clowne, or Shepheard, Countery Wench; An Host, Hostesse; A Hee Baboone, Shee Baboone; A Hee Foole, Shee Foole vshering them in."[sic] Quoted in Iyengar (2007) p. 91. There is a loose constellation of similar personae in the woodland of Shakespeare's *As You Like It*: Jacques as the pedant (who keeps requesting songs but won't dance), the Duke as lord, Touchstone as a fool, Corin as host, Silvius and Phebe as shepherds, and a mysterious lion attacks Orlando. The play also contains cross-dressing and culminates in a dance. Some of these personae also appear in *Taming of the Shrew*, where the noblemen plays a pedant and sends his servant (disguised as a lord) to woo the May-bride Bianca. An old wooer becomes a musician and a traveler becomes a wealthy landlord. Petruchio pretends to be a fool, but really he and Katherina would be the two baboons.

194   Kolkovich (2017) p. 166

195   Philip Stubbes *Anatomie of Abuses* (1583)

196   Christopher Fetherston *A dialogue agaynst light, lewde, and lasciuious dauncing wherin are refuted all those reasons, which the common people vse to bring in defence thereof.* (1582)

197   Modern paraphrase of Graves (1991) p. 398. Robert Graves further proposes that the origin of "Morris" may have been a corruption of "Maris" or "Merry," both of which derive from Mary/Marian.

198   Welsford, Enid (1927) in Eastman (1964) p. 262

199   There's a vein of bestiality jokes in this play, with Helena demanding that Demetrius *"use me but as your spaniel,"* Puck saying *"man shall have his mare"* (the name of Theseus' bride, Hippolyta, literally means "loose horse"), and Pyramus waving a bloody robe crying *"lion vile hath here deflowered my dear!"* See Boehrer (2004)

200   "We add to this that these unmistakably Elizabethan artisans are performing in ancient Greece before Theseus, Demetrius and Lysander, all of whom belong to different centuries." Nosworthy (1982) p. 98

201   Dyer (2017) p. 118

202   The tradition of the *"Whitsun morris-dance"* is mentioned in *Henry V* II.iv.

203   The "Nine Worthies" were generally composed of the Biblical Joshua, David and Judah Maccabee, the Classical Hector, Alexander and Julius Caesar, and the European Arthur, Charlemagne and Godfrey of Bouillon, but there was some flexibility about this. Dyer (2017) p. 118

204   This same Theseus appears in *Midsummer Night's Dream* and Shakespeare and Fletcher's *Two Noble Kinsmen*. I wrote a book about Ariadne, Theseus and the Minotaur, called *Romancing the Minotaur: Sex and Sacrifice and some Greek Mythology.* (2015)

205   Though this does not take place on Whitsun, the girl says *"Methinks I play as I have seen them do / In Whitsun pastorals."* (WT IV.iv)

206   The infiltration of a peasant festival by disguised nobility also has certain ominous undertones – a masked king could use this to identify subversives, and masked royalty could also sew wild oats among the peasants (the disguised king in Winter's Tale suspects that his son has been slumming with a country wench, and if there's any nuptual prospect he plans to nip it in the bud).

207   ...Oh, *now* you check the footnote. Well yes, here's a partial list of what he sells: *"He hath songs for man or woman of all sizes; no milliner can so fit his customers with gloves. He has the prettiest love-songs for maids; so without bawdry, which is strange; with such delicate burdens of dildos and fadings, 'jump her and thump her'; and where some stretch-mouth'd rascal would, as it were, mean mischief, and break a foul gap into the matter, he makes the maid to answer 'Whoop, do me no harm, good man' - puts him off, slights him, with 'Whoop, do me no harm, good man.'"* (WT IV.iv)

208   When the rigid and somber Malvolio shows up in funny clothes making vulgar puns, Olivia calls it *"Midsummer madness."* (TN III.iv)

209   Laroque (1993) p. 272

210   In the opening scene, when Kent argues that Lear has wrongly disowned Cordelia, Lear snaps *"Come not between the dragon and his wrath."* (KL I.i)

211   Asimov (1970:1) p. 482

212   John Stowe *Survey of London* (1598)

213   A certain slim case could be made for the tragic lovers' reunion in the tomb containing some hint of Thesmophoria and/or the Eleusinian Mysteries, ancient Greek holidays celebrating the grain goddess Persephone in the underworld, but I wouldn't stake the credibility of this book on it (If there's any credibility left! But believe it or not, I'm actually pretty cautious about going out on a limb to connect a play with an ancient holiday.)

The Enchanted Forest

214   Shakespeare played various roles in various plays he wrote, but the only two for which we have documentary evidence are Adam in *As You Like It* and the King's Ghost in *Hamlet*. It's likely that Shakespeare had some physical impediment, a limp that confined him to elderly roles, even when he wasn't that old.

215   Actually there are two distinct characters in *As You Like It* named Jaques (a name that does not appear in any of Shakespeare's other works). There's the famous melancholy philosopher Jaques who gives the *"All the world's a stage"* speech. But rival brothers Oliver and Orlando also have a brother named Jaques, who is briefly mentioned at the start and then shows up at the conclusion to narrate the fate of the play's antagonist. He cannot be the same character because

the two men named Jaques have a brief scene together. Ted Hughes explores this two-Jaques phenomenon on the mytho-poetic plane in *Shakespeare and the Goddess of Complete Being* (1992) p. 108-115.

216   That the enchanted forest can transform a man into an *"ass"* (in both senses – a human idiot, and a donkey) is a recurring theme: obviously Bottom's transformation in *Midsummer Night's Dream,* and in *Merry Wives of Windsor,* when Falstaff has been lured into the forest and humiliated, he says *"I do begin to perceive that I am made an ass."* (MWW V.v) Jaques in his song likewise seems to be using the expression *"turn ass"* with both meanings – the hippies have turned into idiots *and* animals.

217   Leontes' description of his childhood bond with Polixenes contains certain homoerotic undertones, and some commentators see a double jealousy – he is possessive of both his wife and friend. The "comic" resolution, in which Leontes' wife, daughter, and friend are restored to him has a dark shadow: his young son who dies of grief at the beginning does not come back in the end. We could say that Leontes *gains* a son when his daughter marries prince Florizel. But in a deeper sense, the replacement-son must be Leontes' future grandchild, also Polixenes' and Hermione's grandchild: Leontes and his friend and his wife will make a baby together.

218   Ted Hughes writes, it's as if the *Tempest* forest were "what remained of the Forest of Arden after the holocaust of the tragedies. (Perhaps one should not make light of the fact that the Mother Forest of those lyrical days...has become a rocky, storm-beaten island of a terrible dead witch and her devil-god)." Hughes (1992) p. 381

219   Coghill (1950) in Eastman (1964) p. 313 We should note, though, that in this interpretation the city of Milan is Eden (humanity's "natural" habitat) and the island is a cursed place of exile. I find this troublesome.

220   Hesiod, Theogony – Works and Days (1999) p. 40

221   Ovid, Metamorphoses (1958) p. 33

222   The Puritan Angelo in *Measure for Measure* tries to lure the nun Isabella into a walled garden to sexually exploit her. But Isabella tells this to Angelo's jilted ex-fiancée Mariana who takes her place, and once she's done this deed with Angelo she publicly shames him into marrying her. Shakespeare will then return to the walled garden in *Winter's Tale,* as the site of an innocent conversation between a Sicilian queen and a Bohemian king. But the queen's husband spies on them and becomes infected with sexual jealousy.

223   Whether Oberon's interest is in match-making in general we don't know. He witnesses Helena's devotion to Demetrius—a slavish, psychotic devotion ("*I am your spaniel; and, Demetrius, / The more you beat me, I will fawn on you. / Use me but as your spaniel, spurn me, strike me, / Neglect me, lose me; only give me leave, / Unworthy as I am, to follow you.*" MND II.i) and he wants Demetrius to accept this deal. This is the kind of devotion he thinks he wants from Titania. So it's debatable whether he cares about helping Helena, maybe he's just feeding his own sadistic fetish.

224   The play does establish that this is an "open" or polyamorous marriage – Oberon has had affairs, including one with Hippolyta, and Titania has had an affair with Theseus. They discuss these openly and dispassionately. Oberon's plan in the play is to make his wife *"dote"* (become emotionally dependent) on a predatory lynx or boar or bear–clearly he's not envisioning an erotic connection, but Puck playfully aims her affections at a hybrid donkey-man.

225   There are two versions of the *Merry Wives* script with some significant differences in Act V scene v–one of them has lines spoken/sung by Puck and the Fairy Queen, the other assigns these lines to characters of the play (Mrs. Quickly, Pistol and Cricket). Sorting out the whole "Quarto vs. Folio" issue would be tedious beyond the scope of this study, I'm just going to guess that assigning the lines to established characters was a later correction. But I'll admit my guess on this is as good as a coin-toss.

References

Akçeşme, Banu and Behiye Çelİk Karahan. "An Ecofeminist Reading of Shakespeare's *The Winter's Tale.*" *International Journal of Languages' Education and Teaching* Vol. 6, No. 1 (2018): 82-95

Archer, Jayne Elisabeth, Howard Thomas, and Richard Marggraf Turley. "Reading Shakespeare with the Grain: Sustainability and the Hunger Business." *Green Letters: Studies in Ecocriticism* 19, no. 1 (2015): 8-20

Asimov, Isaac. *Asimov's Guide to Shakespeare: Two Volumes in One.* Avanel Books, New York, 1970.

Barber, Cesar Lombardi. *Shakespeare's Festive Comedy: A Study of Dramatic Form and its Relation to Social Custom.* Princeton University Press, Princeton, 1972.

Bloom, Harold. *Shakespeare: The Invention of the Human.* Riverhead Books, New York, 1998.

Boehrer, Bruce. "Economies of Desire in *A Midsummer Night's Dream.*" *Shakespeare Studies* 32 (2004): 99-117

Bruckner, Lynne, and Dan Brayton, eds. *Ecocritical Shakespeare.* Routledge, London, 2016.

Bryant, Jerry T. "*The Winter's Tale* and the Pastoral Tradition" *Shakespeare Quarterly,* Vol. 14, No. 4 (Autumn, 1963): 387-398

Calhoun, Howell V. "James I and the Witches in '*Macbeth*'" *Shakespeare Associational Bulletin,* Vol. 17, No. 4 (October, 1942): 184-189

Cotton, Nancy. "Castrating (W)itches: Impotence and Magic in '*The Merry Wives of Windsor*'" *Shakespeare Quarterly*, Vol. 38, No. 3

(Autumn, 1987): 320-326

Diamond, Catherine. "Four Women in the Woods: An Ecofeminist Look at the Forest as Home" *Comparative Drama* Volume 51, Issue 1 (2017): 71-100

Diehl, Huston. "Horrid Image, Sorry Sight, Fatal Vision: The Visual Rhetoric of *Macbeth.*" *Shakespeare Studies* Vol. 16 (1983): 191-203.

Doran, Madeleine. "The *Macbeth* Music" *Shakespeare Studies,* Vol. 16 (January, 1983): 153-173

Eastman, A.M. And G.B. Harrison *Shakespeare's Critics from Jonson to Auden: A medley of Judgments.* University of Michigan Press, Ann Arbor 1964

Estok, Simon C. "Shakespeare and Ecocriticism: an Analysis of 'Home' and 'Power' in *King Lear.*" *Journal of Australasian Universities Language and Literature Association* 103 (2005): 13-36

Feerick, Jean E. "Economies of Nature in Shakespeare" *Shakespeare Studies* (Annual 2011): 32-42

Frazer, Sir James George. *The Golden Bough* (Touchstone, New York 1996)

Frye, Northrop. *A Natural Perspective: The Development of Shakespearean Comedy and Romance* (Columbia University Press, New York 1965)

Frye, Northrop. *Northrop Frye on Shakespeare.* Yale University Press, New Haven 1986

Gleckman, Jason. "'I know a Bank …': *A Midsummer Night's Dream,* fairies, and the erotic history of England" *Shakespeare* Vol. 10, No. 1 (2014): 23-45

Goossen, Jonathan. "'Tis Set down So in Heaven, but Not in Earth': Reconsidering Political Theology in Shakespeare's *Measure for Measure*" *Christianity and Literature* Vol. 61, No. 2 (Winter 2012): 217-239

Graves, Robert. *The White Goddess: A Historical Grammar of Poetic Myth.* Farrar, Straus and Giroux, New York 1991

Green, Roger Lancelyn "Shakespeare and the Fairies" *Folklore,* Vol. 73, No. 2 (Summer 1962): 89-103

Hiscock, Andrew "'Come Now a Roundel and a Fairy Song':
Shakespeare's *A Midsummer Night's Dream* and the Early Modern
Invitation to the Dance" *Cahiers Elisabethains: A Journal of English
Renaissance Studies,* Vol. 97 (2018): 39-68

Hughes, Ted. *Shakespeare and the Goddess of Complete Being.* Farrar Straus
Giroux, New York 1992

Hutton, Ronald. *The Stations of the Sun: A History of the Ritual Year in
Britain.* Oxford University Press, Oxford 1996

Iyengar, Sujata. "Moorish Dancing in *The Two Noble Kinsmen" Medieval
and Renaissance Drama in England* Vol. 20 (Jan. 2007): 85-107

Kakkonen, Gordana. Galić and Ana Penjak "The Nature of Gender.
Are Juliet, Desdemona and Cordelia to their Fathers as Nature is to
Culture?" *Critical Survey* Vol. 27, No. 1 (Mar 2015): 18-35

Kammer, Miriam. "Breaking the Bounds of Domesticity: Ecofeminism
and Nature Space in *Love's Labour's Lost" Shakespeare Bulletin* Vol. 36,
No. 3 (Fall 2018): 467-481

Katz, Leslie S. "*The Merry Wives of Windsor*: Sharing the Queen's
Holiday" *Representations,* No, 51 (Summer 1995): 77-93

Kelley, Sharon A., "Shakespeare's *The Winter's Tale" The Explicator,* Vol. 64,
No. 3 (Spring 2006): 140-141.

Knowlton-Davis, Colleen Marie. "Horned Gods, Horny Men, Witches,
and Fairies: Pagan Remnants in Shakespeare's *The Merry Wives of
Windsor" Journal of the Wooden O Symposium,* Vol. 12 (2012) p25-36

Kolkovich, Elizabeth Zeman. "Women Dancing the Morris in Fletcher
and Shakespeare's *The Two Noble Kinsmen" Shakespeare* Vol. 13, No. 2
(2017): 164-179

Kranz, David. "The Sounds of Supernatural Soliciting in *'Macbeth"
Studies in Philology,* Vol. 100, No. 3 (Summer 2003): 346-383

Lake, H. Coote. "Some Folklore Incidents in Shakespeare" *Folklore,* Vol.
39, No. 4 (Dec. 31, 1928): 307-328

Lamb, Mary Ellen. "Taken by the fairies: fairy practices and the
production of popular culture in *A Midsummer Night's Dream"
Shakespeare Quarterly* Vol. 51, No. 3 (Autumn, 2000): 277-312

Laroque, François. *Shakespeare's Festive World: Elizabethan Season Entertainment and the Professional Stage* (trans. Janet Llord). Cambridge University Press, Cambridge 1993

Lounsbury, Thomas, L.H.D., LL.D., *Shakespeare and Voltaire.* Charles Scribner's Sons, New York 1902

McDonald, Russ. *The Bedford Companion to Shakespeare: An Introduction with Documents.* Bedford Books of St. Martin's Press, Boston 1996

Moorman, F. W. "Shakespeare's Ghosts." *Modern Language Review*, Vol. 1, No. 3 (Apr 1906): 192-201

Myers, Henry Alonzo. "'Romeo and Juliet' and 'A Midsummer Night's Dream': Tragedy and Comedy" from Myers, *Tragedy: A View of Life* Cornell University Press, 1956

Nosworthy, J. M. "Shakespeare's Pastoral Metamorphoses" *Shakespearean Criticism*, Vol. 96 (1982): 90-113

Paglia, Camille. *Sexual Personae: Art and Decadence from Nefertiti to Emily Dickinson.* Vantage Books, New York 1991

Parten, Anne. "Falstaff's Horns: Masculine Inadequacy and Feminine Mirth in '*The Merry Wives of Windsor*'" *Studies in Philology* Vol. 82, No. 2 (Spring, 1985): 184-199

Rawnsley, Ciara. "Behind the Happily-Ever-After: Shakespeare's Use of Fairy Tales and *All's Well That Ends Well*" *Journal of Early Modern Studies* Vol. 2 (2013): 141-158

Shannon, Laurie. "Poor, Bare, Forked: Animal Sovereignty, Human Negative Exceptionalism, and the Natural History of *King Lear*." *Shakespeare Quarterly*, Vol. 60, No. 2 (2009): 168-196

Spens, Janet. *An Essay on Shakespeare's Plays in Relation to Tradition.* B.H. Blackwell, Oxford 1916

Spyra, Piotr. "Shakespeare and the Demonization of Fairies." *Text Matters* Vol. 7, No. 7 (October 2017)

Steadman, John M. "Falstaff as Actaeon: A Dramatic Emblem." *Shakespeare Quarterly*, Vol. 14, No. 3 (Summer 1963): 231-244

Swann, Marjorie. "The Politics of Fairylore in Early Modern English

Literature" *Renaissance Quarterly*, Vol. 53, No. 2 (Summer, 2000): 449-473

Thorne, W. Barry. "Folk Entertainment and Ritual in Shakespeare's Early Plays." University of British Columbia, 1960

Wall, Wendy. "Why Does Puck Sweep?: Fairylore, Merry Wives, and Social Struggle." *Shakespeare Quarterly*, Vol. 52, No. 1 (Spring 2001): 67-106

Wheatley, Henry B. "The Folklore of Shakespeare" *Folklore*, Vol. 27, No. 4 (Dec 31, 1916): 378-407

Wood, James O. "Intimations of Actaeon in *Julius Caesar*" *Shakespeare Quarterly* Vol. 24 (1973): 85-88

Woodbridge, Linda and Edward Berry, ed. *True Rites and Maimed Rites: Ritual and Anti-Ritual in Shakespeare and his Age*. University of Illinois Press, Urbana 1992

Woodbridge, Linda. *The Scythe of Saturn: Shakespeare and Magical Thinking*. University of Illinois Press, Urbana 1994

Zajac, Paul Joseph. "The Politics of Contentment: Passions, Pastoral, and Community in Shakespeare's *As You Like It*" *Studies in Philology*, Vol. 113, No. 2 (2016): 306-336

Character Concordance

Henry IV, 123, 141
Henry the Earl of Richmond, 89
Henry V, 2, 117, 141, 145, 186, 219,
    239 n.161
Henry VI, 47, 50, 123, 229 n.45
Hermia, 106, 108, 156, 184, 187, 201,
    217
Hermione, 60, 61, 86, 87, 94, 95, 130,
    244 n.217
Herne the Hunter, 59, 127, 171
Hero, 108, 109, 112, 129, 204, 231
    n.65
Hippolyta, 164, 197, 200, 242 n.199,
    245 n.224
Horatio, 35, 69, 80, 93, 96, 97, 232 n.73
Hymen, 19, 105, 156–159, 161, 190,
    215

J

Iago, 16, 35, 54, 110, 125, 126, 167,
    242 n.192
Imogen, 33, 130, 160, 227 n.29, 239
    n.162
Iris, 19, 158, 208– 209
Isabella, 130, 227 n.19, 228 n.31, 244
    n.222

J

Jailer's Daughter, 195, 196, 198, 199
Jaques, 34, 113, 213–214, 243–244
    n.215
Jessica, 118, 219, 235 n.104
Joan of Arc/Joan la Pucelle, 39, 40,
    47–49, 62
Sir John Falstaff. See Falstaff
Julia, 28, 160, 203, 227 n.29
Juliet, 2, 6, 7, 34, 90, 91, 106, 108, 110,
    112, 123, 130, 204, 208, 219
Julius Caesar, 52, 53, 88, 91, 92–93,
    104, 128–129, 203, 231
    n.66, 242 n.203
Juno, 19, 158, 159, 190, 208, 209
Jupiter, 19

K

Katherina, 35, 132, 134, 242 n.193
Katherine, 114
Kent, 82, 207, 243 n.210
Kings. See also Hamlet; specific kings by
    name
King John, 52, 186, 229 n.46, 237
    n.126
King Lear, 21, 39, 43, 52, 82, 83, 130–
    131, 135, 143, 207, 212, 229
    n.44, 230 n.52, 232 n.74,
    236 n.120, 243 n.210
King of Bohemia. See Polixenes
King of Navarre, 133, 212, 217
King Richard. See Richard II; Richard
    III
Knights. See specific characters by name

L

Lady Anne, 229 n.45
Lady Capulet, 208
Lady Macbeth, 35, 42, 45, 49, 51, 100,
    121, 227 n.18, 228 n.36, 231
    n.66, 234 n.88
Laertes, 70, 77, 131, 185
Launce, 36
Leonato, 109, 131, 234 n.94
Leonatus, 123, 131
Leontes, 21, 60–61, 87, 94, 110, 122,
    123, 131, 144, 215, 229 n.45,
    244 n.217
Lucentio, 134, 204
Luciana, 175
Lucius, 90, 176, 240 n.163
Lysander, 53, 106, 108, 184, 187, 242
    n.200

M

Mab, 153, 164–167, 178, 237 n.130,
    239 n.158
Macbeth, 16, 20–21, 30, 32, 41, 42,
    43, 44, 45, 66, 68, 93–94,

Q

Queens. *See* Fairy Queen; *specific Queen(s) by name*

R

Regan, 52, 207
Richard, Duke of Gloucester, 50
Richard II, 141, 146, 230 n.48, 231 n.62, 235 n.103
Richard III, 35, 50, 67, 68, 89, 146, 229 n.45, 231 n.60, 232 n.75, 239 n.161
Roderigo, 125
Romeo, 6, 32, 34, 90, 91, 106, 108, 109, 110, 112, 122, 123, 130, 161, 164, 167, 185, 204, 208, 219, 236 n.119
Rosalind, 2, 33, 35, 53, 54, 106, 108, 121, 159, 160, 161, 184, 185, 190, 215, 217, 227 ns.29 and 31, 238 n.148, 241 n.180
Rosaline, 54, 108, 132–133

S

Saturninus, 123
Schoolmaster, 194–198
Sebastian, 73, 113, 203
Servant(s), 61, 118, 120, 160, 175, 191, 198, 227 n.29, 242 n.193
Shepherds and shepherdesses, 115, 205, 216
Shylock, 23, 118, 128, 235 n.104
Silvius, 105, 161, 242 n.193
Sir Toby Belch, 17, 72
Snug, 197
Soldiers, 41, 185
Soothsayers, 52–53, 230 n.49
Stephano, 232 n.77

T

Taborer, 195
Tamora, 90
Theseus, 104, 164, 169, 170, 176, 177, 185, 187, 194–195, 197, 198, 200, 202, 203, 242 ns.199 and 200, 243 n.204, 245 n.224
Timon of Athens, 131, 238 n.143
Titania, 123, 144, 153, 158, 163, 164, 166, 167, 169, 170, 173, 174, 175, 176, 177, 200, 201, 217, 220, 221, 235 n.112, 238–239 n.153, 244 n.223, 245 n.224
Titus, 90
Touchstone, 113, 189, 242 n.193
Tranio, 114
Trinculo, 233 n.77
Tullus Aufidius, 236 n.113
Tybalt, 91, 185

V

Valentine, 191
Viola, 73, 160, 185, 227 n.29

W

Weaver. *See* Bottom
Weird Sisters, 40, 41, 42, 44, 47, 50, 62, 94, 99
Wolsey, 228 n.32

Y

Yorick, 77, 231 n.68

Index

Frazer, James George, 14, 226 n.14,
    237 n.127
"Friar Tuck," 192
Frye, Northrop, 5, 85, 226 n.5, 232
    n.72, 233 n.78, 237 n.125
Funerals, 77–79
    Cymbeline, 77–79
    Hamlet, 77

G

Garden of Eden, 211–221. *See also*
    Enchanted forest
Garter Ceremonies/Garter Knights.
    See St. George's Day
Gender switching, 35, 168. *See*
    also Cross-dressing and
    transvestites
Gerard, John, 55
Ghosts. *See* Afterlife and ghosts
Gods and goddesses
    Ceres, 19, 158, 208–209, 219
    Diana, 19, 44, 130, 142, 161, 163,
        192, 230 n.50, 236
        n.116, 241 n.175
    Flora, 204
    Hymen, 190
    Iris, 19, 158, 208
    Isis, 175–176
    Juno, 190, 208
    Persephone, 20, 128, 163, 204, 228
        n.37, 239 ns.153 and
        154, 243 n.213
Good witches, 58–59
    Macbeth, 59
    Merry Wives of Windsor, 58–59
Graves, Robert, 151, 189, 234 n.88,
    241 n.179, 242 n.197
Green, Roger Lancelyn, 149, 223, 237
    n.129
Greene, Robert, 130
"Green gowns"/Greensleeves, 187–
    190
    As You Like It, 187, 189–190

Midsummer Night's Dream, 187–189

H

Halloween/Samhain, *Macbeth,* 65–67
Hamlet. *See also Hamlet* (play);
    Concordance of Characters
    (preceding Index)
    King Hamlet, 95–98
Hamlet (play), 4–5, 20–21, 233 n.86
    afterlife and ghosts, 77, 80–82, 89,
        93, 95–98, 232 n.73, 233
        n.86
    dramatis personae, 31, 33–34
    enchanted forest, 220, 243 n.214
    fairies, 237 n.136
    fall and winter festivals, 67, 69–70,
        231 n.68
    flowers, 55–56
    folk pageantry, 28, 227 n.23
    funerals, 77
    ghost of King Hamlet, 233 n.86
    Nemesis, 89, 93
    pastoral theater, 25
    purgatory, 80–82, 232 n.73
    ritual, theater as, 14, 18
    royalty, 143
    Shakespearean English, 7, 10, 226
        ns.7 and 8
    Skimmington, 126
    spring festivals, 103–104, 110, 126
    summer festivals, 199
    Valentine's Day l Lupercalia,
        103–104
    witches, 43, 55–56, 229 n.44, 230
        n.55
Harrison, G.B., 226 ns.3 and 13, 227
    n.21, 242 n.198, 244 n.219
Harvest festival. *See* Lammas/
    Lughnasadh
Hecate, 43–45
    Macbeth, 43–45, 228 n.38
Henry IV, Part 1
    enchanted forest, 219

witches, 54, 230 n.51
Ovid, 28, 163, 176, 218, 244 n.221

P

Paganism, 65–67
Pageantry. *See* Folk pageantry
Paglia, Camille, 6, 33, 35, 161, 226 n.6,
     227 n.30, 228 n.33, 238 n.149
Pandosto (Greene), 130
Paradise, 211–221. *See also* Enchanted
     forest
Parten, Anne, 124, 235 ns.106 and 107
Pastoral theater, 25–26
     All's Well That Ends Well, 26
     As You Like It, 25–26
     Comedy of Errors, 26
     Cymbeline, 26
     endings, 28–29
     Hamlet, 25
     King Lear, 26
     Measure for Measure, 26
     Midsummer Night's Dream, 26
     The Tempest, 26
     Winter's Tale, 26
Pentecost. *See* Whitsun/Whitsuntide
Pericles
     fairies, 159
     ritual, theater as, 19
     spring festivals, 130, 235–236 n.113
     witches, 52, 228 n.39, 229 n.47
Persephone (goddess), 20, 128, 163,
     204, 228 n.37, 239 ns.153
     and 154, 243 n.213
Physiognomy, 107
Pixies, 150–154
     Midsummer Night's Dream, 150–
     154
     The Tempest, 237 n.136
Poetry, as charms, 53–54
Pope, Alexander, 227 n.21
Premarital sex, 111, 159, 177–179.
          See also Spring festivals;
          Summer festivals

virginity and chastity, 49, 54, 109,
     130, 135–136, 142, 150,
     159, 187, 230 n.50, 231
     n.60
Protestant Reformation, 190–191, 200
Puck. *See* Robin Hud/Robin
          Goodfellow/Robin Hood;
          Concordance of Characters
          (preceding Index)
Purgatory, 80–86
     Hamlet, 80–82, 232 n.73
     King Lear, 82–83
     penal colony, *The Tempest*, 83–86
Puritans. *See also* Stubbes, Philip
     influence, 200
     resentment, 18–19

Q

Queen Elizabeth, 8, 135, 142–143,
     146, 150, 157
Queen Mab. *See* Mab

R

Reincarnation, 45, 56, 130–131, 239
     n.159
Religion. *See also* Paganism
     Christianization of Britain, 151
     Muslims, 199
     Protestant Reformation, 190–191,
     200
     ritual of, 14, 19
     theatricality of, 27
Resurrection. *See* Easter/Ostara
Richard II
     enchanted forest, 211
     royalty, 141
     spring festivals, 128
     witches, 230 n.48, 231 n.62
Richard III
     afterlife and ghosts, 88–89, 232
     n.75
     fairies, 239n.161
     fall and winter festivals, 67–68

The Sequel

Shakespeare's Goddess

THE DIVINE FEMININE
ON THE ENGLISH STAGE

Coming Soon

I started out writing a book about indigenous English folk beliefs and rituals, and how some of them have mutated and survived into modernity. I quickly found that it's nearly impossible to research English beliefs about witches, fairies, and ghosts without running into Shakespeare, and soon the writing project transformed, as writing projects tend to do.

The result is **Supernatural Shakespeare: Magic and Ritual in Merry Old England.** *As comprehensive as it is, I found when I was done writing it that I was still curious. In addition to fascinating folk beliefs and rituals, Shakespeare's plays also contain many fascinating references to Greek gods and goddesses.*

If you share my curiosity, you'll be pleased to learn that Shakespeare's Goddess: The Divine Feminine on the English Stage will be released in Spring 2022! Here's a sneak peek, an excerpt focused on the story of Diana and Actaeon, one of Shakespeare's favorite myths.

~ *j. Snodgrass*

Diana and Actaeon
LOVE'S LABOUR'S LOST | TITUS | MERRY WIVES OF WINDSOR

In Shakespeare's time, the most popular Greek legend was not about Zeus or Heracles or even Aphrodite, but about the virgin huntress goddess Artemis, whom the Romans called Diana. After a successful day of hunting, a young prince named Actaeon wandered off from his squires and hounds and stumbled into a hidden forest grove where Diana was bathing. The virgin huntress, furious at having been seen naked, transformed Actaeon into a buck, and he was then torn to pieces by his own dogs.

Shakespeare adapted the myth of Actaeon and Diana in various ways, sometimes explicitly but more often with great subtlety. Count Orsino in Twelfth Night uses the image of Actaeon the hart/deer to describe falling in love with the lady Olivia:

> *That instant was I turned into a hart,*
> *And my desires, like fell and cruel hounds,*
> *E'er since pursue me.* (TN I.i)

The conspirators in Julius Caesar are frequently referred to as dogs, and they eventually tear him apart. The forest goddess Diana appears by her alternate name Titania in *Midsummer Night's Dream*, and the ass-headed Bottom stumbles like Actaeon into her sanctum. However, under the spell of a magic flower, she adopts him.

In *The Tempest*, when the drunken clowns Stephano and Trinculo penetrate Prospero's hidden sanctuary (and try on his clothes, symbolically discovering his nakedness) planning to rape his daughter, they are chased away by hell-hounds.

In *Love's Labour's Lost*, the king of Navarre (and his three friends) lodge a visiting French princess and her three friends in a forest adjacent to the castle. The four heroines take up bow hunting deer, and their talk of killing stags for sport segues to the topic of targeting men:

PRINCESS OF FRANCE.
Thus will I save my credit in the shoot:
Not wounding, pity would not let me do't;
If wounding, then it was to show my skill,
That more for praise than purpose meant to kill...
Only for praise; and praise we may afford
To any lady that subdues a lord. (LLL IV.i)

The butler Boyet responds, *"My lady goes to kill horns; but, if thou marry, / Hang me by the neck, if horns that year miscarry." (LLL IV.i)* He bets his life that if the princess marries the king, she'll make a trophy of him and dominate him sexually (he'll be "horny," yearning). The four heroes repeatedly invade the ladies' forest sanctuary, and in the end, the women banish them to a year in exile. This is Shakespeare's only comedy that does not end in wedding and bedding. The virgin huntress in the forest banishes her would-be lover.

In *Titus Andronicus*, Shakespeare's bloodiest play, Titus' son Bassianus and his fiancée Lavinia catch the Roman Empress Tamora having an affair in the forest.

BASSIANUS.
Who have we here? Rome's royal Emperess,
Unfurnish'd of her well-beseeming troop?
Or is it Dian, habited like her,
Who hath abandoned her holy groves
To see the general hunting in this forest?
TAMORA.
...Had I the pow'r that some say Dian had,
Thy temples should be planted presently
With horns, as was Actaeon's; and the hounds
Should drive upon thy new-transformed limbs,
Unmannerly intruder as thou art!
LAVINIA.
Under your patience, gentle Empress,
'Tis thought you have a goodly gift in horning...
Jove shield your husband from his hounds to-day!
'Tis pity they should take him for a stag. (TA II.iii)

Their banter contains numerous Actaeon references–Bassianus contrasts the adulteress with Diana's virginity, Tamora wishes she had the power to make antlers sprout from Bassianus' forehead (and indeed a moment later for the crime of having seen her nakedness he'll be murdered by her two sons). Lavinia wittily responds that the empress's infidelity is turning her husband into a horned cuckold.

Shakespeare again uses Actaeon as a symbol of a jilted husband in *Merry Wives of Windsor*, when the lusty knight Falstaff stalks the wives of two local businessmen. One of the potential cuckolds, the jealous and suspicious Mr. Ford, is warned to:

> *Prevent, or go thou,*
> *Like Sir Actaeon he, with Ringwood [the hound] at thy heels.*
> *O, odious is the name!*
> *...The horn, I say.* (MWW II.i)

Ford fears that, like Actaeon pursued by dogs, he will be hounded by his neighbors with the unspeakable title of cuckold. Later he is amazed that his friend Mr. Page (whose wife Falstaff also pursues) is not suspicious enough, comparing him to:

> *a secure and wilful Actaeon; and to these violent proceedings*
> *all my neighbours shall cry aim.* (MWW III.ii)

And the play is full of *"buck"* puns. When Mrs. Ford mentions *"bucking"* (bleaching) the laundry, her husband sputters about becoming a horned stag: *"Buck? I would I could wash myself of the buck! Buck, buck, buck! ay, buck! I warrant you, buck; and of the season too, it shall appear."* (MWW III.iii)

Most of the Actaeon imagery in *Merry Wives* is applied to Falstaff, the wandering knight whose lust is punished in the play. When the wives are plotting to humiliate him for his lascivious advances, one of them recalls an old legend:

> *MRS. FORD. There is an old tale goes that Herne the Hunter,*
> *Sometime a keeper here in Windsor Forest,*
> *Doth all the winter-time, at still midnight,*

> *Walk round about an oak, with great ragg'd horns;*
> *And there he blasts the tree, and takes the cattle,*
> *And makes milch-kine yield blood, and shakes a chain*
> *In a most hideous and dreadful manner.*
> *You have heard of such a spirit, and well you know*
> *The superstitious idle-headed eld*
> *Receiv'd, and did deliver to our age,*
> *This tale of Herne the Hunter for a truth.*
> *PAGE. Why yet there want not many that do fear*
> *In deep of night to walk by this Herne's oak.*
> *But what of this?*
> *MRS. FORD. Marry, this is our device —*
> *That Falstaff at that oak shall meet with us,*
> *Disguis'd, like Herne, with huge horns on his head.* (MWW IV.iv)

Ancient legends of an antlered man chained to a tree (captive consort to a huntress-goddess) had local variations in numerous European cultures. Sir James Frazer compares various parallel versions of it in his monumental study *The Golden Bough*, where he writes that the myth of Actaeon is one local variant of this archetypal narrative. The primary example Frazer uses is Virbius, torn apart by mares and resurrected by Diana, who adopts him as her consort and stations him by a tree; anyone who manages to kill him gets to take his place. Shakespeare localizes this legend with the name "Herne," from the Old English "Cern" meaning horn (and core name of the European pagan deity Cernunnos).

Falstaff leaps at the proposition of this role play and arrives at Herne's Oak by moonlight. In an early version reprinted in the First Quarto, Falstaff has a full buck's head: *"Enter sir John with a Bucks head upon him,"* and Sir Hugh comments, *"See I have spied one by good luck / his bodie man, his head a buck."* (MWW V.v) The two wives he's been stalking appear there in the wood and excite him with talk of a threesome. He gleefully exclaims,

> *Divide me like a brib'd buck, each a haunch;*
> *I will keep my sides to myself, my shoulders for the fellow*
> *of this walk, and my horns I bequeath your husbands.* (MWW V.v)

But then suddenly, he's surrounded by dancing fairies (village children in disguise) who torture him like Actaeon's hounds.

The Falstaff-Actaeon from *Merry Wives* will be reincarnated in two bodies in *All's Well That Ends Well*: the braggart Parolles (who is hunted and hounded by his fellow soldiers) and the insipid Bertram (who becomes obsessed with deflowering a maiden named Diana in a secret sanctum). Their simultaneous misadventures combine to create the basic shape of Actaeon threatening Diana's chastity and being punished, but Shakespeare puts a fascinating twist on the situation. Bertram fears Helena's powerful eroticism and flees their wedding night. His insecure masculinity longs for the hunt, both in warfare (*"War's no strife /* [compared] *to the dark house and the detested wife"*) and the sexual predation of vulnerable maidens—what some might call "chasing young tail." But he is doggedly pursued by Helena, who stalks and hunts him, and finally catches him by *becoming* the virginal Diana in a darkened sanctum. Bertram-as-Actaeon penetrates Helena-as-Diana's grove, the hunter becomes the prey, and he is captured. And when Bertram finally admits defeat and accepts Helena as his wife, her last line in the play is a threat to hunt *and kill* him if he ever chases young women again: *"If it appear not plain, and prove untrue, / Deadly divorce step between me and you!" (AWTEW V.iii)*

Shakespeare had an obsession with chastity and cuckoldry. Perhaps a little odd for a man who got married six months before his first child's baptism, lived twenty years apart from his wife and then left her his second-best bed in his will. But someone could fill a book with what we *don't* know about William Shakespeare's personal life—and many such books exist! Whatever we know or don't know about the author of these works, this story of the hunter who becomes the prey of a virgin goddess does seem to have struck a deep chord within him.

Other Books by

j. SNODGRASS

Chaos

Chaos, Chaos

Genesis and the Rise of Civilization

Libel: Sex and Sexuality in the Bible

Natives Discover America: An Anthropological Study of the "White Man"

Romancing the Minotaur: Sex and Sacrifice and Some Greek Mythology

Thirteenth Moon: A Star*Lite Fantasy

Turning the Tables: Farming and Feeding in the Gospels

Welcome to Tragedy: A Beginner's Guide to Greek Drama

Words (Between the Lines of Age): Empire, Satire and Revival in the Bible

About the Author

j. Snodgrass studies, teaches, and writes about myth and ritual, exploring connections between mythology and sociology in religions around the world. His scholarly books include four Biblical commentaries, volumes on Greek myth and drama, and a book on Native American perspectives on U.S. history. He has also written a science fiction comedy novel, *Thirteenth Moon*.

The best advice he ever received as a writer was, "Write what you would like to read," to which he has added, "And before writing it, learn it." After many years of merely liking or disliking Shakespeare's plays, he decided to dig in and become conversant on the topic. The book he would have liked to read did not yet exist, so he wrote it.

j. Snodgrass teaches, writes, and lives in Buffalo, New York, with his wife Elizabeth and their four children.

Available at
www.CityofLightPublishing.com
and wherever books are sold.

Become a citizen of the City of Light!
Follow @CityofLightPublishing